December 1997

I saw this and thought of you and your Dad. He was a very intelligent person: This may be an interesting story line especially if you pursue international studies. Love you.

Unc Ron

✧

EINSTEIN'S DAUGHTER

✧

✦

EINSTEIN'S

the search for lieserl

DAUGHTER

✦

Michele Zackheim

RIVERHEAD BOOKS

a member of Penguin Putnam Inc.

New York

1999

Riverhead Books
a member of
Penguin Putnam Inc.
375 Hudson Street
New York, NY 10014

An application to register this book for cataloguing has been
submitted to the Library of Congress.

ISBN 1-57322-127-9

Printed in the United States of America
1   3   5   7   9   10   8   6   4   2

This book is printed on acid-free paper. ∞

BOOK DESIGN BY AMANDA DEWEY

For

Charles Ramsburg,

Ben Zackheim,

Maggie Zackheim,

and

Kathleen Anderson,

with love

EUROPE circa 1900

North Sea

Baltic Sea

DENMARK

Hamburg

Berlin

Elbe River

NETHERLANDS

BELG.

LUX.

Rhine River

Frankfurt

GERMANY

Prague

Munich

Vienna

Danube River

Vistula River

Warsaw

RUSSIA

Budapest

Bern

Zurich

SWITZERLAND

Lake Como

Milan

Venice

ITALY

Zagreb

AUSTRIA-HUNGARY

Sava River

Danube River

Novi Sad

Belgrade

AREA OF DETAIL

BOSNIA-HERZEGOVINA

Sava River

SERBIA

ROMANIA

BULGARIA

Adriatic Sea

Rome

MONTENEGRO

ALBANIA

GREECE

Danube River

CROATIA

VOIVODINA

Novi Sad

Kać

Tisa R.

Sremski Karlovci

Vilovo

Titel

Fruška Gora

⊕ Krušedol

Ruma

Sremska Mitrovica

Sava River

Zemun

Danube River

Belgrade

BOSNIA-HERZEGOVINA

Drina River

Sava River

Šabac

SERBIA

Kijevo

Ionian Sea

0   50 km

0   50 miles

© 1999 Jeffrey L. Ward

Marić

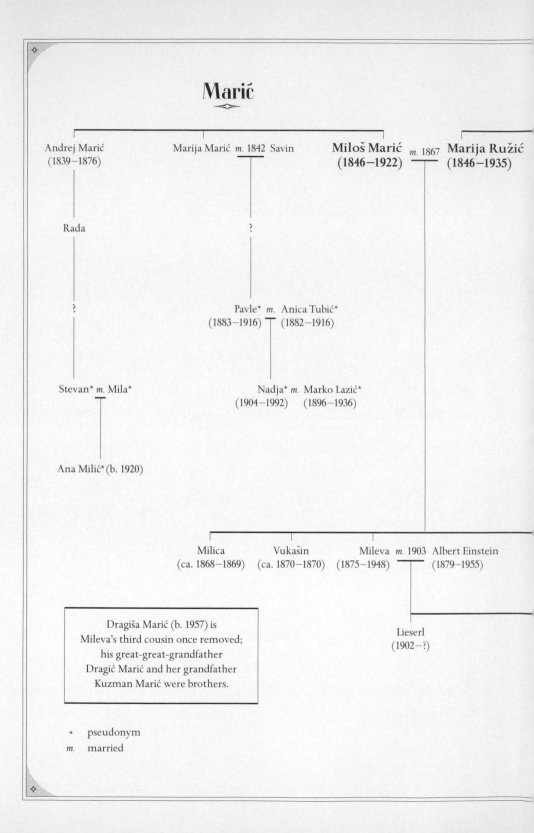

Andrej Marić
(1839–1876)

Marija Marić *m.* 1842 Savin

**Miloš Marić
(1846–1922)** *m.* 1867 **Marija Ružić
(1846–1935)**

Rada

?

?

Pavle* *m.* Anica Tubić*
(1883–1916)   (1882–1916)

Stevan* *m.* Mila*

Nadja* *m.* Marko Lazić*
(1904–1992)   (1896–1936)

Ana Milić* (b. 1920)

Milica
(ca. 1868–1869)

Vukašin
(ca. 1870–1870)

Mileva *m.* 1903 Albert Einstein
(1875–1948)   (1879–1955)

Lieserl
(1902–?)

> Dragiša Marić (b. 1957) is
> Mileva's third cousin once removed;
> his great-great-grandfather
> Dragić Marić and her grandfather
> Kuzman Marić were brothers.

*   pseudonym
m.   married

Ružić

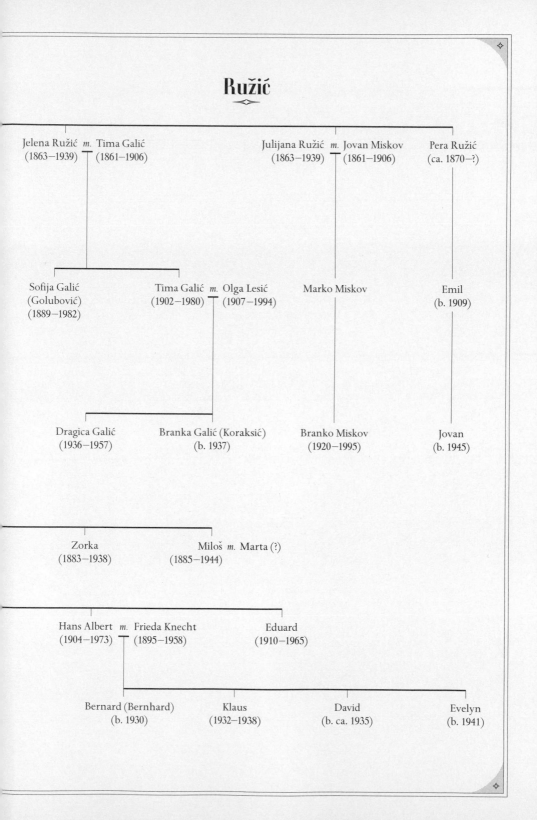

Jelena Ružić *m.* Tima Galić
(1863–1939)   (1861–1906)

Julijana Ružić *m.* Jovan Miskov
(1863–1939)   (1861–1906)

Pera Ružić
(ca. 1870–?)

Sofija Galić
(Golubović)
(1889–1982)

Tima Galić *m.* Olga Lesić
(1902–1980)   (1907–1994)

Marko Miskov

Emil
(b. 1909)

Dragica Galić
(1936–1957)

Branka Galić (Koraksić)
(b. 1937)

Branko Miskov
(1920–1995)

Jovan
(b. 1945)

Zorka
(1883–1938)

Miloš *m.* Marta (?)
(1885–1944)

Hans Albert *m.* Frieda Knecht
(1904–1973)   (1895–1958)

Eduard
(1910–1965)

Bernard (Bernhard)
(b. 1930)

Klaus
(1932–1938)

David
(b. ca. 1935)

Evelyn
(b. 1941)

A u t h o r ' s   N o t e

The search for Lieserl began in an old, gray cardboard shoe box. In that box, tied with faded ribbon, were fifty-four love letters between Albert Einstein and his first wife, Mileva Marić. Mileva had saved them for more than forty-five years, and when she died in Zurich in 1948, her daughter-in-law, Frieda, brought them back to America. Frieda, Hans Albert Einstein's first wife, stored the box on the top shelf of her husband's closet. In 1986, Evelyn Einstein, Albert and Mileva's granddaughter, found photocopies of the letters "folded and scrunched-up in a folder" that had belonged to her mother, Frieda. "Hey, I found some love letters," she told the director of the Einstein Papers Project. By then, Frieda had died. Shortly after Evelyn's discovery, the second Mrs. Hans Albert Einstein turned over the love letters to The Albert Einstein Archives at The Hebrew University.

✧

"1968. Springtime, New York, I wonder if Albert Einstein had a daughter?" I had written in my notebook. *"If he did, was she a genius, too? And why haven't I read about her? Could there be unknown Einsteins wandering about?"* Eventually, the notebook was placed on a shelf in my studio and forgotten.

Almost twenty years later, in May 1987, I read an article in *The New York Times* about the discovery of the love letters between Albert and Mileva. In these letters it was disclosed for the first time that they indeed had a daughter, born in 1902, whom they named Lieserl. But for some reason she had not been written into the Einstein story. Her existence had somehow vanished into history.

It intrigued me to think that hidden deep in the byzantine labyrinth of the Balkans lurked the mystery of Einstein's missing child whose fate remained unsolved. Impetuously, naïvely, I decided that it was time to find her.

I thought I knew Albert. His history is epic. But I did not know Mileva. Her history lies in his shadow. However, to find the child, I knew that I had to know Mileva. And to know Mileva, I had to understand the cultural heart of Serbia.

My research took me on extensive trips to Berkeley, Boston, London, Zurich, Bern, Budapest, Berlin, and three times to Serbia—twice while the country was at war, once when there was promise in the air.

I soon understood that Serbian society is private and intensely loyal. It takes months to cultivate friendship, sometimes years to earn the right to call someone by a first name. One must demonstrate absolute loyalty to be taken into another's confidence. From the beginning, I sought to respect the responsibility that is conferred when a truth is shared. I frequently heard, *dok mi kuca u grudima duša*—*"while my soul beats in my body, I will protect my family's honor."*

✧

I begin the story in 1846, the year in which Mileva Einstein-Marić's mother and father were born. At that time the area where they lived, Vojvodina [*'Voy-vo-di-na*], north of the Danube, was part of the Austro-

Hungarian Empire. The area south of where the Danube meets the Sava was under Ottoman domination until 1882, when it gained independence from the Turks and became the Kingdom of Serbia. At that time, Serbs made up approximately thirty percent of Vojvodina's population; the remaining two-thirds were mainly German and Hungarian.

On the first of December 1918, Vojvodina, along with Serbia, Montenegro, Croatia, Slovenia, Bosnia, and other parts of the Austro-Hungarian Empire were proclaimed the Kingdom of Serbs, Croats, and Slovenes. In 1929 the Kingdom's name was officially changed to Yugoslavia. After World War II, Vojvodina became an autonomous province of Serbia—just like Kosovo. And then in 1989, the constitutions of Vojvodina and Kosovo were transfigured and these regions lost their autonomy. In 1995, Yugoslavia was split again. Now it is composed only of Montenegro and Serbia, which still includes Kosovo and Vojvodina.

Today, in 1999, the most recent war has left the country in ruins. Many of the archives, government record offices, schools, hospitals, and graveyards, where I did much of my research, have been damaged or destroyed. Not one person of the many I interviewed supported the necessity for these wars, and many of them took strong and courageous positions against their government. Now, these kind and intelligent people, some of whom have become my dear friends, have been left stunned and demoralized.

This book is based on more than one hundred interviews and on extensive research into Serbian history, literature, and ethnology.

Here is the story of the destiny of Lieserl, *iz prve ruke,* "from the first hand."

Michele Zackheim
New York City, June 1999

✦

EINSTEIN'S
DAUGHTER

✦

Prologue

On Sunday, May 5, 1901, Mileva Marić and Albert Einstein rendezvoused at the train station in Como, Italy. Albert had traveled from Milan on the St. Gotthard Railway, and Mileva from Zürich on the Gotthard-Bahn. He waited for her "with open arms and a pounding heart." Together, they boarded a bright white steamer and sailed deep into the rocky terrain toward Colico, more than thirty kilometers away. Steep cliffs prevented them from seeing farther than the lake itself. Here and there on the margins of the water slender old white *campanili* stood before Romanesque parish churches, each with its own large bells, which created a musical respite for the fishermen and the voyagers.

The early-spring weather was warm enough to coax the flowering shrubs into startling displays of color. Primroses, violets, hart's tongue, and rusty-red columbine blossomed between moss-covered rocks. Lofty cypresses tossed their shadows against the cliffs while the fisherman pulled squiggling masses of black eels and tiny, slippery gray herrings from the lake.

Lake Como is shaped like a willowy dancing woman. Her head is thrown back toward the east, one leg beginning to *glissade* toward the west, the other *en pointe.* At her waist, on the western shore, is the village of Cadenabbia. Mileva and Albert's steamer moored there for two hours. They disembarked and walked up the Via del Paradiso, a splendid avenue lined with plane trees, to the gardens of the Villa Carlotta. The gardens held many sculptures, including a copy of Canova's *Love and Psyche.* Thrilled, Mileva promised herself to preserve the gardens in her heart. Later in the day, they glided further into the Italian Alps, to Colico, where winter still lingered. They left the steamer and found a *pensione* for the night.

The next morning, they set out on foot to cross an Alpine pass, the Splügen, where they "had to nail [their] shoes deeply in the snow." To their delight, they encountered a storm that created snowdrifts as high as six meters. They hired a coachman and a sleigh that seated two cozily.

"It was snowing so gaily all the time," Mileva later wrote a friend, "and we were driving now through long galleries, now on the open road, where there was nothing but snow and more snow as far as the eye could see, so that this cold, white infinity gave me the shivers and I held my sweetheart firmly in my arms under the coats and shawls with which we were covered."

The coachman stood on a little plank in the rear and prattled to the couple throughout the ride. He referred to Mileva as *Signora,* Mrs., which pleased her greatly.

"Can you think of anything more beautiful?" she asked.

They sleighed until they were famished and then headed back down the mountain. To Mileva and Albert's delight, the sleigh "produced avalanches to properly scare the world below."

The holiday lasted three days. A week later, Albert recalled to Mileva how delightful it had been "when I was allowed to press your dear little person to me in the way nature created it, let me tenderly kiss you for that, you dear, good soul!"

Despite the love that had been growing between them for two years, neither could have predicted the outcome of their Alpine holiday.

PART ONE

Mileva Marić's family lived in Vojvodina, a lavishly fertile region in the southern part of the Austro-Hungarian Empire, on the great Danubian plain. Watered by the second-longest river in Europe, the Danube, as well as the serpentine Tisa and Sava, vast prairies spread for miles in all directions. Where the Marićs lived, there were no hills, only rolling mounds on which a few meager acacia trees grew. Occasionally, a dirt road sliced, unswerving, through the verdant prairies. In spring and summer, green velvet fields unfolded like old damask cloth against the blue horizon. When the year curved toward winter and the earth had turned a deep umber, mauve, saffron, and reddish-colored plants punctuated the landscape.

Mileva's father, Miloš Marić, was born into a peasant family in the village of Kać in 1846, the year Neptune was discovered by Johann Galle in

Berlin and Auguste Laurent determined that the formula for water was H_2O.

At sixteen, Miloš began a military career as a guard in Titel, a thatched village of Serb, German, and Hungarian families fifty-five kilometers from Kać, where the Tisa meets the Danube. Because of the village's strategic military position in the Austro-Hungarian Empire, its guards were called defenders of the gates.

Serbia flowered late. In the fifteenth century, the Ottoman Turks attempted to snatch up Europe through Bulgaria and Serbia, and a characteristically Balkan unofficial but deliberate division ensued. Migration followed migration, and many people resettled in other regions of Eastern and Central Europe. The Kingdom of Serbia, with its own royal family, lay on the south side of the Danube, while the Vojvodina was on the north. When a Serb is asked about the history of his country, he will throw his arms wide as if to embrace the land, shrug his shoulders and say, "It is better to suffer injustice than to commit it."

Serbs on both sides of the Danube have always been a proud people. Reticence is their *modus vivendi*. Yet they are also a people of fury, imagination, and strongly held beliefs. Indeed, until just a hundred years ago, many village Serbs believed that the sky and the earth were linked by gigantic and sublime golden hooks that reached to the heavens from four cosmic mountaintops, rising from the four corners of a square earth. These hooks, they believed, anchored the earth to God.

The Roman Catholic Hapsburg rulers of the Austro-Hungarian Empire practiced a pragmatic religious tolerance. The Serbian frontier guards were allowed to remain Serbian Orthodox and were encouraged to consider themselves a class unto themselves—which afforded them Central European food and comforts, along with the freedom to practice their local traditions. These privileges distinguished the guards from their fellow countrymen—especially the peasants, who remained serfs.

Even though Miloš Marić left the fields for the military, he was still considered a peasant. He did not have the education necessary to advance in Serbian society. He probably never reached the seventh grade. Before he donned his army uniform with its shining brass buttons, he resembled the Bronze-age statues found buried in the fields of Vojvodina. He wore *opanci,* leather peasant sandals unchanged since the Dark Ages, fashioned from rough pieces of hide that curled over the toes and were held in place by straps hooking onto thick knitted socks. His baggy brown breeches and simple high-buttoned shirt were made of homespun flax and wool. On Sundays he wore a shirt with open-work embroidery of *lale,* tulips stitched with red, yellow, and green silk and worsted threads. Over these clothes he wore a waistcoat decorated with tarnished gold braid. Throughout his life, Miloš sported a large, bristly handlebar moustache that dangled loosely to his chin—a beard was rarely seen in the region.

In the nineteenth-century, the military operated much as it had for hundreds of years. At night, straw, food, and wine were distributed to the soldiers to take back to their tents. In the morning, after being awakened by drummers and buglers, the men would sit quietly and "tell their beads"—say their prayers. After a meager meal, they would set to work cleaning their weapons with tallow made from the fat of oxen and sheep—the smell of which would linger with them for the rest of the day.

Miloš quickly learned the language of his Austrian masters. This demonstration of linguistic ability encouraged the military to make him a minor official. The promotion was seminal to his rise in the world—making him one of the first of the Marić family to forsake the farmlands. He worked arduously to escape his native poverty, and eventually he accomplished this through the proverbial back door by marrying up. Miloš—handsome, intelligent, charming—had his pick of available maidens, and he chose Marija Ružić, daughter of a wealthy land-owning family. Miloš was twenty-two years old, and Marija twenty-one. The Ružić family lived on a huge estate, a mile long and half as wide, west of the main road in the village of Titel. In 1867, Miloš and Marija were married in a grand ceremony at the village church, Crkva Uspenja Presvete Bogorodice, Virgin Mary's Ascension.

In rural districts, couples married in order to continue their family lines, not because they had fallen in love. A wife's duty was to move into her husband's family home and cook and clean for his mother, father, and other relatives—in short, to be an indentured housekeeper. But Marija did not. Because Miloš had married into a higher class, he and Marija instead moved into her family's home.

Miloš's adopted village remembered him as a man who attracted notice. He strolled straight as a steeple down Titel's rutted dirt roads. When he was not in military uniform, he sported a *halbcilinder,* a sort of short top hat, and carried an ornate cane. Wearing a sorrel-colored English-style cape flung over Hungarian-style clothes, he appeared flamboyant. But Miloš was aloof and somber.

The Ružić family was devout. As a religious and community offering, Marija's grandfather Ružić ordered two enormous brass bells from Vienna for Titel's newly built church. The bells traveled by train through Central Europe, connecting in Budapest, then passing through the bountiful plains that surrounded Novi Sad and on to Kać, to Budisava, Šajkaš, Vilovo, Lok, finally stopping at Titel. Since the church was three kilometers from the train depot, a team of six oxen, their horns adorned with apples, and a wagon were brought from Ružić's ranch. The bells were loaded onto the wagon in silence. Ružić walked alongside as the small procession commenced its journey to the church. People from the village and countryside lined the dirt road and tossed brightly colored pieces of fabric at them. Ružić and the oxen were covered in color. At the church, the priest gave a *blagoslov,* a blessing, and sprinkled the bells with holy water. The bells were then hoisted up into the tower with ropes and installed by local carpenters. In two hours, they rang out over the village.

In the villages there were still traces of pagan worship of the sun, the moon, and the stars. Serbs believed that each man was assigned his own star, which appeared in the heavens at the exact moment of his birth and was snuffed out forever when he died. But the citizens of Titel understood that Ružić's star was special: His star, like his bells, would live on into eternity. During his lifetime Ružić never acknowledged his gift. Bragging was considered as impolite as speaking about family disgraces.

✧

After Miloš and Marija were married, tragedy ensued almost at once. Their first child, a daughter named Milica, was born in December but died within the year. Marija's visits to the graveyard, up the hill behind the church, became part of her daily ritual. She donned black mourning clothes, which she was to wear for the rest of her life. Her next child fulfilled the fervent wish of every Serb, *Rodio mi se sin,* a son was born to me. According to Serbian legend, witches eat babies, but they cannot attack wolves; so if the previous child had died, the next boy-child would be named Vukašin, wolf. Therefore, Marija's son was named Vukašin. But Vukašin also died—twenty-nine days later.

Mileva, the Marićs' first surviving child, was born in Titel on December 19, 1875, a sunny, bitterly cold day. Although, by then, Miloš was working in Kać, Marija had returned to her parents' home to give birth. Mileva was delivered by the village midwife, the widow Ana Konaček, and was considered a *seosko dete,* a village child, a child of the land. She was born on the birth date of St. Amvrosije the Mediolan. Amvrosije's father, like Mileva's, was a noncommissioned officer, in the service of the ruler of Galicia rather than that of the Hapsburgs. One day while still a child, Amvrosije had a vision that he would make a spiritual contribution to the Christian church. He told this only to his father. Later, on a summer afternoon, while he was sleeping under a shade tree, his mouth open, a swarm of bees landed on his tongue. His *nana* wanted to shoo them away but his father forbade her, wanting to see what would happen. Serbians believe that bees have religious significance. Church candles are made from beeswax—all substitutes are forbidden. The verb used to describe the death of a bee is the same used to describe the death of a man. Not a single bee stung the child. Instead, they left a gift of honey on his tongue. His father was now convinced that his son would become a great man.

Perhaps because their first two children had died so soon after birth, Mileva's parents did not wait the customary forty days to christen her— she was baptized the next day. The ceremony took place in Titel's village church with the glorious steeple that transfigured itself, three-quarters of the way up, into a graceful onion spire. Partly baroque, the little church had only one apse rather than three, on the east end. The altar was directly in front of the apse and hidden by the iconostasis—a tall screen decorated with icons. Suspended from the ceiling was an assortment of brass incense burners, black with age. This incense, known as *Tamjan,* is made from the sap of the Bosuellia plant and was introduced to the region by the Egyptians, who brought it by caravan from Southern Arabia. It filled the church with the sweet and pungent odor of thousands of seeds and grasses and flowers. Mileva was christened by Tanasije Popović, the priest who had married her parents.

Within a few days of her christening, it was evident that something was wrong with the child. When placed on her stomach, her left side appeared higher than her right. The family doctor confirmed that Mileva had a displaced left hip. This particular congenital condition had an endemically high incidence in the Balkans. It occurred in more than twenty percent of the population, primarily females, and almost always affected the left hip. Mileva's hip displacement was made worse by traditional swaddling, in which a child was packed inert, with the hips in extension and the legs bound tightly together—a practice that was believed to straighten the legs and keep the child peaceful.

A month after Mileva's birth, the Marić family moved to Vukovar, 122 kilometers west of Titel, where they lived for two years. By government decree, Miloš had been appointed an administrator for the royal court in the city. The family lived in a square-timbered cottage with a small orchard and a kitchen garden in the back. The timbered house, almost a perfect square, was constructed of small mud bricks packed between wooden uprights and whitewashed yearly with lime from a nearby quarry. *Čuvarkuća,* (a perennial plant with fleshy leaves and dense rosettes of purple and red flowers, which Serbs believed protected their homes from lightning, was planted along the eaves in long narrow wooden boxes.)

By 1877, Miloš was able to purchase a large property in Kać, adjacent to his family home. He bought nearly 642 acres of fields, meadows and marshes. Miloš spent vast amounts of money not only in Kać but also in Banja Luka, a town in Bosnia, where he purchased three farms. In addition, he built three substantial houses—in Titel, Novi Sad, and Kać—and would send all three of his children abroad to be educated. No one was able to identify the source of his wealth, for it was not indicated in the records of the Austro-Hungarian court system nor in any of the pertinent archives. In 1897, he did borrow from a Hungarian bank an undisclosed sum, which was due to be repaid in 1902. Later, he borrowed from the same bank another sizable sum, scheduled to be repaid in 1939. The bank's records show that both loans were repaid many years before they came due.

Soon after the Kać land purchase, Miloš ordered the construction of a summer residence—a large, two-story house with a cupola and ornate wooden embellishments along the eaves and crowning the windows. It was called Kula, The Spire, by everyone in the area and took many years to complete. A large brass bell in the cupola announced to the peasants who worked on the estate that their meals were ready. Surrounded by a fence of hedgerows and dotted with sour cherry trees, the property reminded visitors of a Russian *dacha*. Planted in the fields behind the house were hundreds of tidy rows of onions that guided one's eyes to the horizon.

While engaged in this expensive project, Miloš continued to work as a government official in the district court in Ruma, a city forty kilometers south of Novi Sad, where Mileva's sister, Zorka, was born in 1883. Zorka was also born with a displaced left hip. Two years later, the Marić's last child was born—at last, a living son. He was named Miloš, after his father.

Miloš began teaching his elder daughter nearly as soon as she left her mother's breast. By the time she entered school, at almost seven years of age, she was reading, doing simple mathematics on her favorite quadrille paper, and conversing fluently in Serbian and German. She learned to read music and play the *tamburica,* an ancient lutelike instrument from Asia, upon which she played her father's favorite folk songs. Mileva fit the traditional model of a firstborn—she was quiet and contemplative. She was also her father's favorite. In most Serbian households of the time, men spoke to each other at the evening meal and only the eldest woman present was allowed to participate. But in the Marić household, Mileva was encouraged to think and to voice her opinions, especially at the table. An only child for eight years, Mileva was the center of attention. Everyone in the family acknowledged and encouraged her obvious intelligence, hoping it would one day help her to overcome her physical handicap. When Mileva was with her family, she played without inhibition. But outside her family, she was quiet and withdrawn, keeping to herself, embarrassed by her short leg and the orthopedic shoe she had to wear.

In 1888, after Miloš had received another promotion, the Marićs moved south to Sremska Mitrovica, where Mileva attended the Royal

Lower Grammar School. Here her proclivity for math and physics became apparent. Her fourth-form tuition fees were waived because she was such an excellent student, especially in calculation and physics.

Miloš made one more career move, in the middle of May 1892, when he was appointed to the High Court of Justice. He was transferred to Zagreb, situated alongside the Sava River on the thickly wooded slopes of the Medvednica, "the place where the bears roam." Mileva was admitted to the sixth form of the all-male Obergymnasium, the Royal Classical High School, in Zagreb. She wanted to take a class in physics but was told she was not ready, even though boys with barely passing grades were accepted to the same class. Mileva completed her first year with honors. She was then grudgingly allowed to enter the physics class.

When Mileva finished gymnasium, in 1894, the Austro-Hungarian Empire still refused to allow female students to attend a university. Since she was too intelligent for the provinces and had outgrown all the schools in the Vojvodina, Mileva was sent to school in the West.

In November 1894, her father accompanying her, Mileva arrived in Zurich to study at Höhere Töchterschule, a preparatory school for girls. After two days, Miloš returned home, leaving Mileva as a boarder with the Bächtold family at Plattenstrasse 74. She was almost nineteen years old and completely isolated, not knowing anyone at her school.

Around this time, Miloš finally admitted to a debilitating weariness. Having battled rheumatic fever for many months, he retired after thirty-four years of government service. On January 28, 1896, Miloš moved to his beloved Spire in Kać, on a pension of 616 forints a year, a comfortable but not extravagant, amount.

✧

In Switzerland, Mileva was too shy to make friends, too introverted to enjoy anything except her studies and music. After completing the school year at Höhere Töchterschule in the spring of 1895, she briefly flirted with medicine at Zurich University before returning to her true academic loves, mathematics and physics. She was accepted as a student at the Polytechnikum in Zurich on her first attempt—it took Albert Einstein two. Mileva began in the fall of 1896, one of only twenty women in all the

Prussian and Swiss universities to study natural sciences and mathematics. She was the only woman in the physics and mathematics department at the Polytechnikum. There were four male students and one of them was Albert Einstein.

Mileva Marić and Albert Einstein became friends, attracted by a shared robust intellectual curiosity. Yet they were indubitable opposites. Albert was dashing, loquacious, wildly creative, and proudly proclaimed himself a bohemian. He described himself in the third person as "1.76 metres tall, with broad shoulders and a slight stoop. His short cranium gives the impression of being very broad. Complexion is light brown. A garish black moustache sprouts above his large and sensual mouth. The nose is rather aquiline. The very brown eyes radiate depth and softness. The voice is captivating like a vibrating cello." He also had varicose veins, flat feet, and excessive foot perspiration. Mileva was far more modest and practical. Yet she was also creative, a talented pianist, and a natural free-thinker. But her limp forever shadowed her self-confidence.

They circled each other for more than a year. Albert was persistent; Mileva was hesitant. By the spring of 1898, they had fallen deeply in love. But Mileva was distressed. She had never expected love. She came from a culture that categorized a limping woman as unmarriageable, so she had devoted herself to her studies and sought to succeed as a physicist in order to please her father. Consequently, in October of 1898, she made a dramatic attempt to escape the blossoming relationship. She fled to Germany to study at Heidelberg University, but endured the separation only until the following February, when she was drawn back to Zürich by her heart.

"I am very happy about your intention to continue your studies here again, just do it pretty soon. I am sure you will not regret it," Albert wrote her.

Mileva moved to Frau Engelbrecht's boarding house at Plattenstrasse 50—next door to the building where Johannes Brahms had lived only thirty-two years before—and began to make friends with the other female students who resided there. All of them were outstandingly intelligent women who had been sent by their progressive families to seek higher education. Two of Mileva's best friends were Helene Kaufler, from

Vienna, and Milana Bota, from Kruševac. Milana, in one of her frequent letters to her mother, said "the Marić girl visits us often, she is a very good young woman, but far too serious and quiet. One would not think she is a wise head." Three months later, Milana reported to her mother, "This morning Miss Marić came. She is a very good girl, and very intelligent and serious. She is small, petite, dark, unattractive, and speaks like a real Novi Sad woman. She limps a bit but has very nice manners. Well, that's her picture I'm happy she came."

Photographs of Mileva contradict Milana. They show her to be winsome-looking, with dark upswept hair. She is usually dressed in soft white cotton shirtwaists with high lace collars. Her mouth curves ever so slightly in a smile, and with large black eyes that project intense intelligence, she appears mysteriously pretty. In Serbia, a young maiden is often compared to a tree, as in the saying, "among the brothers was a sister like a fir-tree." Mileva was just five feet tall and as thin as a willow.

In Mileva's eyes, Albert was perfect, the center of "my business and my society." Their notes and letters soon moved from friendship to passion, and they began using pet names for each other. "Dear Miss Marič" and "Esteemed Miss" became "Dear Doxerl," a diminutive for Dolly, and "My dear Johannzel," or Johnnie. Mileva considered Albert her best friend. And sometime during the spring of 1899, their relationship became intimate. Albert was twenty, Mileva almost twenty-four.

They fancied themselves a bohemian couple, true to each other's notions of independence. Albert encouraged Mileva "to be wild like a street urchin," and called her "my wild little rascal," "my little beast." He spoke for them both when he said that they did not like "the philistine life any longer. He who tasted freedom cannot stand the chains any longer. How lucky I am to have found in you a creature who is my equal, who is as strong and independent as I am myself!" Soon after, Albert wrote, "Is this not a journeyman's or even a gypsy's life [that we lead]? But I believe that we'll remain cheerful in it as ever."

Though she desired to embrace progressive ideals, when Mileva surrendered to a sexual liaison with Albert, she was taking an enormous risk. She put her future career in jeopardy and pregnancy would mean being judged a *kurva,* a whore, by her family and friends.

Albert and Mileva devised ways to be alone together. In Frau Engelbrecht's boarding house, Mileva arranged to live by herself on the fourth floor, while her friends occupied rooms on the floor below. After a while the couple's intimacy began to bother Milana, who complained that "Mica [Mileva] and I rarely get together because of that German of hers whom I hate."

At the onset of summer 1899, Albert and Mileva returned home to their respective parents. But they wrote each other love letters filled with sexual innuendo.

"From the series of our joint experiences," wrote Mileva, "a peculiar feeling has formed surreptitiously, which is awakened at the slightest touch, even without the recollection of any particular detail becoming conscious, and which makes it seem each time as if I were again in my room."

Albert tweaked Mileva's modesty, telling her that he "read [her] letter in the quiet little chamber, then twice more and then for a long time I kept reading between the lines with great delight and then I slid it grinning in the pocket." Albert was far more candid about his passion than Mileva, telling her how glad he was to know that she was "home with [her] good old lady, who is marvelously fattening up my little Doxerl, so that she will rest again in my arms plump as a dumpling and healthy and cheerful. . . . I think I have not been able to kiss you for a whole month and I thoroughly long after you."

True to the mythos of Serbian love, Mileva suffered. Serbia's lore is steeped in tragedy and romance—romance of war, of the land, between men and women. The Serbian folktale about Vukosav's wife is emblematic of the ideal of female devotion. Vukosav, a young outlaw, was captured by a Turkish lord. He was put in a deep, moldy dungeon and left to rot. When his wife finally heard of his plight she went to the local barber and told him, "Shave my hair. Leave only a pigtail like those that the warriors wear." Then the wife went home and donned a warrior's red and purple surcoat and shining silver armor. She chose a strong white steed and placed on his back an ornate silver saddle that chimed with bells on his back. She hung a row of pearls and gems around his neck to shine and light the way to her husband. Holding her stave firmly in front of her, she rode off to the house of the Turkish lord. After much travail and elaborate maneuvers, the wife saved her husband from the dungeon and "they kissed heartily and turned their back on the Constantinople road, taking the other one to the coast land. They rode on, gay and happy."

Schooled in the heroic suffering of romantic love, which pervades Serbian myth and literature, Mileva, during her separation from Albert, composed a ballad of her own:

> Quietly the water carries the little boat,
> Further and further away.
> As if through a fog, I still see my sweet native land,
> My sweet native land.
> A cold wind is blowing and makes waves through the water,
> And my poor sick heart is gripped by the cold,
> Gripped by the cold, by the cold.

During the early years of their courtship, Albert supported Mileva emotionally and intellectually. "One kisses equally well as a little doctor and professor," he teased her.

The couple dreamed of becoming a fine pair of scientists, often speaking as one person. "According to *our theory of molecular forces,* there must exist an approximate proportionality between *our constants* Σc_α and the molecular volumes of the liquids," Albert wrote (emphasis added).

They were an ideal team. Albert set sail in his imagination, navigating through inspired concepts, while Mileva had the gift of logic and pragmatic reasoning.

During a visit to his parents in Milan in April 1901, Albert wrote Mileva, "I have an extremely lucky idea, which will make it possible to apply *our theory of molecular forces* to gases as well. I can hardly await the outcome of this investigation. If it leads to something, we will know almost as much about the molecular forces as about the gravitational forces" (emphasis added).

On the same trip, Albert gave "our paper" to Professor Giuseppe Jung at the Istituto Tecnico Superiore di Milano, but signed it with his name only. When later asked why her name was not on some of their collective work, Mileva punned, "Why? We are, two of us only, *ein Stein,* one stone!" In love, Albert declared how "happy and proud I will be when the two of us together will have brought *our work on the relative motion* to a victorious conclusion!" (emphasis added). The work he refers to in this 1901 letter was, in 1905, to become known as Einstein's Special Theory of Relativity.

There is debate among historians about the extent of Mileva's participation in Albert's scientific work. Abram F. Joffe, a Russian scientist, wrote in *Meetings with Physicists: My Reminiscences of Foreign Physicists,* that three original manuscripts, including the one describing the Special Theory of Relativity, were signed "Einstein-Marity." Many years later, Mileva and Albert's son Hans Albert told Peter Michelmore, an Einstein biographer, that Mileva helped Albert "solve certain mathematical problems, but nobody could assist with the creative work, the flow of fresh ideas."

However, Mileva's friend Milana Bota Stefanovic gave an interview to a Belgrade journalist, Misa Sretenovic, in 1929. "[Mileva] would be the most qualified to give information about the genesis of his [Einstein's] theory, since she herself participated in its creation. Five or six years ago, [Mileva] was telling me about that, but with pain. Maybe it is hard for her to recollect those most precious moments, maybe she does not wish to kill the great voice of her former husband."

✧

For Mileva, the new century did not dawn auspiciously. In July 1900, she failed to receive the necessary grade point average of 5.0 for graduation. She received a mark of 4.0, while her four fellow students in the physics and mathematics department scored an average of 5.0 or more. After years of working toward a degree, after all the money her father had spent on her education, Mileva failed. She received the same score as Albert in experimental physics, a 10; he received a 10 in theoretical physics, Mileva a 9; he earned a 5 in astronomy, she a 4. In the theory of functions, however, Albert scored an 11, while Mileva scored only a 5. It was the first significant indignity that Mileva brought upon her family.

Even though Mileva had failed to earn her degree, Albert insisted that they continue working together. "How proud I will be when maybe

I'll have a little doctor for a sweetheart while I am myself still a totally ordinary man," he encouraged her in September 1900.

Mileva persevered. She continued her research and the writing of
her *Diplomarbeit,* a dissertation on the topic of thermoconduction, in the
hope of completing her doctorate, knowing that a Polytechnikum grad-
uate could receive a doctorate from Zurich University without further
examination.

During the same year, Albert received his diploma as a teacher of
mathematics. Now that he was qualified to teach, he would have the
means to marry Mileva. But Albert's mother, Pauline Einstein, had un-
equivocally expressed her displeasure at the prospect. Home for a visit, Albert had "innocently" declared his intention to marry Mileva. His "mama
threw herself on the bed, buried her head in the pillow, and cried like a
child. After she had recovered from the initial shock, she immediately
switched to a desperate offensive, insisting that 'You are ruining your future and blocking your path through life.' " Both of Albert's parents
adamantly refused to give their approval.

"She is a book like you. When you [are] thirty, she will be an old hag,"
Pauline persisted. "She is not healthy."

Albert wanted to please his mother. He wanted to please his father,
too, but he knew Hermann would capitulate if Pauline changed her
mind. And he continued to profess his love for Mileva.

"They both love me and are so disconsolate, as if I had committed the
greatest crime," he complained to Mileva. "[T]hey mourn me as if I had
died. But without the thought of you, I would not want to live any longer
in this sorry human crowd. . . . [P]ossessing you makes me proud and
your love makes me happy. I will be doubly happy when I can press you
to my heart again and see your loving eyes, which shine for me alone, and
kiss your dear mouth, which trembled in bliss for me alone."

Mileva's parents, on the other hand, encouraged the relationship.
After all, in Vojvodina there were roughly eight hundred men to every
thousand women. "They were happy that a beautiful man had fallen
in love with their daughter who had such an ugly defect," a family
friend, Milenko Damjanov, noted. They *expected* their daughter to be
fierce about her love for Albert. But they would not have approved had

they known Mileva had already "given a shirt," an expression derived from a folk song that goes: *A girl. A girl gave birth to a girl | In Banok, in Bjelopavliće. | She called to everyone | To everyone she gave a shirt,* meaning, she had engaged in premarital sex. Marriage was considered a divine sacrament and the only possible condition in which sexual intercourse could take place. The birth of illegitimate children was almost unheard of in the Marić's social circle. Mileva's mother would admonish her, "Better to know how to behave than to have gold."

✧

Deeply committed to each other, the young couple, both residing in Zurich, were forced to live apart, continually nervous about money, about their parents.

"Neither of us two has gotten a job," Albert wrote to their friend Helene Kaufler, "and we support ourselves by private lessons—when we can pick up some, which is still very questionable."

Mileva's father had made it clear to her that he would not support her financially if she did not stay in school. Albert's parents had never supported him at all. His tuition and living expenses were paid by other family members. Now both Albert and Mileva began to look for jobs. She applied for a teaching position in a girl's gymnasium in Zagreb but was turned down. Albert joked about his many applications for employment: "Soon I will have honored all physicists from the North Sea to the southern tips of Italy with my offer."

Perhaps it was because of his job anxiety that Albert became moody. He broke dates with Mileva. He began to flirt with her friends at Frau Engelbrecht's. The couple had been planning a three-day holiday to Lake Como. Mileva had even informed her parents of the journey. Now she was fed up.

Albert went ahead to Como, probably intending to visit his parents first.

"But it is only because of nervousness that I was so awful to you," he protested. "You must absolutely come to see me in Como, sweet little witch." Mileva refused.

Then she received a letter from her parents that "robs me of all desire, not only for having a good time but for life itself." Her parents did not approve of the holiday. They were upset that Mileva was more interested in Albert than in her studies. It was improper for an unmarried woman to travel alone with a man. Instead of furthering her resolve to cancel the trip, the letter from her parents incited Mileva to rebel. She changed her mind. She accepted Albert's apologies and met him at Lake Como. Six weeks later, Mileva discovered she was pregnant.

✧

"[O]ne has to be patient," Albert pleaded. "You just have to be patient! You will see that one doesn't rest badly in my arms, even if it starts a little stupidly. How are you, love? How is the boy?"

Albert teased Mileva about the gender of their unborn child. She wanted a girl named Lieserl; he wanted a boy named Hans Albert.

"If only we could be together carefree and in good cheer for once, without any pressure on us," Albert lamented. "I believe that you cannot imagine yourself in such a situation any more than I can, you good poor girl."

They were *sa jabukom,* with the apple, and not married, and so they decided to keep the pregnancy a secret for as long as they could.

✧

Mileva and Albert had been involved for more than two years, and Albert had yet to meet her parents. This was not the Serbian way. Miloš and Marija began to distrust him. He was a mystery to them. They were afraid of him: He was too clever; he was German; he was Jewish.

Jews were a distinct minority in the villages of Vojvodina. Only in 1867 had the Jews of the Austro-Hungarian Empire, including Vojvodina, been granted equal rights and full legal protection. Although an unspoken separation existed, anti-Semitism was not prevalent among the Serbs. Wherever there was a Catholic majority, especially in German and Hungarian neighborhoods, there were incidents of anti-Semitism, but the Orthodox Church was tolerant and not openly prejudiced against Jews.

In the villages of the Vojvodina, Jews knew their place, and did not participate in the Orthodox citizenry's life. They did their jobs—typically as shoemakers, tailors, doctors, veterinarians, and innkeepers—and kept to themselves, almost always on a *Jevrejska Ulica,* Jewish Street.

In both Titel, where Marija was born, and Kać, where Miloš was born, Jewish families owned the local general stores and often inns or guesthouses. Adjacent to the inns were stables for the horses. And behind each inn was a cave carved into the earth that was used as a natural ice freezer. Each winter, large chunks of ice were chiseled from the rivers Tisa and Danube and transported on wooden flat-bed drays to the mouths of these caves. There, they were cut into smaller blocks and lowered into the storage areas by pulleys and ropes. This form of refrigeration allowed the shopkeepers to preserve food in the summer months. Mileva's family frequented the general stores and were polite to the Jewish families, but they considered them as mysterious and alien as they did Albert Einstein.

✧

Pauline Einstein, meanwhile, was waging a full-frontal campaign against the proposed marriage. Mileva's Balkan ancestors were considered backward by many Central and Western Europeans.

"That woman cannot gain entrance to a decent family," Pauline protested to Albert. She claimed that the Marić family was "common."

Albert's father, Hermann, was quiet and passive. Time and again, his lack of business sense heaped financial burdens on his family. He was hopelessly manipulated by Pauline. Pauline said no to Mileva—so Hermann said no. Finally, Pauline issued a bitter warning to Albert: "If she gets a child, you'll be in a pretty mess." But she would soon learn that Albert had ignored her warning.

✧

In Vojvodina, the age-old principles of morality and appropriate behavior had remained unchanged for centuries. There was no question—if a woman had an intimate relationship with a man, even without becoming pregnant, she had to marry him or be considered a discarded woman whom no man would ever again desire. In contrast, not only was the man not required to marry the woman with whom he engaged in sex, he met with no censure whatsoever.

Mileva had three choices—suicide, a life of perpetual shame, or abortion. Suicide among unmarried pregnant women was not infrequent. Albert begged Mileva not to "get any silly ideas." Shame, *sramota,* was a thorny issue. Serbians fervently believe that "blood is not water"—a family member will never be abandoned or ignored. So Mileva knew her parents ultimately would support her, no matter the circumstances. But the shame that was the price of their support would cripple the family's honor for generations.

At the turn of the century, Serbian women practiced two methods of abortion. The more common one involved drinking a boiling concoction of the strongest *rakija,* a brandy distilled from plums, grapes, or other fruits, and a quantity of gunpowder. Hot bricks or bottles would be applied to the abdomen as the drink was taken. The other method was to drink a boiling-hot distillation of oleander and basil leaves, and then immerse oneself in a scorching hot bath. Mileva may have tried these remedies in Zurich, with no success.

In the end, Mileva desperately needed her mother. Photographs of Marija show a woman with thick, gnarled hands who apparently worked in her own kitchen and helped the servants clean the house. It is thought that she was illiterate. She was certainly not sophisticated, for she wore an old-fashioned *marama,* a kerchief of thick white cotton, low on her forehead, simple black clothing, and practical shoes. Mileva's mother would not have condoned an abortion. In the Orthodox tradition if a woman has an abortion, she cannot take communion. Mileva would have been eternally estranged from God.

No abortion. No suicide. No marriage. There was only one choice. Mileva could only bring shame upon her family.

✧

The previous April, before Mileva became pregnant, Albert had informed her that he had been promised a provisional position in the Office for the Protection of Intellectual Property, the patent office, in Bern. Perhaps the prospect of Albert's employment was the reason the couple tossed caution out the *pensione* window in the ravishing mountains of Italy. They knew the job would solve their problem—it was a good position, with a salary of 3,500 Swiss francs, which meant they could afford to marry without the approval of their parents. It was certainly good enough for two bohemians and a baby. However, it could take months for this position to be approved and advertised. In the meantime, Mileva and Albert fretted themselves into a panic.

"I will look *immediately* for a position, no matter how humble," Albert promised. "My scientific goals and my personal vanity will not prevent me from accepting the most subordinate role. The moment I have obtained such a position, I will marry you and take you to me without writing anyone a single word." In May, he took a temporary position as a tutor at the Technical School in Winterthur.

Even before the two families learned of the pregnancy, they were angry with Mileva and disappointed with Albert. They knew that the couple was spending an improper amount of time together alone. *Majka plače, majka plače,* mother is weeping, mother is weeping, Mileva heard from home. Mileva knew this to be her mother's song of sighs. *Stala zmiji na rep*—Mileva had "stepped on a snake's tail." Even her beloved father told her she must live illegally with him. "You are not to bring the bastard [Albert] home," he was heard to say. Now Mileva was too ashamed to ask her parents for financial help.

While waiting for a permanent position, Albert continued to teach students in nearby Winterthur, eight kilometers from Zurich, and Mileva prepared to retake her final examination, the *Diplom.* She was ill with morning sickness and unable to eat very much. Struggling with her research, she also wrestled with her academic requirements, fretted about her parents, and was obsessed with her relationship with Albert.

"I cannot help but love him very much, quite frightfully much, especially when I see that he loves me just as much," she confided to Helene.

Mileva planned to face her family in Kać in August, after her final exams. By then, she would be four months pregnant.

"My parents are now probably in a better mood," Mileva wrote in July to Albert, who was on holiday with his mother at the Hotel Paradise in Mettmenstetten. "Wouldn't you like to come along, it would make me happy! When they see the two of us in the flesh in front of them, all their misgivings will evaporate."

But Albert declined. "Good luck on your exams," he replied from a veranda overlooking the small mountain of Albis.

While studying, Mileva wrote Albert again, "I am joyfully waiting for Sunday, when I can see you again and kiss you in the flesh and not only in my thoughts, and almost the way my heart commands it and everywhere, everywhere."

But again Mileva failed her exams. Again she scored a 4, while the other four students scored 5 or more and qualified for teaching certificates. Despondent, she terminated her research. In August, she left the Polytechnikum for good.

✧

A few days after receiving her final grades, Mileva departed for Vojvodina, traveling with a friend, Auguste Buček. Auguste, a medical student who also lived in Frau Engelbrecht's boarding house, was returning to her home in Croatia. The late summer was sultry, unbearably hot. A thick mist rose from Lake Zurich as the train chugged past. Their carriage was stifling, and fashion made the heat even more unbearable. Women were laced tightly into corsets. Each day that Mileva appeared in public, she would have had to draw the strings of her corset as tight as possible, the long ivory stays confining her bad hip, making it even more difficult for her to walk.

Yet her corseted waist spared Mileva from having to explain her pregnancy to Auguste, who "does not suspect the mixed feelings with which I am going on this trip." Mileva would alone have to tell her "parents the necessary news, the disagreeable part included."

Thirty-six hours after leaving Zürich, Mileva arrived in Novi Sad, where it was even hotter and more humid. The Marić family's coachman fetched her at the station to drive her to the Spire. As they crossed the edge of the city and headed toward the unfolding yellow plains, the temperature dropped, and Mileva finally had a respite from the suffocating heat.

She told her parents the truth. One can only imagine the scene.

✧

Just over a month later, on September 15, 1901, Albert was hired as a tutor at the Lehr-und Erziehungsanstalt, a private boarding school, in Schaff-hausen, fifty-four kilometers northeast of Zurich. Mileva seems to have faded away. There are no letters between them from the beginning of September until early November, which was highly unusual, as they always wrote to each other when apart. Perhaps there were letters and they were destroyed—but why these particular letters and not others that were in-timate and potentially embarrassing? Perhaps Mileva was with Albert part of the time, traveling from Kać to Zurich to Schaffhausen and back to Kać.

In October on a trip to Zurich, during which she stayed at Frau En-gelbrecht's, Mileva wrote a letter to her friend Helene who was on holi-day in Schächen, Switzerland. She was replying to a letter in which Helene had complained about being pregnant with her first child.

Mileva insisted, "You should be happy, full of joy, not complaining" and went on to lecture Helene: [Y]our little one will mean the whole world to you [even though] she is pushing you around so much inside your belly. Once you have it, everything will be okay again and you will not have much time to be unhappy because you should be happy and full of joy and not feeling sorry for yourself like it says in your letter. What will your dear husband say to that? Now I am starting to shout at you. Those are the kind of problems and nuisances that one has to put up with when you are pregnant and I would really like to be by your side for an hour and talk and chat with you . . . from the heart."

Mileva never mentioned her own pregnancy. Instead, her focus was on Albert. "My dear one is far away from me once again and that is very hard for me, so hard that it makes my life bitter," she wrote. Albert's "let-ters are nothing alive. They do not look at me, they do not say anything like the mouth does, and to that I've gotten used to. Oh, Helene, please pray for me to St. Peter that I can have him all alone for me at once and that I don't need to be away from him ever again. I love him very much."

Mileva concluded the letter once she was back in Kać, declaring that she must "go soon to Switzerland because of a position. If I can arrange it, I will come to visit you in Schächen. My being able to do so depends on a lot of things. I cannot tell you anything for sure." But there was no job prospect. And she had no intention of visiting Helene.

Even if Mileva was planning to travel again from Kać to Switzerland during this period, she certainly would have remained home with her mother, who was very religious, for the autumn holiday of *Zadušnice*—feast day of the dead—that in 1901 fell on October 26.

Traditionally, on the day of the feast, the women of the household rise early, and soon the house is filled with the smell of baking bread. Small, flat, round loaves called *poskurice* are set out on wooden tables and stamped with the Old Church Slavic letters IC, for Jesus, XC, for Christ, HI, for Our Savior—and KA, for the Curse of Adam. The eldest daughter at home walks through the village and distributes the loaves to friends and family members. But Mileva, though the eldest, was six months pregnant and in disgrace. Consequently, her sister, Zorka, would have done the honors. Each time a loaf was given, Zorka would have said, "In their everlasting memory! May God absolve their souls." When Zorka returned home, the Marić family—probably leaving Mileva behind—would have set off for the graveyard. There, Marija would have placed a few loaves of bread, some food, and a bottle of their Kać-grown wine on the family grave. The village priest would have passed among the family graves and recited his blessing for the souls of the dead: "Bless, O Lord, this our food and drink! Come, let us partake of it in memory of all departed souls! Amen."

✧

On approximately November 1, Mileva boarded the Ostend Express once again and traveled two days from Novi Sad back to Zurich. She was unable to remain at home in Vojvodina, unable to stay away from Albert. Instead, she stayed with her friend Milana Bota, at Frau Engelbrecht's boarding house. As was her daily ritual, Milana wrote to her mother, saying that Mileva had "passed her doctorate and is searching for a position in Zagreb."

But Mileva had not passed her doctorate. Indeed, she had formally left the university as a student more than a year earlier. The conflicting stories suggest that Mileva was obscuring the truth from everyone—to her best friend, Helene, to Milana, possibly even to herself. An unmarried pregnant woman in her third term would not have found a job as a teacher in 1901, whether in Switzerland or in Zagreb, where another friend from the boarding house, Ada Broh, ran her own school. No institution would have hired her in her condition. By now, Mileva must surely have been showing. *U laži su kratke noge,* the lie has short legs.

"God only knows why the couple doesn't get married," Milana Bota wrote to her mother on the last line of the first page of her letter. But the next page—and any further comment—is gone. The page is missing from Ivana Stefanovic's personal collection in Belgrade.

Although it appeared that everyone knew about it, Mileva still attempted to hide her pregnancy. Mileva left Zurich again. On Friday, November 8, she arrived in the Swiss village of Stein am Rhein, fifty-four kilometers north of Zurich and eighteen kilometers from Albert who was teaching in Schaffhausen. From a distance, Stein am Rhein looks like a grove of trees. Aged, almost black half-timbered houses with slab-like shingled roofs line both sides of the Rhine waterfront. The village smells of water-soaked wood and melting snow. As one walks into the village, each dwelling is wondrously transformed by an ornate oriel window, a dazzling fresco—even tiny sheds are adorned.

When Mileva disembarked, she crossed Bahnhofstrasse to the moderately priced Hotel Steinerhof. The hotel was a four-story stone rectangle with dormers that made the small rooms on the top floor seem larger than they were. The dormer rooms were for the pension patrons. Mileva was one of those patrons, paying two Swiss francs per night, including meals.

The situation seemed perfect. Albert could easily visit her, arriving after a brief train ride and walking a short distance to her room. In his absence, Mileva could take leisurely walks across the Rhine Bridge to the Rathausplatz, the medieval town center. But soon there were signs of trouble. Albert had agreed to meet her on November 6, but backed out at the last moment.

"I am angry with the cruel fate which ordained that tomorrow I must sit alone," Mileva wrote to him. "Please don't tell your sister, Maya, that I am here, because I am afraid your parents will find out. Only no further tempests, it makes me shudder even to think about it. The present peace and quiet is so nice and beneficial. Tell them I am in Germany."

Mileva had little more to do than read, take walks, and wait for Albert. And because he was teaching every day, his visits were rare.

"I will write to Helene," she suggested in the same letter. "She's surely
got her tiny one by now." And then she added, "I don't think we should
say anything about Lieserl yet; but you too should write [Helene] a few
words now and then, we must now treat her very nicely, she will have to
help us in something important, after all."

Though Helene did not yet know of Mileva's pregnancy, Mileva and
Albert clearly thought they might soon need her help—perhaps in arranging a private adoption. Legal adoption in Vojvodina was almost un-
heard of. More likely, a child would have been absorbed into the fold of
its extended family, raised by relatives as their own. Albert and Mileva may
have hoped that Helene would find a home for their child with one of her
four sisters.

A week later, on November 13, Albert broke another date with Mileva.

"Let me tell you," Mileva wrote in response, "if you are not coming
at all, then I will run away all of a sudden! I have already stored up such
a lot of kisses, if the cup runs over, all will go away." Albert did not change
his plans.

Mileva had no choice, it seemed, but to "run away"—return home—
and this time there would be no hiding her condition from the community. Ultimately, the midwife would know and would report it to the
record office. *Kakva sramota!* What shame! Mileva would bring more grief
and disgrace upon the Marić lineage. *Sve se može oprati, samo obraz ne!* Everything can be washed off, except the stains on one's honor. Nevertheless,
Mileva made plans to go home and bear the stigma alone.

✧

On the morning of Thursday, November 14, 1901, Mileva Marić left the
Hotel Steinerhof in the rain and followed the Bahnhofstrasse to the train
station, where she took the 7:22 Swiss Railway to Zurich. Less than an
hour later, the train stopped in Schaffhausen. Had they arranged to
meet—which seems unlikely given their correspondence—they would
have had only thirty-four minutes together before the train departed
again. Mileva arrived in Zurich an hour later, walked from one side of the

tracks to the other, and boarded the 10:30 train for Vienna. The trip was dreadfully long for a woman in her condition, and the red velvet seats stuffed with horse-hair were quite uncomfortable. She would arrive in Vienna the next morning at 7:50 and have to change, yet again, to an express train, the Austro-Hungarian Railway to Budapest. She would arrive at Budapest's Keleti Station at 2:51 in the afternoon where she would change trains for the line to Novi Sad, thirty-one hours after she had begun her journey—with five more hours of travel before her.

Once outside the Budapest city limits, the train whistled past stilled water mills and empty fields and passed over brown swamps, through groves of willow trees stripped of their leaves and reedy marshlands, toward Vojvodina and the blue-tinted lands of her home. As evening arrived, the porter lighted the cobalt-blue acetylene lamps, casting a cold light upon the compartments until at last, at 7:48, the train pulled into Novi Sad. It was still raining, and the unpaved station yard had turned to mud. With the help of a driver, Mileva loaded her belongings into a *Fijaker,* a horse-drawn carriage with a black leather top that still smelled like the cow it used to be. They drove over the Turkish cobblestones, stopping for the red-and-cream-colored horse-drawn trams. They turned right onto Futoška Street, the creaking of the heavy wagon axles announcing their arrival, proceeded past the synagogue on *Jevrejska Ulica,* to Glavna Street, passing in front of the Serbian Orthodox Church, to Cuřcinska (street of the furriers), and turned left on Kisačka Street—home. Mileva's mother would have greeted her inside the front door, standing before the icon of the family's saint, St. Stefan the Martyr. Mileva was feeling unwell and immediately went to bed.

✧

On the day Mileva came home, a smart, good-looking young man from her region of Vojvodina, engaged to be married to a girl as beautiful as himself, was murdered for making his betrothed pregnant. The killing, probably committed by the girl's family, was unspeakably brutal, yet the young man's father refused to file charges. If he did, he would place his entire family in jeopardy. They too might be killed and their house burned to the ground. Although there were laws against murder, a family could be made to suffer for a family member's "criminal" behavior. Tradition granted a family the right to settle such matters outside the criminal justice system.

Within a couple of days of her return, Mileva wrote Albert to say that her parents had calmed down and were now more willing to trust him and give their blessing to a marriage.

"Their Miezel [Mileva] will get a good husband as soon as this becomes feasible," Albert responded.

Two weeks later, Mileva was still in bed. It was winter, cold, and she was writing to Albert again, softening her condition to alleviate his worry.

"You were so nice to write me from bed," Albert wrote. "But I am not worried at all, because I see from your good mood that the problem is not so serious."

On December 11, six weeks before the child was due, Albert heard that the position at the Swiss patent office was finally advertised. Now he could submit his application—as a formality, for the job had already been promised to him.

"In two months' time," he wrote, "we would suddenly find ourselves in splendid circumstances and our struggle would be over. I am dizzy with joy when I think of it. I am even happier for you than for myself."

A few sentences later, he says, "The only problem that would remain to be solved would be how to have our Lieserl with us." Even if Albert was awarded the position, an illegitimate child could pose problems such as threatening his job or damaging his reputation. He continues, however, "I would not like for us to have to part with her. Ask your father about what to do about the baby, he is an experienced man and knows the world better than your impractical bookworm Johonzel." His reluctance to take responsibility for the child, while engaging Miloš Marić's help, suggests that Albert was coming to regard adoption as a viable option.

Compounding the situation, Albert's parents were now intervening directly. Around this time, the Marićs received a letter, probably written by Pauline but signed jointly with her husband, presumably confronting Mileva's family with their knowledge of the pregnancy. The letter is now lost, but in a letter written to Helene Savić around December 12, Mileva did not complain about her discomforts or anxieties; she complained about the "charming behavior of my dear mother-in-law! That lady seems to have made it her life's goal to embitter as much as possible not only my life but also that of her son. Oh, Helene, I would not have thought it possible that there could exist such heartless and outright wicked people! Without further ado they found it in their heart to write a letter to my parents in which they reviled me to such an extent that this was really a shame." Mileva's use of *sram,* shame, could refer either to the dishonor of the Marić family or to the behavior of the Einsteins.

✧

"Long live impudence!" Albert wrote to Mileva in December 1901. "It's my guardian angel in this world."

His avowed disregard of the opinion of others should have made it easy for him to marry Mileva no matter the circumstances and in spite of his mother's objections. Certainly, it would have mitigated the shamefulness of the situation and made it clear that he truly desired his child. Yet he never came to Novi Sad, nor did he display a willingness to do so. Nor did he follow through on his proposal, made a couple of months earlier, to marry Mileva in secret and present their parents "with the *fait accompli* [to which] they [would] just have to reconcile themselves . . ."

Mileva's tolerance of the situation was likely the result of her reluctance to do anything that could irritate him and jeopardize their relationship. Her physical handicap, coupled with Serbian social conventions, would have made her sensitive to the possibility of spinsterhood and of a life spent in isolation with her family.

As for Albert, perhaps he wished Mileva would simply go away, leave him alone. His future relationships with women suggest as much. But for now, at age twenty-two, Albert would not think of marrying Mileva without his father's approval. He would avoid the marriage as long as Hermann was alive.

✧

On a Sunday afternoon in December, a powerful earthquake centered in Zagreb rocked Vojvodina. Not a house in Zagreb escaped damage. The earthquake was especially strong in the neighborhood of the Stenjevac, the local mental hospital. The upper floors of the hospital started breaking apart, causing a panic among the nuns and inmates. Doctors worked hard to calm the patients and prevent them from running away. And at the moment the quake struck, a soldier's funeral was taking place two hundred and seventy kilometers away in Novi Sad's central cemetery. As the soldier's coffin was lowered into the grave, the earth began to shake, and the mourners became hysterical.

On that day, Mileva traveled to Titel with her mother. (On December 12, Albert wrote Mileva in Novi Sad and asked her to give her parents his warm good wishes. On December 17, he wrote to her in Titel and asked her to give his best wishes to her mother. Had her father been with them, Albert surely would have included him in the greeting.)

A decision had been made, probably by Miloš Marić, for Mileva's baby to be born in the Ružić house where she herself had been born. Even though all three houses—in Novi Sad, Kać, and Titel—were under construction, the one in Titel was the quietest and the most private.

Ancient superstitions abounded in the rural provinces of Vojvodina. Varied and elaborate admonitions were heeded to ward off the persistent threat of bad luck. One should not keep a black cat in the house when it thunders; one should not cut down an oak or cherry tree; one should not hear a cuckoo for the first time on an empty stomach. The sight of a hare could bring evil, as could stepping over the rope of a tethered horse. It was into this provincial atmosphere that Mileva and her mother settled to await the birth of a child conceived in Zurich's richly educated and European society.

✧

On December 18, Albert, having been a legal citizen of the canton of Zurich since February, formally applied for and was awarded the position of Engineer Class II at the Federal Office for Intellectual Property, the Swiss patent office.

"Now there is no longer any doubt about it," he wrote to Mileva. "Our troubles have now come to an end." He made no mention of the baby.

December 19, Mileva's twenty-sixth birthday, was uncommonly

warm. The newspaper reported that "the weather was joking," though locals warned that *vuk nije pojeo zimu,* the wolf did not eat the winter, meaning that the warm weather could not be trusted, for it would not last long.

On the same day, the newspaper reported the flight of a professor and his son from the Austro-Hungarian Empire in a balloon that ascended thirty-five hundred meters above the earth. The professor was ostensibly studying how birds fly; he took three birds up with him in a cage and released them when they reached the proper altitude. But the real reason for his ascent was to study the effects of altitude on his and his son's blood.

While Mileva was reading about such events in the Novi Sad newspaper, Albert read about them in Bern. He missed Mileva's birthday, as he had done in the past, failing to remember it until the following day, when he wrote her a letter, which she would not receive until the twenty-third. Mileva did not seem to mind, and on the twenty-fourth sent him a surprise package of sweets and tobacco.

"Mr. Djurić's apricot tree has blossomed and was flowering today," the Novi Sad newspaper reported the next day. "Such a surprise that this happened right before *Očevi,* Father's Day!" According to the Serbian Orthodox calendar, Father's Day takes place one week before Christmas, which is celebrated on January 6. Miloš probably arrived in Titel in time for Father's Day. On this day, Serbian children traditionally tie their father's hands with soft wool, while he promises them presents if they release him. After much teasing and laughter, the children untie his hands and he gives them sweets, fruits, and money. Father's Day was probably not celebrated in the Marić household in 1901.

Meanwhile, Albert was again in Mettmenstetten, hundreds of kilometers away from Mileva. This time he was with his sister at the Hotel Paradise, enjoying the snow and the silence and an "intimate winter solitude."

"All the time I rejoice in the fine prospects which are in store for us in the near future," Albert enthused in a December 28 letter, the last one written before the birth of their child. "Have I already told you how rich we will be in Bern? 3,500 fr. is the minimum salary the position pays according to the advertisement, but it increases to 4,500." But, he added,

"Ehrat [a friend] thinks, though, that one cannot live on 4,000 fr. with a wife." And still making no mention of the coming child Albert continued, "[Ehrat] talks about [marriage] as about a bitter medicine that has simply to be taken dutifully. . . . How differently people look at one and the same thing, it's very funny, isn't it."

Serbs believed that the new year of the pre-Christian period began toward the end of December, when the sun, having gone far enough into the snowy plains of winter, retraced its steps toward the green fields of summer. The weather was still springlike on Tuesday, January 5, 1902, the eve of the Orthodox Christmas.

On January 6, Božić, Christmas Day, the Marić family gathering was probably small and subdued. Still, according to ancient tradition, beginning at four in the morning, a pig would be killed, cleaned, pierced on an outdoor spit, and roasted. Then it would be served on an enormous wooden platter in the middle of the Christmas table with a bright green, wrinkled autumn apple jammed into its blackened, gaping mouth.

At least nine centuries earlier—on January 9 by the Julian calendar—the Marić patriarch and his family had been baptized into Christianity. The date was not only written in the church records (many of which have since been lost or destroyed) but also passed from father to son and commemorated through the generations. The day the Marić family was converted to Christianity was the feast day of St. Stefan the Martyr. St. Stefan was born a Jew and renowned for his intelligence. When he embraced Christianity, he was chosen to serve poor widows. He believed Jesus was the Messiah and accused his own people of killing him.

"Here," St. Stefan declared, "I see that the heavens have opened and that the Son is sitting at the right hand of His Father."

This enraged the Jewish people of Jerusalem, who expelled him from the city, then pelted him with stones. After he suffered an agonizing death, his body was thrown to the animals.

So each year on January 9, the Marićs celebrated the family's feast day—or *Slava,* meaning glory—to glorify the family's patron saint. A family's feast for its patron saint is the most important holiday in the life of the Serbian Orthodox people, and its celebration is always elaborate.

The day before the *Slava,* the head of the household goes to the *krčma,* the tavern, and buys a bottle of red wine. On the day of the feast he presents it to the family priest as a gift. Friends come by and have a glass of *rakija,* a plum brandy, and a slice of holiday cake. But in 1902, the Marić family celebrated their *Slava* in Titel in seclusion.

✧

The morning of Monday, January 27, looked like night. The newspapers reported that a storm had roared through the town at midnight. The streets of Novi Sad were deserted, and the horse-drawn trams could not function in the raging wind and rain. When people ventured outside, they had to hold onto lampposts to keep from being thrown down onto the pavement or up against the walls of buildings. Some were seen crawling on their hands and knees.

Outside the city, the storm was worse. The violent winds swept between the exposed houses of Titel and soared away over the plains. Red clay roof tiles were whipped around like marbles, smashing against walls and fences. The storm pounded against the Marić house, drowning the voices within as Mileva went into labor.

Surely, because of the pelvic deformity caused by Mileva's hip displacement, the village midwife, Ana Konacek, or her daughter, would have been engaged for the delivery, though Ana's record book, along with most of Titel's medical records from 1902, was destroyed in the Second World War. Midwives knew that with a woman in Mileva's condition it was not uncommon for the head of the baby to be prevented from normally lowering itself into the birth canal during the last few weeks of pregnancy, or even at the onset of uterine contractions. Mrs. Konacek would have to proceed carefully.

They would need water. Indoor plumbing had not yet reached the country, and fetching water in a storm meant a perilous walk across the courtyard to the well. Electricity would not arrive for another thirty years, so candles and gas lamps illuminated the house.

With her pelvic deformity, Mileva was five times more likely to have a breech delivery—a complication that was especially unfavorable for the child. The baby would have to be turned. If Mrs. Konacek's efforts did not succeed, the baby's ankles would present themselves before the head.

A towel would then have to be wrapped around the ankles and grasped firmly, as Mrs. Konacek reached up into the birth canal, inching toward the baby's shoulders. Although the disposition of Mileva's pelvis would have made the application of forceps awkward, midwives would nevertheless have had to use what they called big tweezers to assist in difficult births. When the forceps were locked in place on either side of the infant's head, traction was applied. This was a crucial point in the delivery, when the likelihood of natal injury increased. Slowly, painfully, the baby would be towed out.

Mileva's wish came true—she gave birth to a girl. The infant's first cry would have been made in unison with the raging storm. According to the newspaper, in the faint beginning of the day, everything was eerily silent. For an hour no one heard a sound from the streets. Then, slowly, the village came to life. A murmur was heard. It grew louder and louder as the citizens of the village emerged to view the damage.

But Mileva was sick to the core with her struggle. It is likely that she had lost a lot of blood and that her cervical tissue was shredded. She was weakened by the birth and greatly in need of care. For the first three days, no one knew if she or her daughter would live. Statistically, dying from childbirth was almost as likely as surviving it. More than half of all the women who died [in the region] did so as a consequence of childbirth, and the infant mortality rate was higher than forty percent.

Since Mileva's sister, Zorka, also suffered from congenital hip displacement (CHD), the chances that Lieserl would suffer the same fate increased five-fold. Mileva's mother is also believed to have had a displaced hip, but this is unconfirmed. If Marija did in fact have the condition, the odds of Lieserl's having a displaced hip would jump to approximately sixty percent. The occurrence of this familial cluster of congenital hip displacements makes its genetic origin likely. (Along with CHD, there was an endemically high incidence of other congenital defects in Central and Eastern Europe in the early 1900s, including club foot, cleft palate, Down's syndrome, and cerebral palsy.)

Even Albert himself was thought, at first, to have been born with a deformity. At his birth, "his mother was shocked at the sight of the back of his head, which was extremely large and angular, and she feared that she had given birth to a deformed child. The doctor reassured her, and after a few weeks the shape of the skull became normal. But normal childhood development proceeded slowly, and he had such difficulty with language that those around him feared he would never learn to speak." When he at last began to talk, he continually repeated himself. The Einstein maidservant called him stupid. He was also prone to such ferocious tantrums that his face "would turn completely yellow, the tip of his nose snow white, and [he would lose] control of himself."

✦

Waiting three days, until January 30, Mileva's father wrote Albert from Novi Sad to inform him of his daughter's birth. On February 4, Albert wrote to Mileva.

"Poor, poor sweetheart, you must suffer enormously if you cannot even write to me yourself! And our dear Lieserl too must get to know the world from this aspect right from the beginning! . . . I was scared out of my wits when I got your father's letter, because I had already suspected some trouble. I love her so much and I don't even know her yet!"

His letter suggests that not only did Mileva have a very difficult time giving birth, but that Lieserl suffered enormously, as well:

Albert went on to ask who was nursing the baby, which suggests that perhaps Mileva was incapable of breast-feeding Lieserl herself.

By this time, the decision had been made by Mileva's family not to register Lieserl's birth in the Serbian Orthodox Church record books. Still, it would have been unthinkable not to have the baby christened.

According to tradition, the child would be baptized with a legal, Christian name at the christening and Lieserl would remain her pet name. The descendants of those who knew about the birth claim the child was christened Ljubica, but there is no Ljubica listed in the baptism records of Crkva Uspenja Presvete Bogorodice, the Church of Virgin Mary's Ascension, nor in Titel's public records for 1902. Given the circumstances, however, the baptism probably would have taken place in private, with the tacit consent of the family's priest, Father Bogdanović, not to record the event. After all, Miloš Marić was always quite generous to the church.

✧

Albert rented a room in the home of Anna Sievers, on Gerechtigkeitsgasse 32, in Bern. In a letter to Mileva, he drew a map of his room, which included a bed, a framed picture, a coverlet, a grand chair, a smaller chair, an ornate mirror, a self-portrait, a wardrobe, a sofa, a chamber pot, a window, a door, a stove, a table, and a clock. The room was much too large for him. "One could hold a meeting in it," he joked. And yet, he made no explicit mention of space for Lieserl.

There are two more letters from Albert in February. These letters, written on the eighth and the seventeenth, are missing their final pages. Whether these two pages were lost or destroyed can only be conjectured. However, one thing is certain—neither of the two remaining fragments mentions his newborn daughter.

On February 20, 1902, one month after Lieserl was born, Pauline Einstein wrote to a friend, Pauline Winteler, "This Miss Marić is causing me the bitterest hours of my life. If it were in my power, I would make every possible effort to banish her from our horizon, I really dislike her."

✧

As the quail hid in the tall summer fields, six-month-old Lieserl remained in the Serbian countryside while Mileva returned to Bern. She found a room for herself with the Herbst family at Thunstrasse 24. She was registered as living on "private means." The next day, Albert moved ten doors away on the same street, to number 43A.

The couple was having a difficult time. On June 28, Albert wrote Mileva a note arranging a date a few days later. This arrangement must have followed an argument, for Albert apologizes, "You cannot imagine how tenderly I think of you whenever we are not together, even though I'm always such a mean fellow when I'm with you. . . . We too . . . will make an excursion, and we will leave already on Saturday evening! Then, in the evening and at night, I will kiss you and squeeze you again to my heart's desire."

Albert had begun his job at the patent office. There is no record of what Mileva was doing with her time—perhaps tutoring, studying, or simply waiting to be beckoned. To be with Albert, Mileva had abandoned her child to her family and a wet nurse, hundreds of miles away.

✧

Svoje se meso ne jede, you don't eat your own flesh, is a Slavic saying, and it appears to be a maxim the Marić family embraced. Lieserl would live with her grandparents until Mileva made up her mind about what to do with her daughter.

Mileva knew that if she insisted on keeping Lieserl, she would be forced to return to Vojvodina—without Albert. There, she would be cloistered at home because of the dishonor she had brought upon the family. On the other hand, if she agreed to give up Lieserl, her relationship with Albert could resume. Mileva was determined to find a middle path.

Previously, while she attended the Polytechnikum, Mileva had been living in Zürich on a student visa. But after leaving school, she could stay in Switzerland on a resident visa for only two months at a time. At the end of each two-month period, she was required to leave the country for a minimum of two months, after which she could re-enter Switzerland on another resident visa. On July 11, Mileva returned to Vojvodina, and thereafter her life was a series of comings and goings.

Albert moved his lodgings on August 14, this time to the top floor of Archivstrasse 8. His flat had a fabulous view over the Bernese Oberland and the River Aare. In spite of his credo, "Long live impudence," he conscientiously registered as the law required. Mileva practiced a haphazard civil disobedience. When she was granted a resident visa, she was required to indicate the date on which she planned to leave the country. If she did not leave by that date and did not inform the authorities, she could be deported. But the authorities were often behind in their inspections. By the time they came to Mileva's lodgings, on August 13, she had already gone to Vojvodina without leaving a forwarding address.

A month later, on September 9, Mileva returned to Bern. As to her stated profession, she wrote on the resident permit "will be married." She took up residence with the Suter family at Falkenplatz 9, across the Aare River from Albert. Soon after, to be closer to him, Mileva moved to the home of the Schneider family at Bubenberstrasse 3. Mileva's profession, it seemed, had become following Albert.

Sometime between August 15 and October 3, Albert wrote to a friend, Hans Wohlwend, that he was "in a cheerful, lightheaded mood, because my worries are now mostly gone, except that my father is very ill unfortunately." Albert traveled to Milan to be with Hermann, who suffered from heart disease. It would have been a good time for Mileva to visit Lieserl, but because of the stringency of resident permits, she did not take the chance of being refused re-entry. So she waited for Albert. His father died, in Milan, on October 10. On his deathbed, Hermann finally gave Albert permission to marry Mileva, most likely because he wanted to legitimize his son's daughter.

✧

According to the Bern registry, Albert and Mileva's marriage banns were to have been posted in Novi Sad just after Hermann's death. Church regulations in Vojvodina required that the plea for marriage be announced three times at a church—thirty days before the marriage, then twenty days, then ten days. But the banns would be announced in Novi Sad only if Mileva and Albert were going to be married in the church there, and they had decided not to be. In fact, the banns were never published in Novi Sad at all. Had Mileva given misinformation to the Bern registry? Perhaps she used the impending publication of the banns in Novi Sad as a means of forcing Albert to go through with the marriage.

Once again, Mileva's visa expired, and she returned to Novi Sad on November 9. It must have been during this visit that Mileva was faced with making a decision about Lieserl's fate. She stayed in Novi Sad only five weeks, which meant she returned to Switzerland illegally. Albert and Mileva had probably set a date to marry by then; otherwise, the Swiss authorities would have denied her entry.

No one knew about Lieserl. Yet upon Mileva's return to Bern, friends noticed a change in her attitude and feared her romance might be doomed. Something had happened between the couple, which Mileva would only say was "intensely personal." She was clearly brooding, and

Albert seemed to be in some way responsible. Friends encouraged Mileva to talk about her problem, but she refused.

From the death of Albert's father, in October 1902, until January 1903, there is only one existing letter—a note Albert wrote to a friend, Hans Wohlwend. There is most conspicuously no correspondence from Mileva's family about the well-being of the child.

✧

Mileva and Albert's wedding banns were published on December 17 in Bern and the next day in Zurich. "Albert Einstein/Mileva Marić are pleased to announce to you their marriage, which is taking place on January 6, 1903." They were married in a small ceremony at the Bern registry. It was a simple affair, the official asking them separately whether they wanted to take each other as husband and wife. After "having received their affirmative answer," the "civil registrar proclaimed them married in the name of the law." There was no honeymoon. Their engraved wedding announcement was placed in a black hand-stitched silk case with a magnolia-colored band and braided gold trim. Mileva, who was admired for her sewing, probably had made it herself. It was placed among her most treasured belongings. She had just turned twenty-seven, and Albert was almost twenty-four. They moved to their first official shared residence, at Tillierstrasse 18. They were registered as Mr. and Mrs. Albert Einstein, no children.

On January 27, 1903, Lieserl turned one year old.

✧

Helene wrote to Mileva from Belgrade right after the wedding, congratulating the couple. Mileva replied proudly on March 20, "[W]e have been married for 2 $\frac{1}{2}$ months now—a regular respectable married couple—and that is the true reason why I have not written you for so long. My new duties have taken up my time completely. We have a nice small household that I myself look after. I am sure you can imagine that at least in the beginning until I become accustomed to it, it does not leave me much free time." Mileva, who had come tantalizingly close to having a career as a physicist and mathematician, had never been trained as a homemaker. Nonetheless, she would fulfill the old Serbian proverb: *Kuća ne leži na zemlji, nego na ženi,* the house doesn't rest on the earth, but on the woman. Ironically, Mileva, who had resisted traditional female roles, was living a life not very different from her mother's. But Mileva was too in love to care.

Her passion fit perfectly into Serbian society where, for example, a Serbian man would introduce his wife to a stranger, especially a foreigner, by saying, "This, may you forgive me, is my wife."

"I have become, if this is possible," Mileva confessed to Helene, "even more of a match for my love than I was already during the time in Zürich. He is my only company, and I am happiest when he is next to me."

❖

Mileva had asked Helene for help in finding jobs for herself and Albert in Belgrade, but in March of 1903, she explained that the favor was no longer necessary because they finally had some earnings. She went on to write that it was too bad they could not see Helene in Belgrade that summer. "Albert cannot go before July, and I cannot go away until after July—you know the reason." Helene would be visiting her family in Vienna for the month of July.

Mileva's statement "you know the reason" is the first, and only, indication that Helene may have known about Lieserl. Helene was Mileva's most intimate friend. Perhaps Mileva had described in a previous letter, now missing, Albert's reluctance to see Lieserl or to bring her back to Switzerland. Therefore, "you know the reason" could have addressed the question of why they would not visit the Balkans during his summer holiday.

❖

In the summer of 1903, the Marić family, including Lieserl, loaded themselves into two wagons and left Novi Sad for the country home in Kać. By now, Lieserl was a year and a half old and would have been speaking in two- and three-word sentences. She presumably thought her grandmother Marija or her aunt Zorka was her mother. Since there is no evidence, neither records nor travel documents, that Mileva visited her daughter between November 9, 1902, and August 27, 1903, it may be assumed that Lieserl did not recognize Mileva as her mother.

It appears that Mileva and Albert made a studied decision not to see their daughter. Since her marriage, Mileva could have traveled freely between the two countries. According to Article One of the *Ordonnance du Conseil exécutif de la République de Berne du février 1838 sur la délivrance des Passeports par la police centrale,* every citizen of Bern was required to have a passport in order to travel abroad. Since Mileva, according to the Bernese Civil Code, was now a Swiss citizen by marriage, she was entitled to receive a Swiss passport. Yet there is no record of Mileva ever having had one. Presumably, she was listed on Albert's passport as his wife, which meant she could travel only with him. Unfortunately, Albert's passport from that period has never been recovered. But Swiss citizens could travel freely between the so-called German States—which included Germany, the Austro-Hungarian Empire, and Switzerland—until the First World War therefore, Mileva would not have needed a passport to visit Lieserl. Had she wanted to visit Helene in Belgrade, which was in the Kingdom of Serbia and not included in the "German States," Albert would have had to go to the police and state her destination along with his written permission.

The cost of marrying Albert may have been giving up the child completely.

✧

On August 26, 1903, Mileva received news from her family that Lieserl was seriously ill with scarlet fever. The next day, Mileva left for Novi Sad on the Arlberg train. During a ten-minute stop in Salzburg, at 3:20 in the afternoon, she disembarked to buy two five-heller stamps and an uninspired sepia postcard of Schloss Leopoldskron, a castle near Salzburg, then reboarded her train for Budapest.

Mileva's train arrived in Budapest at 11:41 in the evening. There was tension in the air. The morning's newspaper had reported that a political figure had accused the opposition of interference in the legal affairs of the Empire. The opposition challenged that "now even dynamite can be used to get rid of the people who are attacking the leading politicians." Police patrolled the platforms and the sidings. There was a forty-five minute wait for the next train. In the shadow of the castle, Mileva wrote a quick note to Albert: "Budapest, Thursday, August twenty-seventh, 1903. Dear Jonzerl, I am already in Budapest, it is going quickly, but it is hard. I don't feel well. What are you doing, little Jonzile, write me soon, will you. Your poor Schnoxl." Mileva pasted the stamps crookedly on the card and posted it via the "Post-Fourgon"—a service that took mail directly to a destination without going through the post office. In this way a letter could arrive the same day, or the next day at the latest.

Early the next morning, the twenty-eighth, Mileva arrived in Novi Sad. Her father met her at the station to take her the twenty-two kilometers to Kać. She was still not feeling well. In a week or two she would discover that she was pregnant again.

✧

When Mileva arrived in Kać she saw red crosses, outlined in black, painted on all but two doors, warning people to stay away. An epidemic of scarlet fever had broken out in the region.

"Listen to all this advice," the Novi Sad newspaper cautioned, "and remember this also. When your child gets sick, call the doctor immediately for help. Listen only to him! Don't listen to old women!"

Dr. Laza Marković, a friend of Mileva's brother, Miloš, and of Mileva's, too, had just returned from Budapest with a medical degree. He was probably called upon to treat Lieserl.

Lieserl must have displayed all the symptoms of scarlet fever—a high fever, a racing pulse, and hot, dry, skin. There would have been a parched whiteness around her mouth, and her throat would have been a deep crimson and her tongue a bright strawberry red. She was probably being treated with various home remedies, including quinine, vaseline, and constant dressings of rose water and glycerin mixed with olive oil. Mileva's mother probably would have applied the older folk remedies as well: oil of wintergreen for fever; mint for the itching; monkshood, belladonna, and woodbine combined with wild jasmine and white hellebore to calm the system. Lieserl's chances for recovery were slim.

If a child did recover, mothers were warned, her skin would peel off and lard and sour cream would have to be slathered on her body. As the child healed, she would have to be bathed two times a day with soap and hot water. New clothes would have to be made, and the old ones discarded. The room where the child was ill would have to be disinfected and then repainted.

✧

Around September 14, Mileva wrote Albert from Kać about Lieserl's condition. She also informed him that she was pregnant again, and must have worried about the risk of contagion. On September 19, Albert replied from Bern, "I'm not at all angry that my poor Schnoxl must be on the nest. What's more, I'm even delighted about it and have been pondering whether I should not see to it that you get a new Lieserl, so that you won't be deprived of that which is every woman's right. Don't worry but come back home in a happy mood, and brood very carefully so that something good will hatch out.

"I am very sorry about what happened with Lieserl," Albert continued. "Scarlet fever often leaves some lasting trace behind." Indeed, the illness could permanently affect the heart or kidneys and cause hearing problems, pneumonia, meningitis, even encephalitis.

"If only everything passes well," Albert wrote, and then, curiously, "How is Lieserl registered? We must take great care, lest difficulties arise for the child in the future."

Albert must have thought that Lieserl's birth was not recorded in civil or church records. He may have been concerned that if Lieserl was to live with them, she would need to be registered correctly with the authorities so there would be no problem at the border. According to Swiss law, a child born out of wedlock automatically becomes legitimate after its parents' marriage. But the child's name would have to appear on the passport of the *father* if she was to be brought to Switzerland—which meant that Albert would have had to travel to Vojvodina and escort her home.

More likely, however, Albert had no intention of bringing Lieserl to Bern. Einstein scholars have concluded from his September 19 letter that the couple had decided to put Lieserl up for adoption, based on Albert's concern that the child's registration (or lack thereof) not be a source of trouble for her—or her parents—in the years to come.

"Now come back to me soon," Albert insisted. "Three and one half weeks have already passed, and a good little wife should not be away from her man for longer than that. But our place still does not look nearly as terrible as you may think. You will quickly put it in order again."

Bertrand Russell once said of Albert, "Personal matters never occupied more than odd nooks and crannies in his thoughts." But personal matters were now the whole of Mileva's life. Apparently, in the end, Albert and Mileva agreed it would be best to pretend that Lieserl had never existed. And so, with a deliberate hand, the short life of Lieserl Einstein-Marić was erased.

PART TWO

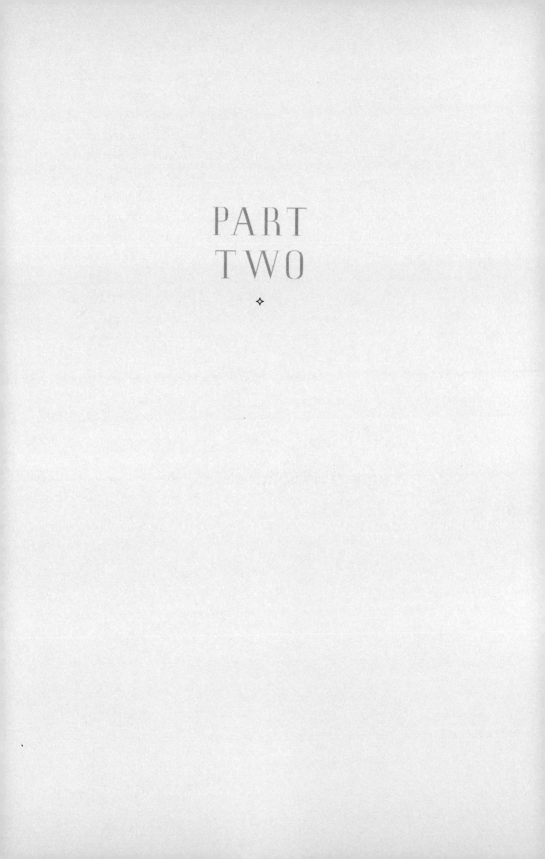

Helene Kaufler was a polyglot. She spoke five languages fluently and studied history at Zurich University. Born in Vienna, Helene was the eldest of five sisters. Her father, who was Jewish, was an attorney. Her mother, probably a Catholic, was a novelist who wrote under the pen name Ida von Banja. As a little girl, she had suffered from a form of tuberculosis that attacked her knee, leaving one of her legs shorter than the other. Like Mileva, she wore an orthopedic shoe all her life. Unlike her father, Helene was a liberal thinker. Indeed, he once slapped her across the face because of her left-leaning politics.

Although tiny (she weighed only 105 pounds), and pretty like Mileva, Helene was the emotional opposite of her friend. In 1900, she married a Serb, Milivoj Savić, who was five years younger than she, and who—at 286 pounds—was a giant by comparison; in fact, his friends, called him a benevolent giant.

Milivoj was born in Užice, in the Kingdom of Serbia, to parents of the *petit bourgeois*. His father was a baker, an innkeeper, and owned a tavern. Milivoj attended university in Graz, Austria, where he studied the industrial sciences. One of his jobs while a student was to sit at a table in the picture window of a local restaurant and eat. The proprietors were convinced that because he so clearly enjoyed eating, he was an advertisement in action.

Albert did not like him.

"Poor little Helene," Albert wrote Mileva in 1900, "she has now fallen for him after all, due to his laudable persistence—now her fine spirit will suffocate in his fat—a sad psychological prophecy. It's really a pity for her. Moreover, I think that in a short time he will be the same scoundrel he used to be." Apparently, although Milivoj was a corpulent fellow, he attracted women easily. And yet, despite her husband's imposing presence, Helene would prove to be the head of the household. In her quiet way, she kept everything under control.

Mileva, a romantic at heart, was delighted. When Helene first told her that she was marrying Milivoj, Mileva was delighted. She assured Helene that her new husband would "carry her in his large hands and make her safe."

"I rejoice with you," Mileva wrote to Helene in 1900 after their marriage, "and am happy that you are so happy and that you have found that which presents your life in the most marvelous light." Albert himself wrote to Helene at this time, assuring her that, in spite of his modern, emancipated notions of domestic roles and his misgivings about her future husband, she would "become a nimble, capable little housewife, for [her husband's] happiness and . . . an example to all the world."

One month after the marriage, Helene was pregnant. Albert cheered her on to motherhood: "Dear Mrs. Savić $(+9\frac{1}{2}$, I hope!)" thinking she was almost ready to give birth.

But Albert was too optimistic. Helene must have miscarried soon after, because within six weeks she was pregnant again.

Her daughter, Julka, was born in October 1901, while Helene and Milivoj were living in Reutlingen, Germany, a center of the textile industry. Julka's birth was registered in Tübingen, a university town eleven kilometers from Reutlingen. Her birth certificate, supplied by the records office in Tübingen, reads: "A child was born at the women's clinic at the university in Tübingen, to Helene Savić, born Kaufler, wife of Milivoj Savić, engineer, of Catholic faith, resident of Reutlingen (allegedly a man of Serbian nationality) on October twenty-eighth, in the year nineteen hundred and one. It is a girl and was born at ten forty-five in the morning. The child has not yet been given a first name." Fourteen days later it was entered that "the child of the married couple Savić has been given the first name of 'Julka.' "

(Oddly, just a week before her daughter's birth, Helene was in Schächen, 208 kilometers from Tübingen. But it is unclear why Helene, who not long before had complained to Mileva that she was not feeling well, would be so far from her husband and her doctor so late in her pregnancy especially since she had already lost a child.) At the last minute, she must have taken the train home to have her baby.

✧

Just after Julka was born, the Savićs moved to Belgrade, where Milivoj rose quickly in the Ministry of Commerce and Industry. He was one of the primary strategists of the economic development of Yugoslavia and went on to write six books on the subject. The house was always filled with family, friends, and students. Unlike most Serbian men of that era, Milivoj loved to shop for food and was known to serve mutton cutlets to anyone who walked through the door at dinnertime.

Helene gave birth to a second daughter, Zora, in Belgrade on December 28, 1902. On March 20, 1903, Mileva wrote that she "was so pleased to hear the news about the arrival of your little daughter.

"I haven't written you for so long," she continued, "even though I have already received such nice letters from you." (There are no known existing letters between them from December 1901 until this letter.) "Your little Julka is such a delightful . . . thing. Can she walk and speak a little already? You must be very happy with her. I can't think otherwise. Have you not had your picture taken with her? I would love to see you as a mother and even if it would only be in a photograph."

Toward the end of the letter, Mileva talks about Albert as being unhappy with his position at the patent office. Then she asks, "Do you think people of our *type* could find some sort of job in Belgrade? We could lend ourselves to teaching German in a school." Here, Mileva may be speaking for herself. In actuality, Albert probably would not have entertained this idea seriously. He focused his ambitions on Western Europe rather than provincial Serbia. Mileva might have been imagining positions for them that would have made it possible for her to see Lieserl more often. In any event, such a prospect never materialized. The couple stayed in Bern, and Mileva gave birth to Hans Albert Einstein on May 14, 1904.

Apparently, it was the first time in Mileva's family history that a Marić baby was not born at home. Mileva delivered her baby in a clinic, this time with Albert by her side. On May 15, Albert wrote Helene and Milivoj a glowing birth announcement, saying that Mileva was fine. She was not.

A month later, Mileva wrote Helene that she "was very weakened by the birth. . . . When [Hans Albert] was born, he was so big and strong that the doctors in the clinic wondered how such a small mother had such a big child." But she was delighted with her "little treasure. You have no idea how much joy he gives me when he laughs so happily when he wakes up." Albert must have shared Mileva's delight, because in the same letter she writes, "Albert assumes quite a fatherly dignity!" There are no letters from Mileva's family in Vojvodina congratulating the couple upon having a son. The only evidence that they were still in communication is a postal coupon sent from Miloš Marić to Mileva—but the date on it is April 1905, almost a year after Hans Albert's birth.

In 1905, Albert's position at the Swiss patent office was made permanent. Though his salary was raised to 3,900 francs, it was still not enough for a family of three to live on comfortably. He was working feverishly on four different papers—his doctoral dissertation, *A New Determination of Molecular Dimensions; On a Heuristic Point of View Concerning the Production and Transformation of Light; On the Movement of Small Particles Suspended in Stationary Liquids Required by the Molecular-Kinetic Theory of Heat;* and *On the Electrodynamics of Moving Bodies: The Special Theory of Relativity.* This last paper was completed on June 30, 1905, and by the end of the summer, he submitted to *Annalen der Physik* a shorter paper that postulated that mass is a function of energy and vice versa.

Mileva must have been happy—thrilled with Albert, her son, their life together, a legitimate family at last. Still, the Marićs had yet to meet Albert or Hans Albert. In fact, when they left for their Balkan holiday in late August 1905, the Einsteins rode through Novi Sad on their way to Belgrade without stopping to see her parents at all. Such behavior was contrary to Serbian family custom. Whatever the cause—pressing business or deliberate rudeness—they traveled by train directly to the Savićs, where Albert saw the little Savić girls for the first time.

✧

The Einsteins stayed in Belgrade at the Savić house on Katanićeva Street, and the next morning they all departed for Kijevo, a tiny village on a lake outside Rakovica. Chugging toward the village on the Beograd-Niš line, they passed over low red-hued hills carpeted with blue periwinkles that rolled southward, away from the river. As they neared the resort, Mount Avala—511 meters high—rose before them, covered with spiky shrub oak and outcroppings of stone. The train snaked around the mountain and soon came to a stop. The two families stayed at a small hotel on the lake.

After a week with the Savićs, the Einsteins finally paid their respects to Mileva's parents. During Mileva's first few days in Novi Sad, she introduced her new family to old friends, including Desana Tapavica, who had married Dr. Emil Bala, soon to be Novi Sad's mayor. Mileva told both Desana and her father that "just before we left for Novi Sad, we finished some important work that will make my husband world famous!"

While Mileva socialized with friends, Albert discovered the Erzsébet Királyné Kávéház, the Queen Elizabeth Café, part of a hotel of the same name owned by Lazar Dundjerski, one of the wealthiest men in the region. Dundjerski also was owner of a theater behind his hotel, which he had built from the ruins of an older theater. Under Austro-Hungarian rule, plays and operas in the Serbian language were not allowed to be performed publicly. So Dundjerski constructed this somewhat obscured space in 1895 for Serbian dramatists.

In fact, there were two cafés managed by the hotel. The front café was under a rectangular, tentlike structure set away from the wall of the hotel with a waist-high, filigreed wrought-iron fence around the perimeter. Customers sat on unforgiving black metal chairs at tiny marble-topped tables that were only big enough to hold two coffee cups and an ashtray. As the sun moved around the café, white cotton curtains were unfurled to protect the customers. In 1911, when the red-and-yellow electric streetcars were installed, it became too noisy to chat. But it was still the best place in town to sit and watch people stroll by.

When Albert held court, or when he just wanted to be quiet and read by himself, he would walk through the hotel to the patio in the back. There, he sat with his books and newspapers spread out on a round wooden table in the shade of potted white lilacs and miniature plane trees. Even today, Novi Sad residents tell stories about Albert's loquacity and laughter. It was on this patio that Albert was remembered to have said he was "not against moderate alcohol consumption."

"Voilà," he exclaimed, "the Serb drinks from birth until death. When he is born, as he matures, when he travels, when he gets married, when he gets buried—and yet Serbs are a nation of geniuses. That is how I perceive them, based on my wife." At the end of the day, he would return on foot to the Marić house on Kisačka Street, just a few blocks away.

Although Lieserl would have been three and a half years old in 1905, there is no evidence of her presence during this visit.

✦

In January 1906, Albert finally received his doctorate from Zurich University. Two months later, he was promoted again at the Swiss patent office and received another pay raise, this time to 4,500 francs.

More than a year had passed since their trip to Belgrade when Mileva wrote Helene in December 1906 to thank her for the "friendly reception" in Kijevo. And she did so only after being "properly embarrassed" by a postcard from Helene.

"I often think with pleasure of your lovely children, dear Helene," Mileva wrote. "What an intelligent child your Julka is already." Here too, Mileva committed a social blunder. It was considered impolite to remark about one child and not the other.

By summer 1907, Albert was so busy with his job and his many projects that Mileva went alone with Hans Albert to visit her parents. She very much wanted to see Helene, but she could not.

"I do not have a passport," she wrote, "and here in Hungary [the Austro-Hungarian Empire] it is too difficult to get one. Can you perhaps smuggle me across the river or can we meet one afternoon in Zemun [on the Austro-Hungarian side of the Danube]? So, very happily I will wait for your instructions."

✧

The years of 1907 and 1908 were an active time for the Einstein family. Although there is little information available about Mileva, presumably she was busy with her son and her household, which included student boarders for whom she cooked and did laundry. In January 1908, Albert submitted to the Philosophical Faculty II of the University of Bern his *Habilitationsschrift*, a thesis called *Consequences for the Constitution of Radiation of the Energy Distribution Law of Black Body Radiation*. In February the faculty approved the position of a *Privatdozent* (lecturer) for Albert at the University of Bern.

The family took a week's holiday in August 1907 and traveled to the rustic village of Zweisimmen in the Bernese Alps. They hiked along the River Simme, now quiet after the energetic springtime runoff. Soon they entered the Simmental Valley, with its Alpine flowers and steep, echoing cliffs. By the time they reached the tiny village of Lenk, they had climbed to 1,400 meters. In the center of the village was the only hotel, the Hotel Hirsch, a traditional wooden chalet with eaves that almost touched the ground on the north side. Lining all the road-facing windows were white windowboxes with trailing red geraniums. Even with her bad hip, Mileva hiked along with everyone else, taking turns with Albert carrying their son. Within a week of returning home, Mileva left again with Hans Albert to visit her parents in Novi Sad. Again, she was not able to see Helene, who was visiting her family in Vienna.

✧

In March 1909, a crisis erupted in the Kingdom of Serbia over Austria's annexation of Bosnia-Hercegovina. A coalition of Serbs and Croats had become threatening to the Austro-Hungarian Empire because they opposed the annexation. They wanted Bosnia-Hercegovina for themselves. War was in the air.

At first, Helene considered moving to Bern with her family to get away from the impending military activity, and wrote to Mileva for help. On March 29, Mileva replied on a postcard. She was concerned and felt "very bad for the poor men. I would be happy if your dear ones would come here."

Mileva had taken the initiative and turned to a few estate agents and newspaper advertisements to find a boarding house or a furnished apartment for the Savićs. She did not know if Helene's "little ones would feel very well in a boarding house," and worried that the food would not be up to Helene's high Austrian standards.

In the end, Helene and her family decided to go to Vienna instead. Two months later, she wrote Mileva about her poor health.

"I was very distressed to hear," Mileva replied, "that you were sick once again and I hope that this time it is not as serious and that you will not have to have an operation." Mileva offered to take "one of your children, although I do not want to separate them from their Mama." She said that Helene should decide which little girl to give to her as "our guest."

In another, undated letter from 1909, Mileva offered to take Helene's orphaned niece. She promised, "You can trust me with little Mara, and you can leave her nanny at home. My little Albert has an enormous longing for other children and he would be endlessly happy.

"I can reassure you, dear Helene, that the little I know of your children I love them very much and it would be a great pleasure for me if one time they will stay at my house for a couple of years."

A couple of years! Mileva was apparently responding to a letter in which Helene had expressed her concerns about the well-being of her children during her illness. Whether she asked Mileva to keep the children for a long period of time, we do not know. But Mileva's letter suggests that Helene was worried about what might happen to her and her family; it also demonstrates Mileva's devotion to her friend.

"I don't need to tell you," Mileva reassured Helene, "that you are a very good friend of mine and that obviously my friendship to you extends to your dear girls." And then she adds, somewhat mysteriously, "But my deepest wish is that we can all together share them."

By September, the threat of war had faded, and Helene and her family were back in Belgrade, and Julka who was eight years old, was back in school. Mileva complained to Helene about how difficult it had been to locate her.

"I wrote you in Vienna and expected you to write to me if you were still there so I could see you on my return," she groused. "I waited in vain for a sign of life from you."

Three more sentences follow; the fourth is crossed out by a different pen.

When I came upon the deletion, I went over to the window and held the photocopy of the letter up to the glass. In the diffused light, I could read, "I always try to comfort myself about my dec[Entschei . . .]—" Did she mean her *Entscheidung*—her "decision"—about relinquishing Lieserl? Who crossed out the sentence? By now, such incidents were becoming routine—a page missing here and there—an incorrect date penciled in.

✧

Meanwhile, Albert had begun to flirt openly with other women. When he responded too enthusiastically to a note from a former girlfriend, Anna Meyer-Schmid, Albert ended up apologizing to Anna's husband.

"I am sorry that I caused you distress by my careless behavior. I answered . . . too heartily and thereby reawakened the old affection we had for each other." Much later, in 1951, Albert complained to Anna's daughter that Mileva's jealousy was a trait of her "uncommon ugliness."

Five months after this incident, Albert wrote to his best friend and lifelong correspondent, Michele Besso, that he had not recovered the "mental balance" of mind that "M" had made him lose. The Einstein-Marić marriage, it seems, had begun to unravel.

Albert accepted a position as Extraordinary (associate) Professor of Physics at Zurich University. In October the Einstein-Marićs returned to their beloved Zürich, where their romance had begun. They took an apartment at Moussonstrasse 12.

At that time of year it was common for a fierce northerly wind to roar down the city streets. Inside the Einsteins' apartment building, however, it was warm. Mileva was relieved to be living in Zurich after "seven bitter and difficult years," but life was not any easier financially. Zurich was dearly expensive, and a great number of the couple's arguments centered around money. To make ends meet, they again rented rooms to students. And Mileva did all the housework, climbing up and down four flights of stairs and cooking three meals a day for her family and boarders. Her roles as mother, housekeeper, cook, and wife began to take their toll on her physically. She was often tired and out of sorts, and Albert's ebullience about his work seemed only to magnify her misery. A photograph of her taken at this time shows her wearing an old, unbecoming, patterned house dress with a wide round collar trimmed with lace. Her face looks as if it were squatting on a plate. Her once luxuriant hair is sheared short, drooping and lusterless. In one of her rare intimate letters from this period, she shared her despondence with Helene.

"You see, all that fame does not leave a lot of time for a wife. I read between the lines some impishness where you write that I have become jealous of science. But what can be done, one person gets the pearl and the other just gets the shell? Your first letter made me so happy, it made me feel so good to see what a high opinion you have about me—and that you like me. I often ask myself whether I really fit this opinion, or am I, on the contrary, a person who feels deeply and passionately, who fights a lot. What concerns me the most and makes me suffer is that, because of pride or perhaps due to fear of other people's glances, I put on a mask of pride. And I have to ask you that if the latter were true, even if deep down in my soul I stood before you with less pride, would you still love me? See, I long for love very much and I would be happy to get an answer from you. I almost think that the damn science is to be blamed. I can happily accept your smile when you read that."

In September, Mileva thanked Helene "for the photograph of your children. They look very different externally. However, there is something very endearing in their expressions."

Julka did not look like either of her parents. She was a mysterious-looking child with a heart-shaped face, large dark eyes, and a small, full mouth. Zora, in contrast, was blond with a broad-cheeked face, a long thin mouth, and small, uncompelling eyes. She looked like Helene, but lacked her mother's vitality.

Mileva complained to Helene that she felt "sorry that [Hans Albert] has neither a brother nor a sister. So we more or less have decided to take a child into our home of approximately the same age as he, maybe an orphan, if only we could find a nice one." However, before this surprising suggestion could be acted upon, there would come news of the family's growth.

In a subsequent letter Mileva informs Helene that she is again pregnant and that "we expect a third ally approximately in August." Was Mileva counting as allies the unborn child, herself and Hans Albert, and notably excluding father Albert? Or could the third ally be Lieserl, the first of Mileva's three children? Whichever was the case, there is no exhilaration in her announcement—it is noticeably more detached-sounding than the way she usually spoke about children. Indeed, Mileva precedes her news with an update on Albert's new position and his publications.

✧

When Mileva discovered she was pregnant with Lieserl, she seemed to be secretly delighted. She and Albert would be bound in their love for each other by parenthood. During her first pregnancy, she was sick much of the time. She told Albert, "[H]ow much I am suffering now, and this afternoon I had such a severe headache that I had to lie down." But she tried to make light of her condition, saying she had "already become such an utter whiner of a little mother."

Having a congenital disorder herself, Mileva, now that she was pregnant again, must have been fearful for her new baby. Albert may have been concerned too. Many years later, Albert wrote Hans Albert, "You know yourself what dangers result from your mother's heredity."

Mileva's hip displacement seems to go back a number of generations. There were also indications of mental instability. Her sister, Zorka, also suffered hip displacement and capitulated to psychosis, escalated by alcoholism. Her brother, Miloš, was always considered a notch more eccentric than acceptable, and according to interviews with people in Novi Sad and Kać, her father was thought to have battled depression.

✧

Eduard Einstein was born in Zurich on July 28, 1910. Albert sent a brief announcement to Helene. Mileva also wrote a note to Helene when Eduard was approximately seven months old in which she proudly declared, "I nursed him myself up to two weeks ago."

In 1910 Marie Curie (with André Debierne) isolated metallic radium, for which she won her second Nobel Prize for chemistry. Mileva had thought she would be sharing her husband's world of science and discovery. Instead, she sat alone in the old armchair by the window on Moussonstrasse. The winter season passed for her in one long, bleak stretch of time. Albert was spending most of his time at the university. He often attended lectures and concerts with his friends. One of these lectures was on "love and its effects on the subconscious." Afterward, at a café on Bellevueplatz, he showed enormous interest in two Slavic sisters "of rare beauty and charm."

✧

Helene's marriage also changed. "It is not what it used to be," she complained to Mileva. "I have reconciled myself, but with regret."

Despite her troubles, Mileva was trying hard to make everything work. Even with two small children, she still managed to find time to attend most of Albert's public lectures. She also supported his passion for music. Before they married, many evenings had been spent with Mileva at the piano, Albert playing his violin, and invited friends contributing their own musical talents. Now Mileva made sure that Albert's cherished musical evenings at home continued.

Then Albert created another crisis. He accepted a position in Prague at a higher salary. Mileva did not want to go. Despite her objections, they moved in April 1911, and her letters to Helene became scarce, although just before they left Zürich, in February 1911, she griped about their imminent relocation: "I worry about the children growing up in disagreeable conditions." Later in the same letter, she compared men working in the outside world to women staying at home with the children. "I think," she continued, "that we women cling to the memory of that remarkable time that is called youth longer than men and we would like that it always be like that. . . . Don't you find that men reconcile themselves easier with the here and now?"

In Prague, Eduard's health began to deteriorate almost immediately, the beginning of a lifetime of mysteriously induced headaches and repeated inflammations of the middle ear.

"Little Eduard, once a flourishing and healthy child, is rapidly going downhill. He is showing signs of rickets," Mileva wrote to Helene in 1913. "The hygienic conditions are hard. There is no drinkable water, the milk is of dubious quality, there is soot everywhere, there are no gardens, no free space for children to play."

For medical and psychological pediatric information Mileva often relied on her friend Dr. Laza Marković. By now he was well known in Novi Sad not only as a physician but as a writer and playwright; his written work addressed cultural and health issues. One of his plays, a morality play called *Marriage: Or How Will a Nation Achieve Good Progeny?* was about marriage and children. In it, Milan, a farmer whose daughter and grandchild are sick, asks if insanity and nerve diseases are hereditary.

The doctor replies, "Well, the predisposition for insanity [and] mental and nerve diseases is hereditary. Even those members of the family who do not become insane are also not of a good constitution. They are often irritable, mean, and march to their own drum; they are strange."

Then the farmer asks, "Can these children regain their strength?"

"With good care and a good, healthy, and temperate life, even the weaker children can improve. However, if they are bad since conception, they cannot improve," the doctor replies. "If a child is born with a sick brain or nerves, it will be difficult to prevent the disease from coming out. The terrible illness already lies in these children, and it is often awakened by the smallest thing. It is easy to set on fire a barrel full of gunpowder."

As Eduard grew more sickly, Albert grew more emotionally distant from his wife. Later, in 1915, he was to complain to his friend in Zürich, Heinrich Zangger, that "my youngest has unfortunately turned out a bit weak." After another year he wrote to Michele Besso, "I am depressed by the condition of my young one. It is out of the question that he will grow to full manhood. Who knows if it would not have been better if he could depart the world before he really knows this life."

Fortunately, it did not take long to convince Albert to leave Prague. By January 1912, the family had returned to Zurich, happy that they "had shown their backs to Prague." This time they were able to afford a pleasant six-room flat on the sunny side of the Zurichberg. Albert was heartily welcomed into his new position as Professor of Theoretical Physics at ETH (Eidgenössische Technische Hochschule), formerly the Polytechnikum. His salary leapt to 11,000 Swiss francs.

✧

In April 1912, Albert traveled to Berlin to meet with other leading physicists. During this trip he met two of his cousins, Paula Einstein and her sister, Elsa Einstein Löwenthal. Elsa had been divorced since 1908 and had two daughters, aged fifteen and thirteen. Albert took an immediate fancy to Paula. But he soon became bored and turned toward Elsa, beginning an intimate relationship that would last for the rest of her life. He later told Elsa that "Paula's behavior displeased me very much. It is hard for me to understand why I could have taken a fancy to her." Then he answers himself, "But it is in fact simple. She was young, a girl, and complaisant. That was enough."

By October 10, Albert wrote to his cousin that his wife did not "underestimate how important" Elsa was to him. In a subsequent letter he complained to Elsa that Mileva "is the most sour sourpuss that ever existed. I shudder at the thought of seeing her and *you* together. She will writhe like a worm if she sees you even from afar!"

It is not difficult to imagine how Mileva heard about the affair, since Albert was known not to be able to keep things to himself. He, most likely in a fit of anger, simply blurted it out—that was his way. Mileva must have been devastated. She had two small children to care for, and she was still deeply in love with her husband. Her silences caused Albert to accuse her of being "by nature unfriendly and mistrustful." As Mileva grew more and more melancholy, Albert became convinced that Elsa was his salvation.

Meanwhile, Montenegro, Bulgaria, Greece, and Serbia had gone to war against Turkey. The First Balkan War had begun. It was over by December. But by the end of June 1913, the Second Balkan War had broken out, with Bulgaria attacking Serbian and Greek positions. As a result of these upheavals, mail delivery became unreliable. There is only one known piece of correspondence from this time—a five-page letter to Helene, posted at the beginning of 1913. In it Mileva had written, "If you were happy you would not have sent all those sad letters to me before." Clearly there had been more letters between the two women—now lost. And yet, something appears to have gone awry in their relationship, deterring Mileva from responding.

"To tell you the truth," Mileva wrote Helene in the same letter, "I wanted to write, but I thought that you did not want to hear from me. But your letter from yesterday, with all its admiration, makes me ashamed of myself."

There is no indication of what the quarrel with Helene had been. Mileva proceeds with a poignant display of her private dilemmas. "My great Albert," she wrote, "has become a famous physicist, extremely respected and admired by his colleagues. He works hard on his problems. I can plainly see that he lives only for them. I have to confess with some shame that we are a bit unimportant to him and that we take second place."

On the back side of the fifth page, obviously having not read Mileva's letter, Albert appended a postscript, sending "a greeting to the Serbian heroine," telling her that "we were very glad that you made it well through these upsetting times." He most likely was referring to Helene's work as a medical volunteer during the war.

✧

Mileva's health now began to decline. She had been almost thirty-five years old when Eduard was born, and the weight of a full-term baby might have caused the start of a lifelong battle with rheumatism, compounding her hip problem. Even walking could be excruciating, which must have made it difficult for Mileva to chase after two small children.

Mileva had planned to accompany Albert to Paris, where on March 26, 1913, he was giving a lecture on the law of photochemical equivalence. But on March 14, Lisbeth Hurwitz, the daughter of family friends, wrote in her diary that she and her mother had visited Mileva and were shocked to see Mileva with her face badly bruised and swollen. Albert explained that it was caused by a dental problem. Mileva would not answer her friends' inquiries. Albert traveled to Paris alone.

By this time, Albert and Elsa had been seeing each other in secret for nearly a year, and he was regularly receiving love letters from her at the university. Albert told Elsa, "I treat my wife as an employee whom I cannot fire. I have my own bedroom and avoid being alone with her." He complained of an "icy silence" in their house and told Elsa that Mileva "is an unfriendly, humorless creature who does not get anything out of life and who, by her mere presence, extinguishes other people's joy of living."

Even so, Mileva persisted in trying to hold her marriage together. In mid-September, the entire family visited The Spire. Albert spent some of the time either on a bicycle or driving a donkey-drawn buggy to the village. One early evening, he went with Mileva to the local café. He asked the musician to sing his favorite song about peasant girls: *Even though my eyes have seen all the men in Novi Sad, | I made a mistake. | I fell in love young. | And I had never even spoken to him before we married.* Einstein was delighted by the song and asked the musician to repeat it several times.

On Saturday, September 20, Albert wrote to his friend Henrich Zangger in Zurich that he and his family "have been staying here [Kać] since Monday in bucolic tranquility at my in-laws'. The journey was smooth but tiring. It's terribly hot here. One does not see any sign of cholera. Tomorrow I will leave with my wife for Vienna."

Late that same Saturday afternoon, the Marić and Einstein families left Kać and returned to the main residence, in Novi Sad. Mileva and Albert had intended to continue on together to Vienna, where he was giving a lecture to the annual meeting of the Society of German Scientists and Physicians on the twenty-third. Hans Albert and Eduard were to remain in Novi Sad, where Mileva would fetch them after the conference. But instead of returning to Zurich from Vienna, Albert also planned to go on to Berlin, where he was negotiating a new position at the Prussian Academy of Sciences and where, of course, he would see Elsa. He had written before his trip to Vojvodina, promising that, "at the end of the next month, I will visit your family, i.e., you."

According to interviews with Marić family members, in the very early evening of the twentieth, Mileva and Albert had a terrible argument in the presence of her parents and their children. Hans Albert, seemingly accustomed to such rows, remained silent in the face of them, which had earned him the nickname of "Steinli," Little Stone. Albert left that night on the 7:50 train to Vienna, alone.

✧

During the visit to Kać, Hans Albert had been ill with a painful inflammation of his middle ear. In a letter written in 1970 to a longtime Marić family friend, Djordje Krstić, Hans Albert recalled, "[T]here was a big thunderstorm with a strong rain and all the gutters in the street were overflowing with water. . . . I remember that we both, my brother and I, were baptized Greek Catholic [sic] at that visit. It was in a local church, and I remember the beautiful singing."

Mileva, although herself quietly devout, raised her children neither Christian nor Jewish. She followed the traditional Serbian woman's path, expressed in the poem by Knez Rogan: "What a woman does is an ever-smiling wonder / In creeds she bothers nor of 'which' and 'what'; / A hundred times she'd change her faith; / So she might have the longing of her heart." In other words, Mileva did as Albert desired, which meant there was no organized religion in their home. But Mileva's father, it seems, had decided the time had come to introduce his grandsons to God.

Nikolajevska, St. Nicholas, the oldest church in Novi Sad, was constructed in the baroque style around 1730. Inside, the walls are decorated with gold filigree that catches the light coming through the stained glass windows and from the hundreds of flickering candles. The patriarch of the church, Father Teodor Milić, was a famous singer, preacher, political radical, and a personal friend of Miloš Marić's.

The family arrived at the church after the liturgy. Immediately, little Eduard started running in circles. No one could control him. Mileva's brother, Miloš, grabbed him as he headed behind the iconostasis, where no one but the priest is allowed, and brought him to the apse. There, a small cross, a silver bowl filled with oil, an etched crystal goblet filled with water, and a *Sveto Pismo,* the Bible, stood on an oval-shaped marble table. Soaring above them was a vaulted ceiling, frescoed with God and cherubic angels.

Mileva's friend Dr. Laza Marković, nicknamed "Mrgud," meaning grumpy, was appointed the children's *kum,* godfather. He held two large beeswax candles tied with blue ribbons. Father Milić, dressed in a red velvet robe with a thickly embroidered gold cross on the back, said a brief prayer and placed a white cloth on each of the children's shoulders. The priest then turned to face them and lifted a handful of water, sprinkling their head three times and saying, "The children of God are christened, Hans Albert and Eduard, in the name of the Father amen, and the Son amen, and the Holy Spirit amen." Father Milić crossed himself then anointed each of them with small crosses on the right sides of their foreheads, eyes, nostrils, mouths, ears, hands, legs. He repeated the ritual on the left sides of their bodies. Then Dr. Marković, along with the priest, led the boys around the marble table three times. A few strands of hair cut from each child's head were placed in a ball of wax and given to their grandparents whereupon all those in attendance crossed themselves and said amen.

On Monday, September 22, *Zastava, The Banner,* a Novi Sad newspaper, published an announcement of the christening.

LITTLE SWISS OF SERBIAN ORTHODOX FAITH

Yesterday in the local Serbian Orthodox Church, were baptized two little Swiss, sons of Albert Einstein, grandsons of our esteemed friend and fellow citizen, Miloš Marić. Little Albert and Eduard were baptized in the Serbian Orthodox faith according to the wishes of their grandfather, Miloš.

✦

By April 1914, as the fox-trot swept the Continent, Albert sashayed into a job in Berlin. He was appointed to the Royal Prussian Academy of Sciences.

"Tell me," he teased Elsa, "how did it come about that you knew of the impending appointment and were able to help bring it about?"

Again, Mileva did not want to leave Zurich. Moving to Berlin meant living near Albert's mother and all his relatives—including Elsa. Elsa, at Albert's urging, even offered Mileva her assistance in finding an apartment. Mileva turned her down. Incredibly, Albert could not understand why. He told Elsa that "my wife goes there [Berlin] with very mixed feelings. She is afraid of the relatives and probably most so of you (rightly so, I hope!)"

But Mileva had no choice. By now the marriage was in a terrible state. Albert decided that if Mileva wanted to stay married to him she would have to obey his rules:

"A. You will see to it (1) that my clothes and linen are kept in order, (2) that I am served three regular meals a day *in my room,* (3) that my bedroom and study are kept in good order and that *my desk is not touched by anyone other than me.* B. You will renounce all personal relations with me, except when they are required to keep up social appearances. In particular you will not request (1) that I sit with you at home, (2) that I go out with you or travel with you. C. You will promise explicitly to observe the following points in any contact with me: (1) you will expect no affection from me and you will not reproach me for this, (2) you must answer me at once when I speak to you, (3) you must leave my bedroom or study at once without protesting when I ask you to go. D. You will promise not to denigrate me in the eyes of the children, either by word or by deed.

Ever since you have been in Berlin, you have become quite nasty. You should know that people take an interest in the way the great man behaves."

Elsa and some of Albert's German colleagues freely shared their unpleasant feelings about Mileva, and Albert cheerfully encouraged them. Mileva could not contend with the gossips. While Albert had the strength to fight over money, belongings, and when and where the children could see him, Mileva was traumatized and barely functioning. She lasted only a few months in Berlin before taking the children back to Zurich.

Albert promptly moved into a bachelor flat around the corner from Elsa. On his own, Albert was thriving.

"Life without my wife," he wrote to Zangger in April 1915, "is a veritable rebirth for me personally." He struck the same note with Zangger three months later: "In personal respects I have never been so at peace and happy as now. I am living a very secluded and yet not lonely life, thanks to the loving care of my cousin, who had drawn me to Berlin in the first place, of course."

Albert was in love. His work was being recognized by the most esteemed scientists in the world. He was making more money. The better things went for him, the worse they became for Mileva. Her gloomy moods stretched out for days at a time, then weeks, and finally they became her, forever.

✧

On a peaceful, sunny summer day, June 28, 1914, Archduke Franz Ferdinand and his wife were assassinated in Sarajevo by Gavrilo Princip, a Bosnian Serb nationalist. The archduke's death was the occasion for the Austrian ultimatum one month later, which led directly to the declaration of the First World War. The Austro-Hungarian Empire declared war on the Kingdom of Serbia by sending them a telegram.

"All the powers are to hold the ring while Austria quietly strangles Serbia," the British Under-Secretary of State for Foreign Affairs Sir Arthur Nicolson noted. A day later, on July 29, as the bombardment of Belgrade commenced, the Savić family fled to Paris and Milivoj Savić took up a new occupation—procuring supplies for the Serbian army from Western Europe. Helene continued her work, in yet another war, with a rehabilitation program for wounded Serbian soldiers.

✧

On December 2, 1914, Belgrade was occupied by the Austrians. The Serbs had run out of ammunition. But Savić and his colleagues were hard at work. Thirteen days later, the Serbian army was quietly rearmed as they were bivouacked across the Sava River. On December 16, in a terrible blizzard, they attacked and retook Belgrade. More than 100,000 Austrians and as many Serbians were killed in the campaign.

✦

On November 25, 1915, the Serbian high command ordered a retreat across the mountains to the Adriatic coast. Their King Peter was carried on a stretcher during the exodus.

Serbia was overrun by the armies of the Central Powers. In Belgrade, women were fighting in the streets, caring for the wounded, burying the dead. Evidence was found of 306 women massacred by the Austrians in the Mačva, the northwestern part of Serbia.

Although Mileva was in Zurich, far from the war, she was still trying to retrieve her furniture and household items from Berlin. And at the same time, Albert was insisting that she was hoarding her dowry. In fact, she was using her dowry funds to meet her financial obligations. In January 1916, Albert promised Mileva that he would always take care of her and provide generously for the boys. However, he also made it clear that he found her "constant attempts to lay hold of everything that is in my possession absolutely disgraceful. Had I known you twelve years ago as I know you now, I would have viewed my responsibilities toward you at that time quite differently."

Mileva also was trying to find ways to make it easier for Albert to have a relationship with Hans Albert, since the correspondence between father and son had ceased. "I remember so well," she reminded Albert, "how much you used to love this little Albert, and consider it impossible that you would not want to help me remove bitterness from his life, and not increase it."

Her pleas on behalf of her son softened Albert and even might have had the effect of making him resist marrying Elsa. "The attempts to force me into marriage," he protested to Zangger in November, "come from my cousin's parents. . . . If I let myself be trapped, my life would become complicated . . ."

Finally, Albert took to his bed. After finishing the *General Theory of Rel-*

ativity he broke down, suffering from acute exhaustion. But as soon as he regained a little stamina, he was on the offensive again, demanding a divorce. Mileva still hoped that he might come back to her. Perhaps she thought that the longer he remained on his own, the better chance there was of finding a peaceful solution and keeping the family intact. After all, he had told her that he liked being a bachelor and that his autonomy "revealed itself as an indescribable blessing to me." She could not believe that he was now asking for a divorce—it could only mean that he wanted to remarry.

At the news, Mileva suffered a complete physical and emotional collapse and was hospitalized. Albert backed off—but not for long. By February 1916, he asked once more to "turn our now well-tested separation into a divorce." A month later, he was pushing her hard, offering ideas for a settlement. Then in April he came to Zurich to see his boys for the first time in seven months. At first the visit went well. But when Hans Albert, who was then twelve years old, asked his father to see Mileva, Albert refused and, in turn, Hans Albert refused to see him again during his stay. Albert accused Mileva of influencing the children against him. And yet, only ten days earlier, he had praised her for not alienating him from his children.

In July, Albert wrote to his friend, Michele Besso, who was also truly protective and helpful to Mileva and the children. "Now I see you developing a bitterness toward me for the sake of a woman who has nothing to do with you. Resist it! She would not be worth it, even if she were a hundred thousand times more in the right! . . . We men are deplorable, dependent creatures, this I admit gladly to anyone. But compared to these women, every one of us is a king; for he stands more or less on his own feet, not constantly waiting for something outside to cling on to. They, however, always wait for someone to come along who will use them as he sees fit. If this does not happen, they simply fall to pieces."

Hans Albert and Eduard, who was now six, needed their father. But at the end of July, Albert told Hans Albert that he could not "get away from here [Berlin] just now because I have too much work to do." In a postscript he suggests that perhaps Aunt Zorka could come and care for them, even though he knew that Zorka was eccentric and had been displaying strange and disturbing behavior.

Then Albert took another baffling sidestep. On the same day he wrote to Hans Albert that he could not come to see him, he wrote the opposite to Zangger. He said he would see the children, "Without hesitation, to keep the boys company throughout the day when they return from holiday, so that they do not get the feeling of being alone." He also contradicted himself when he said that he "would come by all means. I have no requisite duties in the near future."

At the beginning of August, Helene came to Zurich, taking a break from her war duties, and anxious about Mileva. Finding her in bed, unable to care for the children, Helene packed the children's bags and bundled them off to Vilars sur Beaumont, near Lake Geneva, where the Savićs had rented a country house. Mileva would have some quiet time alone to try to recover while Helene and the boys joined Julka, Zora, and two of Helene's nieces, Mara Maslać and Stana Košanin, for a holiday. Julka was fourteen years old, with deep-set eyes emphasized by dark circles. She was extremely introverted and shy, and excelled in school, particularly in the sciences and mathematics. Added to the five children in the Savić house were eight more in the vicinity. The children formed a tribe and built a secret shed of branches in the woods. Hans Albert marked the overgrown path to their hideout by notching the trees with his own axe. Indeed, Helene had to pay a fine to the landlord for scarring the timber.

During the holiday, Helene tried to cajole Hans Albert into writing to his father, but he refused.

"I believe," Albert wrote Michele Besso toward the end of August, "that [Hans Albert's] negative attitude toward me has fallen below the freezing point." And then, as if trying to appease everyone, he continued, "in his place, under the given circumstances, I also would probably have reacted in the same way." In a rare compassionate moment, he even admitted to Zangger that he was "very sorry for the woman, and I also believe that her difficult experiences with me and through me are at least partly to blame for her serious illness." Nevertheless, he still did not see the boys, although he now promised not to trouble Mileva "any more with the divorce."

September 1916 was unusually warm in Europe. People were uncomfortable and irritable. The Battle of the Somme was in progress. In six weeks, the Allies had advanced only a couple of miles, and the death toll was beyond comprehension. Hans Albert and Eduard were both in school in neutral Switzerland. Mileva still could not cope with day-to-day household duties and paid a maid to look after her children. The doctors thought she might be suffering from cerebral tuberculosis.

On September 8, Albert wrote to Helene about his sons. He complained that they did not understand him and, consequently, felt only anger. He added that indeed it might be better if "their father does not see them anymore." He asked Helene not "to feel sorry for me; despite my external troubles, my life goes by in perfect harmony."

Albert detested Mileva now as much as his mother ever had. In the same letter to Helene, he wrote that Mileva "*is* and *will* forever remain for me an amputated limb. I will never again be close to her. I will finish my days far from her, feeling this is absolutely necessary."

Around September 10, Mileva collapsed again and was admitted to a Catholic sanatorium, the Theodosianum, on Asylstrasse in Zurich. She was suffering from severe anxiety and had an excruciating case of periostitis, an inflammation of the membrane covering the bone—in her case, the spine—which had not, until now, been diagnosed.

After almost five weeks in the hospital, Mileva wrote Helene a short note, trying to assuage her concerns. "I will most probably return home soon and continue there to attend to my health."

Meanwhile, Albert urged Hans Albert to write again to his aunt Zorka because "she is very worried about Mama and is not allowed to visit now."

But two weeks later, he wrote in a fit of pique, "Your father's path was not always strewn with roses like now, but rather with thorns! Just ask your mother to tell you about the early days sometimes." Albert, it seems, was goading Hans Albert to challenge the bedridden Mileva about her past. This dare might have led to a devastating revelation to an impressionable child already overburdened by the family's troubled state of affairs.

✧

Mileva battled illness all through the winter and into the spring. "Why I have to suffer so much, I do not know," she wrote Helene on January 1, 1917. In May 1917, she was back in the hospital. She took Eduard, who was ill with a lung inflammation and a persistent high fever, with her. She sent Hans Albert to the Zanggers. After a month the family reunited. Eduard was feeling better, but Mileva was still struggling with her health.

Albert decided to take Hans Albert out of Zurich. At first he considered bringing him to Berlin, thinking he would educate him at home. Then he changed his mind and thought about sending him to live in Lucerne with his sister, Maja. But Albert apparently did not have the courage to approach his own sister with the request—he asked Michele Besso to do it for him. In the meantime, he weighed other options for Hans Albert, each one farther away from Mileva—perhaps to live with a former student in Frauenfeld, or with Besso's son in Glarisegg.

"My wife," Albert wrote Besso, "must not be considered in this matter, but rather only what is advisable for the boy." It was only through the determination of Besso and Zangger that Hans Albert remained with his mother.

For the month of July, Albert took Hans Albert and Eduard to the Swiss Alpine village of Arosa. Sloping against granite cliffs at an altitude of 5,900 feet, the village also edges the shore of Lake Obersee. Albert delivered Eduard to the Pedolin Sanatorium for Children in the older part of town for a planned year's convalescence, and then he and Hans Albert explored the thick fir woodlands and lakes of the Schanfigg Valley.

In August, Mileva was back in the hospital, and Albert became seriously ill with stomach catarrh, then duodenal ulcers. He lost fifty-six pounds in two months. To be better cared for, in September 1917, he moved to the flat above Elsa's on Haberlandstrasse 5, in the district of Schöneberg. Because of the war, it was hard to feed him properly; there was scarcely any food in Berlin. The bread was almost inedible; the rations were inadequate. Lard, meat, and sugar were virtually nonexistent, and only cabbages were readily available. But somehow Elsa managed to find food and mother her "Albertle" back to health.

All the while, Albert insisted that Eduard be returned to Zurich because he could not "come up with the money" to keep him in the sanatorium. Anyway, he said in a letter to Besso, "I do not believe in the new medical magic with X rays. I am at the point where I only trust *post mortem* diagnoses, nothing else."

Finally, in October, Mileva's sister, Zorka, came to Zurich to care for her at home. It proved to be a disaster. Albert's friend Zangger wrote that he was hoping "the sister would assume the domestic chores. However, she has become melancholic and had to be attended to in an asylum." Zorka was admitted to the Burghölzli Psychiatric Clinic in Zürich, where she remained for two years.

Meanwhile, another catastrophe befell the Marić family. Mileva's brother, Miloš, who had been serving as a battalion doctor for the Austro-Hungarian army, was captured by the Russians and reported missing, presumed dead.

✧

On March 4, 1918, Mileva was readmitted to the hospital for two weeks—while Eduard was transferred to another high-altitude sanatorium, this time in the canton of Appenzellerland—and Hans Albert was invited to stay with the Zanggers.

Once more, Albert applied to Mileva for a divorce. He pleaded with her, "Just put yourself in my place. Elsa has two daughters, of whom the elder is eighteen years old [she was in fact twenty], i.e., of marriageable age. This child, who is already handicapped through the loss of her eye, has had to suffer from rumors that have been circulating regarding my relationship with her mother. That weighs upon me and needs to be remedied through a formal marriage."

Albert was not being honest. By May, he had made it clear that he wanted to marry Elsa's daughter Ilse. Ilse reported to a friend, Georg Nicolai: "Yesterday, suddenly the question was raised about whether A. wished to marry Mama or me. . . . Albert himself is refusing to take any decision, he is prepared to marry either Mama or me. I know that A. loves me very much, perhaps more than any other man ever will, he also told me so himself yesterday. . . . [But] I have never wished nor felt the least desire to be close to him physically. This [is] otherwise in his case—recently at least. He himself even admitted to me once how difficult it is

for him to keep himself in check. But still I do believe that my feelings for
him do not suffice for conjugal life. . . . In the end, I would feel like a
slave girl who has been sold. . . . You must admit, this is a somewhat unnatural thing for our sensibilities nowadays. . . . (Although A. asserts that
these are social prejudices.) . . . A. also thought that if I did not wish to
have a child of his it would be nicer for me not to be married to him. And
I truly do not have this wish. . . . I do not know whether it really would
be fair—after all [my mother's] years of struggle—[if] I were to compete
with her over the place she had won for herself, now that she is finally at
the goal. It will seem peculiar to you that I, a silly little thing of a twenty-
year-old, would have to decide on such a serious matter; I can hardly believe it myself and it makes me also feel very unhappy. Help me! Yours,
Ilse."

At the top of the letter, Ilse had written, "Please destroy this letter immediately after reading it!"

Shortly after Ilse wrote this letter, Albert wrote Mileva and told her
that he had changed his mind about coming to see the boys in the summer. Instead, he had decided to go to Ahrenshoop, a remote village on the
Baltic Sea, with Elsa, Ilse, and Ilse's younger sister, Margot.

In September, Mileva was once again in the hospital.

"How the children are managing is a mystery to me," Albert wrote
his mother. Actually, it was thanks to the constant attentions of Zangger
and Besso that the family managed. Zangger was angry with Albert, char-
acterizing his "renewed divorce offensive as a knife at the throat without
advance warning." Finally, it was too much: Mileva's unconditional devotion to Albert was shattered. She seemed determined to heal herself—
and to embrace the future of her children.

✧

For both Mileva and Helene, 1918 was a year of terror and death. Helene's
sister, Marija (Kaufler) Doublier, died of cancer, leaving behind two little
girls.

After commiserating with Helene, Mileva wrote, "I cannot tell you
how much I suffer because of my sister, who has been sick for ten months
already and does not get better at all. There is nothing more terrible than

to see somebody whom you love in such a condition and to feel how much she also suffers."

During the war, Mileva even in her incapacitated state, had tried to help Helene. Helene had inherited money from her family in Vienna and had given it to Mileva for safe-keeping. Mileva placed the 674 Swiss francs, along with 200 Swiss gold francs in a bank in Zurich and kept at home two Austrian pierced ducats and an undisclosed amount of silver money. Whenever Helene needed money, Mileva sent Hans Albert to the bank with the necessary papers to facilitate a money transfer.

By September 1918, the end of the First World War was in sight. Helene and her family returned home to Belgrade, but they found that their house had been confiscated by a German officer. He had broken into the safe, looking for money, jewels, or silver. According to Helene's grandson, Milan Popović, Helene found the safe ajar and some of Mileva's letters missing.

✧

"I am very eager to see which will take longer, the war or our divorce," Albert wrote Mileva. As it happened, the divorce was the longer contest. On Valentine's Day 1919, Albert and Mileva's marriage was officially dissolved. As the defendant, Albert declared to the court in longhand that he had "no accusations against the plaintiff. The real reason for the dissension lies in the differences of personalities. Since June 1914, we have lived completely separate. During the marriage there have been numerous scenes because of differences of opinion where on the part of the plaintiff verbal and physical abuse occurred to which I in a state of irritation . . . responded. . . . It is true that I committed adultery. I have been living for approximately four and one-half years with my cousin, the widow Elsa Löwenthal, and since then I have had intimate relations with her. My wife, the plaintiff, has been informed that I have had intimate relations with my cousin since the summer of 1914. She expressed her indignation to me."

According to Swiss law, in the case of adultery, the guilty party cannot remarry for one to three years. In the Zurich divorce court, a ban was placed on Albert preventing him from remarrying for two years. Damning the "philistines," Albert married Elsa at the Berlin registry office five months later, on June 2. Although he had always mocked the bourgeois lifestyle of Berliners, he settled comfortably into Elsa's quiet, conventional, middle-class life.

Mileva never remarried. Albert, on the other hand, was only just beginning his romantic exploits. He continued his pursuit of women and his extramarital affairs long after his marriage to Elsa. It is believed that all of Albert's letters to and from his intimate women friends were "destroyed at his request."

✧

On September 22, 1919, Albert was delighted to discover that experiments conducted by British scientists during the solar eclipse of May 29 confirmed his theory of relativity by successfully measuring the bending of light. The press treated it as an enormously newsworthy event—as if Einstein had been competing with Sir Isaac Newton and had won. Part of Einstein's theory of relativity involved disproving Newton's claim that light is deflected from the sun at 0.87 second of arc by proving that light is deflected by 1.7 seconds of arc. On November 6, the Royal Astronomical Society in London officially confirmed his findings. Overnight, Albert became a twentieth-century legend.

And yet, being the most famous man in the world neither changed nor solved his personal problems. Albert was still griping about Mileva. And Mileva was still struggling emotionally, even though her health was improving. Because of Albert's unpleasantness, Mileva was reluctant to allow Hans Albert, now fifteen years old, to visit him. In any case, Hans Albert did not like Elsa. Indeed, much to Albert's chagrin, he was openly rude to her. In an effort to persuade Mileva to allow the boy to visit, Albert promised, "[My] wife will keep in the background. I can even take meals with him alone, if you like. But these are minor details. A man should not have to go to such lengths on account of you women."

Clearly, Albert had no patience with and very little respect for women. The only female scientist to whom he accorded a modicum of respect was Marie Curie, and even that he could not do without qualification: "She has a sparkling intelligence," he wrote Zangger, "but despite her passionate nature she is not attractive enough to represent a danger to anyone."

Even from Elsa, he kept his distance. Once when she referred to the two of them as "us," Albert retorted, "talk about you or me but never about us." This was the man he had become—a far cry from the romantic who freely wrote about "our" work in his letters to Mileva when they were young lovers.

The only female Albert had a difficult time denying was his mother. In January 1920, soon after Albert and Elsa married, Pauline Einstein came to die in her son's new home.

Pauline was terminally ill with abdominal cancer and moved into Albert's study, where she was attended by a Hungarian-born physician, János Plesch. Until he was expelled from Berlin by the Nazis in the summer of 1933, Dr. Plesch was Albert Einstein's personal physician. He was also a close confidant for the rest of Albert's life.

Oddly, he may even have met Mileva many years before. In September 1894, two months before Mileva left for school in Switzerland, János Plesch was stationed in Novi Sad as a member of the Royal and Imperial Army of the Hapsburg Empire, not to fight, since there was no war, but to uphold a "seignorial loyalty to the House of Hapsburg and its traditions." Plesch spoke elegant, polished German and was gregarious, inquisitive, and a lady's man. Such a man probably socialized with the local gentry, where he may have met members of Mileva's family, if not Mileva herself.

Plesch went on to establish one of the most successful medical practices in Germany. He was connected, professionally and privately, with all the right people—including Marlene Dietrich, Samuel Goldwyn, Josef von Sternberg, Arturo Toscanini, Richard Strauss, Max Liebermann, Oskar Kokoschka, and Marie Curie. The famous director Max Reinhardt was a friend to both Plesch and Albert.

Plesch tried to make Pauline comfortable, although he feared she would endure long months of excruciating pain before death took her. To everyone's surprise, Pauline died in February, only a few weeks after moving into her son's home. Albert was "saddened but not heartbroken."

✧

At the end of 1920, just as Mileva was settling into her new life, Albert decided that she and the boys should move to Darmstadt, a German city halfway between Zürich and Berlin. As a result of the postwar economy, Albert claimed that they "could live better in Darmstadt than in Zurich" and that it had a good polytechnic institute for Hans Albert. Mileva, asked to uproot her sons from their familiar surroundings and herself from the comforts of home and friends, not surprisingly refused. "Your opposition to this move is so unnatural," Albert complained, "that I am often reproached for neglecting my responsibility to you."

Meanwhile, Albert would go his own way. In the spring of 1921, Albert and Elsa made their first trip to America and were astonished by their reception. Reporters and photographers swarmed over the arrival pier in New York. Airplanes circled above them, trailing bright banners and welcoming messages. Flowers and colorful confetti were tossed from open windows as the city's official car, a two-year-old black Packard Twin Six with a broken headlight and a bent license plate, proceeded through the city. Driving in front of them was another car with an enormous placard that read, "This is the famous Albert Einstein."

In spite of—or perhaps because of—all this attention, Albert expressed his disdain for America. He declared after his visit, "the excessive enthusiasm for me in America appears to be typically American. And if I grasp it correctly, the reason is that the people in America are colossally bored. After all, there is so little for them there.

"Above all things are the women who, as a literal fact, dominate the entire life in America. The men take an interest in absolutely nothing at all. The women do everything which is the vogue, and now, quite by chance, they have thrown themselves on the Einstein fashion."

✧

As Mileva grew healthier, she must have become increasingly preoccupied with thoughts of Lieserl. In 1924, Mileva wrote to Helene, "How are you and your family, your grandchildren! Mara and Stana are of course hardworking students. Aren't any of them willing to study in Zurich for a while? I have such good memories about this flock of girls that I would be so pleased to get to know some of them better."

Over the next few years, at least five young women from Belgrade paid visits to Mileva in Zurich—Julka and Zora Savić; Stana Košanin and Mara Maslać, nieces of Helene Savić and the "hardworking students" mentioned by Mileva; and Milica Stefanović, the daughter of Mileva's school friend Milana Bota Stefanović.

"You are familiar with my unfulfilled wish to have a daughter," Mileva continued to Helene, "I would be such a——" Again, maddeningly, there the page ends.

Mileva's "unfulfilled wish" may suggest again that Helene was aware of the loss of Lieserl. Or perhaps we should draw the opposite conclusion—that Helene believed Mileva never had the daughter she longed for. Only one thing is certain: If Helene did know about Lieserl, she kept the secret all her life.

✧

As Julka Savić grew older, her face changed, becoming square-shaped and appearing to sit plumb on her wide neck. She still had the charcoal-ringed eyes and the quiet, mysterious smile, and she still bore no resemblance to her sister, Zora. As soon as she finished her university schooling, she married a Serb, Novak Popović. Right before Julka's marriage, Mileva and Helene spoke confidentially. Mileva wrote to her friend:

"What you have confided to me in the last hours of our getting together moved me very much and gave me a lot to think about. It would have been reassuring to you, and made you happy if your child [Julka] had her heart's wish fulfilled. But whether she would have been happier because of it, who can know? Who can know what fate has planned for us? Think of the fate of your one friend [Mileva] and in a smaller measure, also of your other friend [she probably refers here to Milana Bota, who died of cancer], and I think that you can look quietly into the future and entrust Julka to her bridegroom, who seems to be a splendid person."

It is difficult to determine what Julka's "heart's wish" could have been—perhaps not to marry, perhaps to attend university in another city. Almost immediately she became pregnant with her first child, Jelena, who was born in May 1923, followed by a son, Milan, in November 1924. Julka and her husband lived with her parents, on Katanicéva Street, rather than with his. But staying at home was not Julka's way. She began medical school soon after the births of her children and worked straight through, without a break, until she finished. She began practicing in 1926 as a volunteer at the General State Hospital in Belgrade and also taught at the university. Helene remained the matriarch of her extended family. Her grandchildren were especially close to her. Since Julka was utterly involved in her work, Helene was very much their surrogate mother.

✧

In early summer, 1933, before Albert emigrated to America, he and Helene Savić may have seen each other in Novi Sad where Helene was visiting friends. But Albert's alleged trip to Novi Sad is much disputed. Non-Serbian historians take that position because there is no factual proof that Albert was not there. Serbian historians are unyielding in their conviction that he was indeed in Novi Sad at that time. Two well-known and highly esteemed citizens of Novi Sad, Dr. Aleksander Moč and Dr. Kosta Hadži, maintained that they spoke with Albert that summer at the Queen Elizabeth Café. Dr. Moč, for one, had known Albert for many years. The three gentlemen reportedly sat at a table near the sidewalk, talking about the postwar situation in Germany.

But why would Albert have been in Serbia without a professional agenda, just prior to seeking refuge in America? In the absence of official documents, itineraries, or academic appointments, the only aspect left to consider is that his mission was a personal one—a leave-taking in which he sought a form of closure.

✧

Helene Savić's eighty-two-year-old aunt Caroline and her cousin, Malvina, both Jewish, were isolated in Vienna when the Second World War broke out. Malvina was first thrown in jail and then into a concentration camp. Albert, meanwhile, was safe in Princeton, New Jersey, and receiving requests for references from Jews stranded in Europe. Some letters addressed to "Herr Albert Einstein, America" actually reached him.

In 1939, Helene wrote to him. She pleaded with him formally: "You, most honored Herr Professor, have so often helped many unfortunates who have found themselves in this same situation. Is it possible for me to hope that also my relatives can be saved through your noble help and position?" Helene reminded him of their happy "hours together in Zürich and Vienna and on your dear visits to Kijevo and Belgrade." She closes the letter, "Sincerely yours, Helene Savić née Kaufler, Katanićeva 10, Belgrade, Yugoslavia."

Albert answered Helene briefly. He was "only helping to bring out younger people," he said. "The replanting of older people must take second place." Both Malvina and Caroline perished in a concentration camp.

✧

In 1932, Milivoj Savić lost his job with the ministry, probably because of his outspokenness and political leanings.

"It made me quite sad to hear that your husband lost his position," Mileva wrote Helene. "I can imagine vividly what that means to him. The other matter of which you write me has distressed me no less. Unfortunately, a large part of all troubles in this world comes from women. And it is sad to say that just those women who know very well how to work their way through the dark often have quite a lot of luck." It seems the women suspected that Milivoj was having an affair.

A few weeks later, Mileva wrote again and asked Helene if Milivoj had "reconciled himself with giving up his position. I well understand," she further empathized, "that for such an industrious person as he is, the most difficult thing is to give up his work."

After this, something must have happened between Mileva and Helene, because their lifelong friendship abruptly ended. There are no further letters between the two friends. Indeed, when Milivoj died of a stroke, in 1940, Mileva did not send Helene a letter of sympathy. Rather, she conveyed her condolences through Helene's niece Stana Košanin.

"I am very sad that [your] Uncle Savić has left us forever," she wrote. "I remember many escapades from our youth and I am sorry that another good friend has left us. Please give my greeting to Helene and tell her that I am sorry that she has lost her companion. But perhaps it is good that he was able to calm down and will find some peace. . . ."

By 1941, Julka's husband too had died. In April, the ferocious bombardment of Belgrade forced the extended Savić family together under one roof on Katanićeva Street. The burden of supporting the family fell on Julka. Although by now a lung specialist, she did not earn very much money. To see her patients she had to travel by overcrowded trams, carrying heavy equipment, including a machine for treating tuberculosis. Most people in Belgrade had family in villages who sent them food, but the Savićs had none. They struggled along for another three years. By then, the situation had grown even more desperate. There was very little food, no heating fuel, few of the fundamental human necessities. Helene was rail-thin and slowly becoming a shadow. Eleven years after Mileva's last letter to her, Helene died of pneumonia and starvation. Even in her estrangement from Mileva, she held to the loyal Serbian way and left the earth with her friend's secrets unbetrayed.

PART THREE

R umor in Serbia always embraces a fragment of truth," my friend Slavica Dokmanović wrote to me. "Come to Serbia, I will show you. We will work together to find the missing daughter. It will be an adventure."

The fortitude it takes to track down information almost a century old in a country that had suffered four major wars between 1912 and 1944 can be summed up by the Serbian adage: *Be patient as an ox, | as brave as a lion, | as industrious as a bee, | and as cheerful as a bird.* In 1995, Serbia was embroiled in yet another war, and I was to find myself forty kilometers from one of its enemies, Croatia, and sixty-five kilometers from its other enemy, Bosnia— and struck numb by the pity of it all. I set out on my journey, knowing I should wait until the war was over, but there was no sign of when that might be.

Slavica is a lawyer and the director of the Clinic of Gynecology and

Obstetrics in Novi Sad and the mother of a Serbian student, Marija Dokmanović, whom I had befriended in America. Months before I met Slavica in person, she began to navigate for me the circuitous routes toward
obtaining the official documents that would assist me in my search for
Lieserl. Slavica lives with her husband in Sremski Karlovci, once considered the intellectual heart of the Vojvodina. Now it is a downtrodden
town, struggling to survive the latest conflict.

"Not to worry," she said, "we will move around the war."

Slavica's promise and her optimism lured me overseas to retrace Mileva's path and to learn what became of her daughter.

✧

I flew to Bern on September 7, 1995. For two days I adjusted to European
time and explored the city, photographing the areas where Mileva and Albert had lived. The morning of the third day was cool and gloomy. At a
few minutes after seven, the street lights were still lit. As I walked to the
train station, I kept my head down against the mist, but my face was
damp, my body chilled. I boarded the 7:45 to Zurich and arrived exactly
on schedule, seventy-two minutes later. After buying the *International Herald Tribune,* I boarded the 9:33 to Vienna. Almost to the minute, this was the
schedule and route Mileva had taken in 1901 when she returned home to
give birth to Lieserl.

My compartment was empty, and I situated myself as I have done for
years, according to my own particular working ritual. I placed my notebook on the small folding table under the window and set my camera and
the first of many Swiss chocolate bars on the plush red seat beside me. I
took off my shoes, put on my Chinese slippers, and settled in.

Looking out toward the front of the train, I could see the conductor
dressed in a natty dark blue uniform with gold and red braid around his
collar and cuffs of his sleeves. He was standing at the very edge of the
platform, leaning toward the tracks, holding a round white sign with a
red circle painted in the center, "the poached egg." He waved the sign back
and forth in a wide arc, and we silently glided out of the station.

The train moved through a still, frozen landscape, skirting the high

Alps bordered with autumnal colors, golden villages and russet farms. For a few moments the clouds parted, and a faint half-moon appeared.

Abruptly, the train came to a screeching halt. Across the tracks and down the embankment through thick snow, a black-and-white mother dog and her two pups stumbled toward the edge of a dense pine forest and disappeared behind a row of trees. The train lurched onward.

At dusk, I changed trains in Vienna, and finally arrived at Budapest's Keleti Station at 10:33 in the evening. A Hungarian friend in Budapest had made arrangements with a commercial van company to take me the next day directly to Slavica's home, not far from Novi Sad. I had been warned that the trains to Serbia were unsafe and had recently experienced a slew of robberies and murders. To make matters worse, neither credit cards nor travelers checks were accepted in Serbia. I was wearing around my waist a money belt with eight thousand dollars in twenty-dollar bills to pay for interpreters, housing, food, gifts, and transportation. I was also carrying money from a feminist humanitarian organization in the United States for the Serbian branch of an organization called Women in Black. This group had been standing silently in protest on the streets of Belgrade every Wednesday since the beginning of the war. They were also operating a rape hotline, a rape crisis center, and an outreach program for women and children refugees.

The following morning, I found myself seated in the most dilapidated, cigarette-smoke-dingy minivan imaginable. It was apparent that the driver slept in the van while waiting for his passengers. There was only one other traveler besides me, a Serbian woman from Chicago whose only English word was "shit." Finally, we left for the frontier in a puff of black-leaded petrol exhaust.

We drove through flat expanses of farmland and vineyards in western Hungary. Thousands of little sticks used to mark grape seedlings were standing at attention like wooden soldiers. Winter wheat was throwing its first haze of green across the fields. Where the earth was newly plowed, steam rose from the dirt, creating a chessboard of gray clouds and light green vistas.

After riding for two hours, I began to notice something odd. One

Serbian bus after another was coming toward us, filled to overflowing with men. I thought maybe they were headed across the border into Hungary to find work. But I learned from the driver, with the aid of my Serbo-Croatian dictionary, that they were smugglers. The international embargo was forcing thousands of men to find a way to supply goods to the people of Serbia. Granted, some were scoundrels, but most were just trying to make a living by buying food, clothing, books, cigarettes, alcohol, and medicine in Budapest and returning home to resell them.

"These men, they are not thieves," the driver insisted. "They are in a terrible situation. We have a saying, 'Life gives to every slave an empty glass to fill either with his tears or with hope.' We are the slaves of Milo˘sevi´c and his mafia."

When we reached Kelebija, a border town of the former Yugoslavia, a number of vehicles, including our minivan, were waved to the side by a female Serbian guard with brassy yellow permed hair and red ruby lipstick. I watched as dollars and German marks were slipped into passports, identity cards, bills of lading. The driver told me that the guards who work here can afford to retire and open small businesses after three months. The female guard, who was toting a serious-looking pistol on her hip, was going from car to truck to car, leaning into the drivers' windows and smiling prettily while she was handed the stuffed documents. We handed over our cushioned documents. None of us said a word. With a flick of her ruby red nails, we were waved through.

It was dark and raining when we arrived in Sremski Karlovci. The town was engulfed in a clammy fog. Every light shining through a window or on a street corner was using the least wattage possible. Even the headlights of the few cars on the road were so dim that I had to strain to see the vehicles themselves. We looked for Slavica's street, *Železnička ulica,* Railroad Street. After driving along the highway that followed the railroad tracks, we came to a dark ochre house with brown wooden shutters and lace-curtained windows. Slavica was waiting by the gate, under an umbrella.

Slavica has the face of Balkan memories—broad, open, and oval-shaped with a wide forehead. She has Slavonic eyes, gray, turning almost black when she is angry. Her hair is also gray, thick and wavy, trimmed short. Later I was to learn that it is unusual in sophisticated urban areas of Serbia for women not to color their hair as they grow older. It is a sign, an unspoken declaration, that a woman has a mind of her own if she allows her hair to go gray. A few months earlier, I had asked Slavica's daughter, Marija, if her mother was a feminist.

"Not a lot of people are aware of feminism, nor is feminism much discussed in Serbia," Marija told me. "But knowing my mother and knowing her thoughts, I would say she is a raging feminist!"

Slavica reminded me of the Serbian proverb, *Seeing, suffering, and death are the three teachers of people. Seeing makes people wise, suffering makes them wiser, and death makes them wisest of all.* I could see that Slavica had lived a life very different from my own. She kissed me the traditional three times, and then we embraced like old friends.

✧

Slavica already had a connection to Mileva because her mother-in-law had been a friend of the Marić family. She even had heirlooms from Mileva's family: Four postcards, one from Mileva and three from her sister, Zorka—and an original, unpublished photograph of Mileva, Zorka, and their brother, Miloš.

"But this is our most precious," she said, showing me a tiny white fluted teacup with deep-pink painted flowers and a gold handle. "This is the cup that Albert Einstein always requested when he came for tea."

After a supper of *palačinke sa mesom,* a thin rolled pancake filled with ground meat and topped with sour cream and bright red *ajvar,* paprika paste, and *kisela čorba,* a soup made with carrots, rice, chicken, lemon, and vinegar, Slavica took off her apron.

"You sit there," she said, directing me to a seat at the long dining room table, "and I will sit here." She sat down across from me and planted her elbows on the table. Between us she had placed our correspondence, books, a pot of coffee, and sweets.

Slavica believes fiercely in family. When the war created economic collapse in 1994, she foresaw the plight her loved ones would face before anyone else did. She bought twenty chickens and four turkeys and put them in her backyard. She planted vegetables and stockpiled flour. She was ready for hard times, and hard times came quickly. By the end of the year, no one was drawing a salary. Her father-in-law, a retired priest, who lived on a pension, was shocked one day when he tried to buy a tube of toothpaste. The cost was three months' worth of his pension. He thought he would buy an egg to cook for his dinner instead. To his chagrin, he found that four months' pension bought only half of an uncooked egg.

Slavica's husband, Nikola, is an engineer for a sugar company and fortunately was paid in sugar. This he bartered for a little petrol here, food from a friend's farm there—and they managed, but just barely. Like most people in Serbia at this time, they made their home a safe haven. They knew the comfort within their walls gave them a false sense of safety, but they had to believe in it or flee their country. In fact, I had written to Slavica before my arrival, begging her to leave, and had arranged for a place her family could stay in Budapest.

"Thank you very much for your kind letters," Slavica had responded. "Thank you for taking care of us. The situation here is miserable. The crisis is reaching its peak. My salvation is my faith in God. Your escape plan to Budapest is a big relief for me indeed. However, I do not think of escaping into a foreign country or anywhere because of these two reasons: I cannot live on welfare, and I have a duty to defend my property, for the house would be robbed.

"I had a grandfather whom I liked very much. He died twenty years ago. I heard these words from him, 'God give us peace and good health and all of our plans will be realized.' These words represent a great truth. We are longing for peace, peace of our souls and peace in our countries. But the war is spreading. I ask you. Who is fighting whom?"

Now, months later, at her table, Slavica explained to me, "We are becoming more and more unstable every day because there is no way out. At least, we do not see the way out. This creates depression and sorrow. Most of the population does not deserve to lead such a life or end up in such a life. Until the pain touches you with its little finger, you do not know what pain is." I could feel Slavica attempting to calm the air around us.

"We are going to find Lieserl. Remember," she continued, patting the table with the palms of her hands, "we are a country of women who are only one generation away from the farmlands, the pastures of our ancestors. We are also educated and curious and intuitive and can reason the circumstances. I am convinced this search is something that can be put on the daylight."

"What do you mean, 'on the daylight?' " I asked.

Slavica laughed. "Shine the light on the question and you will be able to find the answer in the dark."

"Then maybe you can tell me why Mileva would give up her child in a society that prided itself on a close family tradition?"

"Try not to forget," she persisted, reaching across the table to pat my hand, *"Zaklela se zemlja raju da se tajne sve saznaju,* the earth pledged to paradise that all secrets will be revealed."

I commented on the sprinkling of Serbian proverbs throughout Slavica's speech. She smiled. "It is part of our custom to use adages," she said. "I think you will better understand my country through a direct translation of my mother tongue. It is preferable for our work together, rather than using the American vernacular."

That first night, Slavica attempted to educate me about how a Serbian woman would think through a problem.

"We take all the ingredients and roll them around in our minds. Then like a ball of dough, we knead it, like this." She pantomimed kneading bread dough. "We push it here, roll it there, until we can lift it off the table without it sticking to anything. We let it rest for a while. When it has expanded with ideas, we bake until our answer is firm."

By one in the morning, we had developed a plan. We would focus on as many of the Marić family members and friends as possible—especially the women, who held the memories, kept the letters, passed on the legends—and to find records of the Marić family history. We needed to locate people who knew the truth about Lieserl. But most of all, we needed to find witnesses. There is a heroic pride in telling the truth among the Serbian people.

Later, as I was trying to sleep, a crowd of men gathered outside my window, boisterously drunk. Slavica went outside and asked them to be quiet.

"Go home," she said.

"We cannot go home," they answered. "We have no home."

They were refugees from the Krajina who were camping behind the little shop across the dirt road from my bedroom window.

✦

In the morning, more refugees were moving down the road, many on foot, carrying large bundles on their heads or strapped to their backs. Pots and pans were attached to the bundles with string, rope, and old leather strips, clanging against one another. Some of the refugees perched on tractors that had run out of petrol and were being pulled by horses, cows, and oxen. One wagon had been resourcefully outfitted with eight bicycle wheels and was being towed by a milk cow. The cow's teats were swollen, swaying, and knocking against her back legs. Each time they hit her legs, she made a pathetic whimper.

"Where are they going?" I asked Slavica.

"They are heading for nowhere," she answered, and then the telephone rang. A few moments later, I heard her gasp.

"Da, da—da, da," she said, and put down the receiver. She began to pace. "A historian from Novi Sad has heard about your search," Slavica said incredulously. "He told me not to bother any longer, that you, the *Amerikanka,* should go back to America, that he has found Lieserl!" She stopped pacing and sat down. "He is going right now to check the village's record office and will call us back. I do not believe him."

As we were letting this upsetting news sink in, the doorbell rang. Slavica's niece and sister-in-law had arrived. Coffee and cakes were served, and since everyone spoke English, however haltingly, we chatted about my trip. Slavica's sister-in-law, Miroslava Djordjević, is a doctor of gynecology and obstetrics, and her daughter, Aleksandra, is a biochemist. I was anxious to show them some photographs that had been loaned to me by Evelyn Einstein, the daughter of Hans Albert, who lives in California. There was an especially interesting picture of Zorka, Mileva's sister, sitting on a balcony, holding a baby on her lap. I asked the three women if they could determine the child's gender.

"First we must see if the child is wearing earrings," Miroslava said.

At the turn of the century, when a girl was born, the midwife would wrap the baby in her apron and bring her into the yard. There, she would pass the baby through a hoop and swing her toward the east three times, after which she would stand on the doorstep and ask the mother three times, "Do you see the sun or the moon?" The mother, hidden behind the door, would say, "The sun!" Then the midwife would pierce the child's ears with a thin razor or a needle and loop a silk thread strung with antique silver coins through the holes. The child would wear the coins for one, three, five, or seven months. Then, on a day set aside for the ceremony, the same midwife who placed the coins in the child's ears would remove them and throw them into a clear running stream or a fire. Afterward, the midwife would take the baby girl to a rock and sit down. Here the baby would be breast-fed three times by a woman from the village whose every child had survived.

In a simpler version of this rite which is still practiced today, a baby girl's ears are pierced one day after birth. A string is threaded through each ear, dangling a small gold coin. The coins are worn until the thread breaks, and then they are replaced with gold studs. "In this picture," Slavica showed us, "the child is without earrings. I understand from our relative that Mileva's mother wanted to do the traditional piercing but Lieserl's grandfather Marić forbade it. He thought it was old-fashioned and pagan. And he was the master."

Then they looked at the style of dress, which was quite ornate, with rows of lace and tiny tucks at the bodice.

"This is definitely a picture of a girl," Aleksandra said.

"In our country one does not confuse the genders of a child," Slavica explained. "A little boy is dressed in a miniature man's clothing and a little girl in a miniature woman's. This child may indeed be our Lieserl."

The phone rang again, and Slavica answered. "*Dobro*, okay," she said, "*čekaj, čekaj,* hang on, hang on." She put her hand over the receiver and turned to me. "It's the historian who claimed he found Lieserl. He said he was mistaken." Slavica winked. "She is not registered in the village. He asks if we can work together. What do you want me to tell him?"

I made a sour expression, and Slavica laughed. In her best singsong voice, sounding as if she were saying yes, she said, unmistakably, "No."

✧

Later in the afternoon, when Slavica and I were alone, we decided to look up every notable woman in Serbia said to have been born around 1902, the year of Lieserl's birth.

"Mileva and Albert's child would not have been ordinary," Slavica claimed. "She would have been unique in some way. Here, you look through this book and I will look through this one."

She handed me the big Prosveta Enciklopedija [The Educators' Encyclopedia.]. We looked under the last names Marić, Marity, Mariti, Maritz, Einstein, Ružić, and Ajnštajn, which is Einstein in Serbo-Croatian. Serbia, historically a patriarchal society, was slim on noted women. We found one name, Ljubica Marić, who fit our requirements. She was a composer and a member of the Serbian Academy of Science and the Arts. Her most famous composition was *The Threshold of a Dream.*

"This is perfect!" I almost shouted. "I cannot believe it!"

"Good. Do not believe it," Slavica replied. "Here, look at this. Ljubica was born in 1909. This is much too late. A woman of her status would have no need to lie about her date of birth. No, this is not Lieserl."

So we decided to begin our interviews with the remaining members of Mileva's immediate family. As custom dictated, we had to listen to the men first.

The next day was sunny and warm, with the smell of drying leaves in the air. We left for Kać with the car windows down, on our way to visit Dragiša Marić, a second cousin of Mileva's, once removed. We drove over the *Stari Most,* the Old Bridge crossing the Danube, skirting Novi Sad, and continued through villages that were so small they could not be found on the map.

Vojvodina villages are very much alike. The architecture is baroque, and the buildings are painted a pale ochre or a limestone white. They have clean, wide streets lined with acacia trees sometimes clipped into the shapes of globes. Most windows are hung with lace curtains or covered by wooden shutters. Toward the center is a school and a town hall. The heart of the community—the market square—is used for parades, concerts, and speeches and the sale of food, livestock, and other products. There is always at least one Serbian Orthodox and one Catholic church, with white marble facades that have turned a pale golden hue with age.

Weathered wooden buildings are sometimes all that remain from the various military occupations.

The village of Kać has faded mauve, pale blue, and tan houses standing wall to wall along the road. Dragiša Marić lives with his family in a more modern house that looks like a *vojvodjanska gradjanska,* the home of a middle-class Vojvodina family. It is typically situated, in the middle of its own vegetable and flower garden, and located at the end of a long, narrow road. The house is made of brick, stuccoed and painted a soft, dusty pink. The roof is covered with red clay tiles. A porch runs along one side of the house.

Slavica explained to me that Dragiša, the self-appointed genealogist of the Marić family's Kać contingent, had lost his job teaching agriculture at the technical school because of his political affiliations.

"Since men have unequivocal power in Serbian households," Slavica said, "it must have been very difficult for him. Ironically, Dragiša's wife is working to support the family."

I had already seen women lower their heads when walking past a man, sometimes stepping out of his path in deference. I also saw a woman kissing the hand of the *domaćin,* the head of the household, and even one woman putting on her husband's shoes while he sat reading a newspaper.

Dragiša greeted us at the door with one of his three children, a ten-year-old son. The boy was the mirror image of Mileva's father, Miloš—the same long, square jaw, close-set eyes, high forehead, and skull broadening at the temples. He was wearing a pair of blue sweatpants with dirty knees. "Self Control" was written on one leg in English.

After coming inside and shaking hands with everyone present, we were invited to sit in the living room around a low wooden table. Four members of the Marić family, all *porodica,* blood relatives, were there: Dragiša, his son, and Dragiša's elderly mother and father. Dragiša was dressed in dark pants, a threadbare blue shirt, and a tweed jacket that was a little small for his large person. I handed out the gifts that had been suggested by Slavica, in keeping with the tradition of a visit by a foreigner—a twenty-dollar bill for each child and Turkish coffee, Nescafé, and Swiss chocolate for the rest of the family. Dragiša gave the American money to his son, who sat on the sofa examining it with great interest.

"I am going to buy books with my part," he said, and his father and grandparents smiled proudly.

"The love for mathematics by our esteemed family member Mileva Einstein-Marić runs in our family," Dragiša said. "My son will show you." And while we sat politely, his son recited his numbers from one to one hundred in German, English, and Serbo-Croatian.

Serbs are known for, and are proud of, their remarkable ability to recall their history for at least nine generations. So when Dragiša told us a story about Albert Einstein, we believed him. "One summer day in Kać," Dragiša said, "while visiting my esteemed cousin Mileva's family, Professor Einstein decided he was tired of getting up and letting in the family's mother cat, father cat, and their many kittens. To avoid being bothered, he sat down on the porch and designed two cat doors, one for large cats and one for babies. Since the professor was not at all handy with tools, he had a servant cut two rectangles out of the door, side by side. Over each opening was tacked a thick hide from a goat. The servant could not understand why there had to be one door larger than the other. Our professor patiently explained that one door was for the large cats, the other for babies.

"The servant shook his head and asked, 'Should you not make a third door for Mileva's father's pet skunk?'

"The professor looked at him as if he were a little crazy and said, 'Of course not, the skunk can very well use either of the two cat doors!' "

While we were laughing at this anecdote, Dragiša's mother left the room. She returned with a silver tray of food and drinks. Pungent Turkish coffee was offered in tiny white cups, and poured from a brass *džezva,* a long-handled coffee pot. Because of sanctions, it was difficult to buy many ingredients for baking. So instead of the traditional *makovnjača,* poppy seed cake, there was a tasteless stale white coffee cake supplied by UNPROFOR (United Nations Protection Forces). None of us could eat it. Then came the *šljivovica,* a delicious, thick yellow brandy, home-brewed from plums grown on the family farm. I knocked it back like everyone else.

"You have left some at the bottom of your glass," Dragiša pointed. He waited while I swallowed it, then he poured another.

"Oh, no," I protested, "it's too much!"

"Three times is Serbian," he said pleasantly. "And *bog ti dao zdravlje,* may God grant you good health."

He filled my glass one more time, we clinked once more, and drank. Smoking, which is almost as much of a tradition as the brandy, came last.

Just as we were finishing, there was a knock on the front door. Dragiša went to answer it. We could hear his laughter in the hallway. He came back holding a blue envelope.

"I have just received my instructions to report to the army, yet again. Again," he said, "I will refuse. I served once and was turned away from that form of violence for good. It was ridiculous—I could not determine who was the enemy!"

Then Dragiša's mother, who had been sitting quietly, said, *"Izvinite me,* excuse me." We all turned together, as if on swivel stools, to look at her.

"I have something to say to you. I have a relative who was born in 1905. Many years ago she told me that there was a little Lieserl, although she remembered that the family called her Ljubica. You see," Mrs. Marić said, entwining her fingers, "Ljubica is a name for the flower, a violet."

"It can also mean 'love,' " interjected Slavica. "Ljubica was a name often given to a child born out of wedlock."

I held my breath.

"This relative," Mrs. Marić almost whispered, "she has Zorka's nature. Excuse me, I will be soon back." Mrs. Marić got up and left the room, leaving Slavica and me on the edge of our seats.

✧

Einstein historians have always maintained that mental illness and depression ran in the Marić family. In 1916, during the First World War, Zorka was visiting Fiume, now Rijeka, on the Adriatic coast of Croatia. One day, as she was walking down a road alone, she was attacked and raped by a gang of soldiers. Zorka stayed away from men forever after that. The years went by, but the trauma and the accompanying shame seemed to become so profound that she slowly descended into alcoholism and eventually lunacy.

In the late summer of 1919, Miloš, Mileva and Zorka's father, who was already quite ill, sold one of his properties in Banja Luka. In Vojvodina, there is a tradition of people keeping their money at home. Banks are scorned as being collection stations for politicians, so Serbs have false-bottomed cabinets, secret drawers in kitchens; they stuff important papers into pillows, behind removable ceiling tiles—anything to keep their valuables out of the bank. Miloš Marić was no different. He decided to bank his Banja Luka real estate money in an unused winter stove at the Novi Sad house. One day, in the autumn of 1922, Zorka lit the stove and burned all the money.

It was at this point that Zorka's behavior became particularly bizarre. She adopted every stray cat in the neighborhood, but rarely let them outside. Her little house, facing the courtyard on the Kisačka Street property in Novi Sad, became squalid, nearly uninhabitable.

✧

Mrs. Marić returned with more coffee.

"I would like very much to meet your aunt," I said as gently as I could.

"No, it can never happen," she replied firmly.

"But why?" I asked.

"No, never," she vowed.

"Where do you think I should look for Lieserl?"

Mrs. Marić shrugged, turned her palms up, and said, *"U istoj vodi dva puta ne možeš plivati jer reka bez prestanka teče.* Because the river is always flowing, you cannot swim two times in the same water. She could be anywhere. Remember, they tried to keep the story of Lieserl at home—they tried to stop the river from flowing. But I would not count on the river stopping its flow. I would not count on the secret staying hidden."

With that, the entire family stood to say good-bye.

As we were gathered on the porch, shaking hands once more, Mrs. Marić took my hand. She leaned over and kissed me on one cheek, then the other. As she leaned to kiss me a third time, she stopped, still holding my hand. Speaking quietly she said, "One day in 1903, a German-speaking woman from Belgrade came and took away your Lieserl." She winked.

Slavica overheard her. "Could it have been Helene Savić?" she whispered as we moved toward her car. "Her native tongue was German. And didn't she have a daughter about the same age?"

✦

Dragiša had offered to drive with us to the outskirts of Kać and show us the way to The Spire. After we had gone a few kilometers, he proudly declared, "There is the land," as he pointed everywhere. Inherited by Mileva's father in 1895, the land extended as far as the horizon—and then to the right, to the left, and behind us, seemingly without end. Mileva's family was wealthier than I had imagined. But nothing was left of The Spire except a rectangular mound of earth that framed the original foundation and a lonely acacia tree bent by the wind, far off to the south.

"Imagine, if you will," Dragiša continued. "The house was set well back from the road. It was shaded by a grove of sour cherry trees and a few large chestnuts. Surrounding the house was a rough wooden fence and then a bit further out was a thick wall of hedgerow. Now nothing, nothing."

The house had been destroyed by the partisans during the Second World War. They ravaged everything owned by wealthy people who were unable, or refused, to give provisions to the army. After the war, the land was taken over by local farmers and cultivated according to "Serbian tradition," which meant that once a farmer had worked a piece of abandoned land for twenty years, it was his. Because of war and family catastrophe, no one in the immediate Marić family had returned to claim their land. Now, more than fifty years later, it was too late.

There is one remaining photograph of the Spire, which I saw at Slavica's house. When I examined it with a magnifying glass I could see a woman dressed in turn-of-the-century clothing, leaning toward a small child with a white dog in the foreground. It was either early spring or late fall, because the trees had very few leaves and some were even bare. It is difficult to determine the age of the child, but it appears to be about two years old. This child could not be either of Albert and Mileva's two sons, because they had visited the Spire only when the trees were in leaf. But it might be Lieserl. When I searched for the original photograph and its negative, it had disappeared from its archive in Zurich.

✧

The search for a child who disappeared so young and so long ago is primarily a process of elimination. To begin the hunt, I had to track down all possible legal documents. Death certificates are a treasure trove of information. Besides the date of birth, they cite where the person was born, the name of the parents, godparents, midwife, and most important, the next of kin. Next of kin are often still alive. But even if they were dead, I could find *their* next of kin. Problems would arise however, if the next of kin had only female children, because when a woman marries in Serbia she takes her husband's name.

I had already searched the Novi Sad area for Lieserl's death certificate, without success. It was time to go to Budapest and search the municipal archives, the chief repository of the records for Vojvodina region during the Austro-Hungarian Empire.

✧

Because of the international sanctions, I had to change trains at the Yugoslav-Hungarian border for the Pushkin Express to Budapest. Almost three hours later, as my train rounded a gentle bend in the Danube, I could see Buda on the west and Pest on the east, silhouetted in a lavender-tinted twilight. Glimmering white stone buildings soon came into view, and the exquisite spire of St. Matthias's Church towering over a cluster of splendid parliament buildings.

I had arranged for an interpreter, Katalin Thury, to help me research archives in five districts. I had three premises in mind: One, that Lieserl's birth was recorded in Budapest; two, that Lieserl had been brought to Budapest to be treated for scarlet fever and died; and three, that Lieserl was adopted and her case had been recorded in Budapest, as were many such cases prior to the First World War. We gave each office the surnames Marić, Marity, Mariti, Maritz, Einstein, Ružić, and Ajnštajn. We also gave the name Štrangar, which had shown up on a court property document for Miloš Marić in 1871. (As it turned out, a court clerk had accidentally written in the name Štrangar, who was the owner of the house that Miloš and Marija were renting at the time.) We gave as first names Erzsébet, Lieserl, Jelisaveta, and Ljubica.

The next morning we left for our first office—a large nineteenth-century apartment building, mustard-colored with white trim, that had been renovated after the Second World War. On either side of it were buildings whose exteriors had been pockmarked by bullets, remnants of the war and the 1956 uprising.

Katalin told me to wait in a café across the street. When she returned forty-five minutes later, she looked relieved. "Now we can go to the Central Registration Office to file a form requesting Lieserl's birth and death certificates using this 'letter of permission,' " she said, waving the paper at me.

Every record office we visited was in a renovated building that was stunningly baroque on the outside, ugly and modern on the inside. Large leather-bound books were pulled from the shelves. We were not allowed to touch, or even look at, these books. We had to stand three feet away and avert our eyes, according to the law.

In District II, the woman searching for the names looked up and shouted, "I found it, I found it!" Katalin and I surged forward, but the woman drew back.

"Oh, please, *please,*" begged Katalin. The woman used her little finger to beckon us closer, and with a grand flourish, turned the book toward us. Karolina Marić had died of cancer in March 1903 at the age of four. Her mother's maiden name was Fischer, her father's first name was Károly— there was no way to make even a fanciful connection there.

In a crumbling, musty book at the New Public Cemetery, the clerk found an Erzsébet Eisenberg. Lieserl is a diminutive of Erzsébet. But Erzsébet had died in June 1902 at the age of two—again, not our Lieserl, who would have been only six months old at the time.

Next was the Wolf Valley Cemetery, in District XII, where there had been a large Serbian section. No longer. If a grave was not paid for year by year, the body was exhumed and disposed of in a garbage heap. Before the First World War, Serbs had their own section of the graveyard and their own record books. There was no possibility of finding Lieserl, even if she had been buried there, because all the records from before the war had been destroyed by bombs.

Then came the hospitals. St. László was the largest in 1903, and it had a children's contagious-disease section. We drove to an outlying district and found the hospital near Nagyvárad Square—a sprawling series of dirty gray buildings, almost neoclassical in design. The clerk at the front desk showed us to the records office. Four bored-looking women were sitting at their desks. By the time Katalin had finished telling them the story, they had all gathered around her, animated with questions. Then the secretary to the director bustled in, and all four women told our story to her.

The secretary said that most of the records had been destroyed in the war. "But I will check with the director," she promised. "Also, you need to check the hospital, Rókus Kórház."

Rókus Kórház, also known as Semmelweis, was once a hospital for poor people that included a children's wing for contagious diseases. It was located near the Keleti train station, where Mileva had sent Albert a postcard on her way to see Lieserl when the child was ill with scarlet fever.

However, the hospital's records had been destroyed in a fire that had injured many children on August 25, 1903. Mileva's postcard was sent to Albert on August 27—two days after the fire. It was unlikely that Mileva would have journeyed on to Novi Sad if her daughter was already in a Budapest hospital.

✦

I had been dreading a trip to the old state asylum, Országes Pszichiátria és Neurologiai Intézet, the State Psychiatric and Neurological Institute. Yet as Katalin and I approached its library, I was surprised at how beautiful the garden was, a cheery oasis in the center of gloom. The librarian who was assigned to help us took us upstairs, where we found a book that listed the female patients discharged from the hospital between 1898 and 1912. But the records listed only the name, the date of arrival, the illness, and the date of departure. There were no further details—not the names of those who had admitted the patients or the patients' dates of birth.

We looked for all the Erzsébets who had been committed between 1902 and 1912. We found two interesting records.

N. Erzsébet. Arrived: 19 July 1903. Taken to Nagykalló, Hungary on 18 January 1907. Illness: Born Stupidity.

B. Erzsébet. Arrived: 23 October 1903. Left: 13 May 1905. Illness: Acute Stupidity. Taken to Sátoraljaújhely, Hungary.

The librarian then brought us down to the cellar, where crates of old case records and some photographs were stored. It was very strange, rather creepy, being in the cellar of an old mental institution. The walls of the dim corridors we walked along were crumbling, the floors were uneven and dirty, and bare lightbulbs lit our way. To my surprise, we passed by scores of vendors lining the corridors, selling cheap goods like secondhand clothes, perfumes, seeds, food.

"It is because in Hungary the salary of the nurses and doctors is very low," the librarian explained. "The goods sold here are much cheaper than those in a normal shop."

The crates were covered with years' worth of dust. We found some of the boxes from 1903, letters A through C and R through Z. We looked through them all but could not find any of the possible children. Unfortunately, we did not find the carton marked N for the unnamed Erzsébet N. Nor did we find the carton marked E for Einstein, or M for Marić. And in the B, no Erzsébet. The librarian did find a book that said eleven children were admitted to Hungarian mental hospitals in 1903, but they were not mentioned by name.

✧

For a week we traipsed through one record office after another, combing through musty old books. We interviewed elderly clerks who might have remembered the Serbian community during the Austro-Hungarian era. We researched adoption laws. We went through old newspapers. We found nothing.

Katalin telephoned Father Magyar, a priest of the Greek Orthodox Church in Budapest. The church had accepted some Serbian records for safekeeping, and he agreed to go through them, including adoption records and records of children with disabilities. But the next morning he told us he found nothing.

"I suggest you visit Stojan Vujičić," Father Magyar advised. "His father was head of the Serb community in Budapest. And now Stojan maintains many of those records in his home. He is a walking encyclopedia of Serbian history in Budapest!"

A writer well known in Budapest, Vujičić looks like a handsome, Serbian-Hungarian version of Orson Welles. We sat in a café next door to his office at the Association of Writers and had coffee.

"After you called I looked through all the books and found only one child who died in 1903 or 1904," Vujičić said. "A little boy who succumbed to a 'snake in the throat,' meaning *torokgyik,* or diphtheria.

"Adoption was very rare," he continued. "It occurred only when a child was orphaned and had no family left whatsoever. Even then, if the adoption took place before the First World War, it was not necessarily recorded. To find Lieserl you have to look in paradise. That is where she is. That is where she belongs."

✦

I flew back to Belgrade, where I was to meet Slavica and begin our search for Julka Savić, the leading contender for Lieserl. The plane landed on a runway sprouting grass and *puzavica,* a crawling vine similar to Spanish Lace. Since the beginning of the war, the air terminal had fallen into disrepair. White stuffing oozed out of the seats. Passengers stumbled over bubbled and broken industrial rubber tiles. The concrete floor around the baggage claim area was punctuated with small craters that had to be carefully navigated. Lights in the terminal were turned off most of the day, no matter how overcast and dark it was outside.

NATO forces were bombing only forty-nine kilometers away from Slavica's house. She met me at the airport, visibly upset.

"I will tell you about it when we get to your hotel," she said. "It has nothing to do with our work together or with your family. It is the war." She was silent for the rest of the drive.

After I got settled in my room, Slavica and I sat down on two chairs facing the window, looking across the red-tiled roofs of Belgrade.

"When I arrived for work at the hospital yesterday morning I was called to the waiting room. A woman was in labor. She was from Croatia, a refugee with no papers. I learned that as her family was trying to escape, their caravan of people on foot, cars, trucks, and animal-drawn wagons, was bombarded. The woman's husband was in one car, she and the three children in another. As the woman and children were watching, a missile hit his car and killed him. Eight days later, she arrived with her children across the border into Serbia."

Slavica stood up and paced the room, agitated, wringing her hands.

"Some way or other, she found her way to our clinic. She was taken to the delivery room. Her labor was normal. Her vital signs were good. She gave birth to a healthy little girl. But then the woman died. She just took a last breath and died, right there on the delivery table. Nothing could be done to save her. The last thing she could do in her life—the last piece of energy she had—was to give birth to a promise, to a living being. We located some of the relatives in Serbia and delivered the children into their hands. What a struggle they all have in front of them. It breaks my heart."

I could not help but think: Here was a mother who had mustered every last ounce of strength to bring her daughter safely into the world—and there was Mileva who, it seems, at first fought ferociously and then did not fight hard enough.

✧

Belgrade, called Beograd in Yugoslavia, was named the White City—*Beo* for white and *grad* for city. But in 1902 it was not very white. Its gutters were overflowing with refuse. The old Turkish quarter was sullied by decay and desolation. Worn cobblestones, and more potholes than one could avoid, prevented quick passage, particularly by the horse-drawn wagons and droves of oxen moving at a sleepy pace. Perched on a hill at the confluence of the Sava and Danube Rivers, the city looked out over mud flats in all directions. Along the banks of Belgrade's streams and rivers, reeds sprouted like a roughly woven carpet and willows cast their spiky-branch shadows against a watery sky. To the east, one could see the wooded Gypsy Island, to the north, the low, hazy hills around Zemun, and the Danube was easy to imagine following all the way to the Black Sea. On a clear day, even Romania was visible.

Belgrade is regarded as a crossroads of the West and the East, and the frontier outpost of Central Europe. When Lieserl was born, it still retained its Turkish influence. A handful of minarets, white and needle-like, dotted the skyline. Men wearing red fezes were still seen in its cafés. Some women dressed in ankle-length chadors could be seen lifting their hems to jump over the puddles and rubbish. There were sixty thousand people in Belgrade, mainly Orthodox Serbs, a dwindling population of Muslims, and a small but vibrant colony of Spanish-speaking Jews.

✧

Vida Ognjenović, Yugoslavia's leading woman of letters, who lives in Belgrade, first depicted Mileva's inimical behavior in a play she wrote in 1972. Recently she was commissioned by Serbian television to write a new version, incorporating the love letters between Mileva and Albert.

In 1989 she was appointed artistic director and general manager of the National Theatre, located in the heart of Belgrade. By law, her position as general manager also held her responsible for the actual building. In 1995, her book of short stories, *The Poisonous Milk of Dandelions,* won the Ivo Andrić award, the Yugoslav equivalent of the Pulitzer Prize.

The three-party opposition to the Milošević regime had organized a rally for March 9, 1991. The regime ordered that the rally take place on the banks of the Danube, away from the city, so it would not be noticed by the press or attract a large audience. Vida thought they should use the National Theater's balcony, overlooking the *Trg Republike,* Republic Square. She offered her theater as a stage and "opened the door to the revolution." Sixty thousand people appeared to see and listen to the leaders of the opposition parties. The rally was terminated by the police and the army. Vida was fired by Milošević two years later.

By 1996, the national protest had taken root. Republic Square, now called Freedom Square, was the site where hundreds of thousands of Belgrade's citizens congregated to protest Milošević and his government. Also, at seven o'clock each evening, throughout Serbia, people would go into the streets and clang garbage-can lids, pots and pans and blow whistles for one minute. Making themselves heard once every day was their form of civil disobedience.

Slavica and I drove to Vida's flat on Ulica Pariske Komune, next door to the first McDonald's in Serbia. The day felt like night. We needed to turn on the headlights so we could see through fog, coal-heating pollution, and cascading rain. After we parked, I had to use my traveling flashlight to find the number on her building.

Vida works in a corner of her book-lined living room. Taped to the glass door of one of the bookcases is a photograph of her old friend the writer Danilo Kiš.

When Kiš died, in 1989, he was mourned as a true hero who represented everything positive about Yugoslavia. Hundreds of people attended his funeral, each carrying one dahlia in silence. Kiš requested that there be no eulogies. At the end of the afternoon his grave was blanketed with red and gold dahlias, and the footsteps of mourners left a path in the crushed autumn leaves.

Vida had prepared a freshly baked apple cake and Turkish coffee for us. As she spoke, her hands were in constant motion—caressing the rings on her fingers, the fabric covering her knee, the delicate coffee cup.

Slavica was being unusually quiet. Abruptly, she put down her cup and said in an exasperated tone of voice, "I have been searching all the cemeteries in Belgrade, and I can find no such person as Julka Savić Popović. It is Serbian custom to bury family members together in the same tomb, or at least in the same cemetery. So where is Julka Popović? Is she really dead? Was she or was she not Helene's natural child?"

Indeed, Slavica *had* looked everywhere for Julka's death certificate—in every district of Belgrade and its environs, in every church record office, in every graveyard—and had come up with nothing. To make matters more confusing, volume one of *The Collected Papers of Albert Einstein* states that Julka died in 1985, while volume five gives the date as 1986. The state records office contains no registration of the death of Julka Savić Popović on either of those dates.

"I do not understand," Slavica said. "They were able to give me her sister Zora's death certificate with no problem."

"I will help you in any way I can," Vida said. "But you should get a lawyer in Belgrade who can help you get at the truth." And then she declared, like every Serbian woman I had met, "Mileva would never have given up her child for adoption, this I know."

"Ni dlaka s glave ne pada bez razloga, not even a strand of hair falls from your head without a reason," Slavica said as we walked back to our car.

✧

Slavica returned to Sremski Karlovci while I stayed in Belgrade to engage an English-speaking lawyer who could help me track down Julka's legal documents. One lawyer asked me, "Who cares about the truth after eighty years? I must be very careful until I see your credentials. You might be an insurance-fraud investigator." Finally, I retained an attorney because he had an interesting response to my inquiry.

"As it has been related to me recently by common friends," he told me over the telephone, "Dr. Milan Popović claims that his mother, Julka Savič, burned some of Mileva's letters before her death. I suspect that those letters may have contained clues as to Lieserl's identity. Some of the letters allegedly survived and are in the possession of Dr. Popović, who has promised to publish them. Now, since the love letters between Mileva and Albert have been found, people in the University of Belgrade's faculty of philosophy joke about Dr. Popović being Einstein's grandson. The idea is, I suppose, that Dr. Popović's mother was actually Lieserl, adopted by Dr. Popović's grandmother Helene Savić."

The Belgrade intellectual community has always taken pride in the relationship between Helene and Mileva—it is part of the lore of the city's intelligensia. Since the existence of Lieserl was first revealed, in 1985, rumor within this community has had it that Helene had secretly adopted the child herself and the girl raised as Julka was in fact Lieserl. It would certainly make sense. Ostensibly born two months after Lieserl, Julka had been seriously ill immediately following her birth. Most significant, Helene was Mileva's best friend, and in Serbia, a best friend is the equivalent of family. I made an appointment to meet the attorney two days later.

When I telephoned Slavica, she was amazed. "Remember, my dear, the love letters have not been translated into Serbo-Croatian, nor are they available in our bookstores in English—so few people here know that Lieserl actually existed."

Robert Schulmann, director of the Einstein Papers Project, had given me Popović's telephone number. I called him from the hotel.

"I am sorry. I do not have time to meet with you," he said after I identified myself. "Good-bye." And then he hung up.

✧

When Albert Einstein died, in 1955, he bequeathed all of his "manuscripts, copyrights, publication rights, royalties and royalty agreements, and all other literary property and rights, of any and every kind or nature whatsoever, to my Trustees hereinafter . . ." His trustees were Otto Nathan, a distinguished economist at Princeton University who had helped Albert with his financial concerns, and Helene Dukas, Albert's private secretary of twenty-seven years.

Albert had stipulated that when his trustees died, all rights were to pass to The Hebrew University of Jerusalem. In 1971, the Princeton University Press and the Einstein estate signed an agreement to publish his writings. So far, the Project has published eight of the projected twenty-five volumes of *The Collected Papers of Albert Einstein*.

In 1976, John Stachel took an extended leave from Boston University's physics department to become the editor and director of the Project, then housed at the Institute for Advanced Study, in Princeton. Robert Schulmann was hired in 1981, first as staff historian, later becoming associate editor. At that time, because of lack of space for the growing Project, the papers and the staff were relocated to the offices of the Princeton University Press.

Shortly before Helene Dukas died, in 1982, she and Nathan decided to carry out Albert's desire to transfer his estate to Jerusalem. At this point, The Hebrew University entered into a partnership with Princeton University Press. The Albert Einstein Archive, along with Mileva's letters to Albert, Helene Savić, and other mutual friends, was copied, and the originals were sent to The Hebrew University for permanent placement.

In 1984, the Project was moved to Boston University. Robert Schulmann replaced Stachel as its director in 1988.

✧

Before I left for Serbia for the first time, in 1995, I met with Schulmann, a tall, rangy man, in his office at Boston University. I asked him about Mileva's letters to Helene that had been reprinted in *The Collected Papers of Albert Einstein*. Schulmann explained that since the Project is interested primarily in those segments of the letters that shed light on Albert's story, the bulk of the letters from Mileva to Helene have been overlooked, save for those containing Albert's cordial but pedestrian postscripts. I had known before my meeting with Schulmann that there were many more letters than I had seen in the volumes, and I also knew that Milan Popović, Julka's son, was the fierce guardian of them all.

"You want to know what Popović says about the letters?" Schulmann asked, leaning back in his chair with an ironic grin. "He told me that years ago, when he came back from his honeymoon, he decided to have a look at them. That's when he discovered that many of them were missing. He asked Julka where they had gone, and she said they were so private that she didn't want anyone to read them."

"Did she burn them?" I asked.

"We don't know for sure, but if the letters aren't there, then somebody did something with them!"

"Will you show me copies of the ones that exist?"

"I can't," he said. "I promised Popović that the Einstein Papers Project would not allow anyone to see the letters without his permission."

"Are the letters sealed then?"

Schulmann shrugged.

✧

The unavailability of Mileva's unpublished letters to Helene was disconcerting. When I returned home to New York in 1995, I decided to investigate further. I found that in the fall of 1985, when the existence of the letters became known, John Stachel had traveled to Belgrade and acquired photocopies of the letters from Popovic, with an understanding concerning access to the letters. After my repeated attempts to gain access to the letters through Stachel and Schulmann failed, I couldn't help but feel I was being stonewalled and that Popovic was responsible.

In fact, I had already found many direct quotes from those sealed letters in several published books and articles, including *Einstein, History and Other Passions* by Gerald Holton; "Of Love, Physics and Other Passions: The Letters of Albert and Mileva," an article Holton had published in *Physics Today; The Private Lives of Albert Einstein* by Roger Highfield and Paul Carter; and *Einstein Lived Here* by Abraham Pais.

I was also aware that Popovic himself was planning to publish something on the subject. When I asked Schulmann about Popovic's motives, he confirmed that Popovic, then at work on an essay of his own, was also looking for Lieserl and was "closing in on her identity."

"It is obvious he views you as competition," he said.

I decided to confer with an attorney. I was advised that Popovic's control over the physical letters—the paper and ink, as opposed to the content—did not mean that he controlled the right to publish or copy them. He did, however, control access to the letters.

Schulmann agreed to telephone Popovic on my behalf to ask if I could read the letters. Popovic refused, saying he would allow access only when he was ready. I asked Schulmann if he would send me a copy of the side of the missing fifth page of Mileva's December 1912 letter to Helene that contained Albert's postscript, "a greeting to the Serbian heroine." But Schulmann told me that he "could not comply, as the agent of the purchaser of the love letters asked us not to hand out copies, at least not until volume eight is published. . . . Sorry." This made no sense to me. What did Mileva's letters to Helene have to do with the love letters between Albert and Mileva? They are an entirely different corpus.

And there is a problem. The citation in volume five of *The Collected Papers of Albert Einstein,* edited by Martin J. Klein, A.J. Kox, and Robert Schulmann, published in 1993, states that "only the first four pages of the five are available. . . . [Albert's postscript] is on the verso of the fifth page." If only the "first four pages of five are available," then how did the Project get Albert's postscript on the fifth page? According to Milan Popović, the postcript copied on a separate piece of paper. I can only assume that Helene destroyed or removed the fifth page because it contained something she did not want anyone to read.

✧

Soon after my fruitless request for the missing page, in November 1996, Popović was interviewed about Lieserl in a Belgrade television broadcast.

"My mother, Julka, told me that there is something about [her] birth that cannot be brought to light," he said. "I think that my mother had heard about Mileva's secret pregnancy. I made some research about Lieserl, and I have the following results. First, she was born in Vojvodina. Second, she had scarlet fever. Third, she was adopted. But knowing Mileva as a mother, I cannot accept that she gave her child away for adoption. To me, Lieserl's destiny is still a secret."

✧

The day after Popović hung up on me, I was walking down the Bulevar Revolucije in Belgrade and realized that I was in his neighborhood. Feeling courageous, I decided to telephone and ask to see him again.

"Of course," Popović said, much to my amazement. "Come now."

I found my way to his house on Kataníćeva Street. The house was purchased by his Savić grandparents in 1903, and although today it is situated in the middle of a busy metropolis, it was then edged by rolling fields of wheat and maize. I entered through a black wrought-iron gate and walked past a small stuccoed house, which looked as if it had been built to protect the larger house behind it from outsiders. The main house, also stuccoed, was built in the fashion of an urban Turkish fortress, its windows set high and curtained with lace.

Popović is a psychiatrist, formerly president of the Serbian Physicians for Peace, who was involved in treating refugees in camps throughout Serbia. He has always protected himself and his family, including his Aunt Zora, from researchers. Zora had lived in the small house in front of Popović's for many years. He claimed that she was blind, a little "cuckoo," and unable to remember anything. Everyone who came to see him was firmly shepherded past her house on their way to the street. She died in 1992, at the age of ninety.

We sat in his study and began a game of cat-and-mouse, each of us trying to learn how much the other knew.

"Do you know where Helene's letters to Mileva are?" I asked.

Popović shook his head. "Do you?" he replied.

"No," I answered, "but Evelyn Einstein thinks they may still be in Switzerland—maybe in the closet of Aude Einstein, her brother Bernard's ex-wife."

"Then why don't you go to Switzerland and interview her?" he asked.

"By the time I learned about the closet," I said, "it was too late. Another writer had claimed Aude Einstein as his own private source, and she would not talk to anyone else. She won't even talk to Schulmann."

"So now," I asked, "can you be candid with me?"

"Yes," Popović answered, a placid expression frozen on his face.

"Do you know what happened to Lieserl?" I asked.

"I suppose, but I am not sure," he answered.

"But you think you know?" I asked.

"Yes," he answered.

"Do you have proof?" I asked.

"Do I have proof to support my thinking? Yes and no, yes and no. I'm not sure. Maybe, maybe. If I was sure, I would publish it. I am a man of science. I have a hypothesis about Lieserl, but I cannot tell you this. Not yet. They look for Lieserl in my family also, you know. She is not my Aunt Zora. Pity."

Popović said that he needed to go to Budapest to look for Lieserl's birth or death certificate. I told him that I had already been there and found nothing. He became quiet at this disclosure and turned away from me.

"Anyway," I said, addressing his back, "Mileva would never have given up her child."

"No," Popović answered and turned around to face me again, "No, she was so devoted to children, it is not possible."

I figured that either Popović knew what had happened to Lieserl, or he did not know much more than I did, perhaps even less. He went on to

tell me that he was writing a five-part essay about the relationship between the Einstein and Savić families for *Politika,* a Belgrade newspaper. He
promised to give me permission to read Mileva's letters in the Einstein
Archive after the essay was published. I knew that Popović had been talking about publishing this essay for many years. I did not confront him
with the access issue at this moment because I was not ready to shut
down our conversation. I was trying, hoping, somehow to make him see
me as an ally, not an adversary.

"I did find some interesting letters written in German," he offered.

"Who are they from?" I asked.

Popović shook his head. "I will give them to you after I have published," he said flatly.

Our meeting had come to an end. He asked his son, Bojan, to show
me out. When we arrived at the front gate, Bojan looked at me with a
sneer. I did not know why I needed a personal escort to walk past Zora's
house. She had been dead for more than a year.

✧

The Belgrade attorney I had retained had an office tucked behind the
fancy facades of the buildings that surround the National Assembly. I
found his address, climbed two flights of stairs, and was welcomed into a
bright white suite of offices with newly finished light wood floors. He was
a middle-aged man, trim and dapper, dressed in an elegant gray business
suit, holding a cigarette between tobacco-stained fingers. Over Turkish
coffee, we made plans to visit the government records office in the morning.

Because the majority of children were born at home in the early part
of the century, Julka's and Zora's births would have been registered by
taking their christening records to the government records office in Belgrade. There, in a large, brown leather-bound ledger, the clerk would
have written the child's name in ink, as well as the hour, date, and place
of birth, parents' names, their dates and places of birth, their citizenship,
and their present address. Similarly, when a person died, his death was
first registered with the church and then recorded by the government.

In order to obtain a formal birth or death certificate, one must file a written request or go to the records office in person, whereupon a clerk will locate the correct ledger, find the name, and fill out a standard form with the information.

Slavica had secured copies of Julka's and Zora's birth certificates and Zora's death certificate through the mail from the government records office in Belgrade. But the birth certificates she received had listed both as being born in 1902, which did not match the birth dates noted in *The Collected Papers of Albert Einstein,* which placed them at 1901 and 1903 respectively. And we still had not been able to obtain a death certificate for Julka. The attorney and I decided to apply again for their birth and death certificates.

The records office was situated on Ulica Miloša Velikog, a wide boulevard with hundreds of plane and chestnut trees and embassies of most countries of the world parading up one side and down the other. The government building was new and ugly, constructed of poured concrete. Inside, four clerks stood behind the counter. When our turn came, my attorney said, "I am looking for the death certificate of Zora Savić Karakašević. Karakašević is her married name."

"I gave the answer to the court," the clerk shouted rudely. "I cannot give you the death certificate." Then he turned brusquely and walked through a door behind the counter. We were stunned. We did not even have a chance to ask for Julka's death certificate. The thought that Popović might have arranged for its disappearance occurred to me.

"There is nothing we can do now," my attorney told me, "but wait and see if I can approach colleagues who are higher up."

We went to another room in the same building and immediately were presented with Julka's and Zora's birth certificates.

The copy of the birth certificate sent to Slavica by the same office stated Julka's birthday as October 15, 1902. According to this one, she had been born on the same day and month, but a year earlier—October 15, 1901. And the copy of the original birth certificate from Tübingen, Germany, which I had obtained through the mail, dated Julka's birth on October 28, 1901. Similarly, the copy of Zora's birth certificate that Slavica had received in the mail showed her birthdate to be December 28, 1902, but this one stated her birthdate as December 28, 1903—a year later.

"You must know that to try and solve the mystery of Lieserl, you have to understand our calendar situation," the attorney said. "When Lieserl was born, the old Julian calendar was still being used in the Balkans. In other words, dates on the new Gregorian calendar are two weeks ahead of the old calendar. For example, the first of January in the new calendar is December 18th in the old."

We took this confusing information with us to the Belgrade parish of the Temple of St. Sava, where we hoped to locate the Savić girls' christening records. These are a more detailed source of information than birth records. At the turn of the century, every Serbian Orthodox child was christened. If they were not, it was usually because they died soon after birth or because they were illegitimate and the parents were too ashamed. The christening form was filled out by the priest who performed the ritual, and included the date and place of birth, the date and place of christening, the parents' names and ages, the child's placement in relation to any siblings (first, second, and so on), whether the child was a twin, illegitimate, or had defects, and the name of the attending priest and godparents.

In the church's records office, we requested both sisters' christening papers. The clerk found Zora on page 241 in one of the ledger books. Zora's entry placed her birth on December 28, 1902, which corresponded to my research. Julka was found on page 153. It was stated that she was born on October 15, 1901, by the old calendar.

My attorney tried to untangle the confusion. "At that time, the only official document you needed to prove your legitimacy was a christening paper. Helene must have simply taken Julka's christening paper to the government record office and used it to enter her birth as October 15, 1901.

"However," he said, "what is obvious here is that a child's true identity could effortlessly be manipulated. Helene could have easily and deliberately told the priest a date different from that of the actual birth.

"Also, something else I find interesting is that according to the christening paper, Julka was christened at home, which in the upper-class society of Belgrade at that time was highly unusual. Something must have been wrong—she may have been sick. Babies were usually christened with a flourish forty days after birth, during which time a mother was not supposed to leave the house. She was thought to be impure and therefore inadequately protected from evil spirits. For some reason, Julka had not been christened until she was eight months old."

✧

The following day, on the bus from Belgrade to Slavica's house in Sremski Karlovci, eighty kilometers away, I felt as if I were traveling through a black-and-white motion picture. Serbia was enshrouded in a soot-colored veil. The only colors that stood out were the plastic canisters of black market petrol on the hoods of private cars parked on the side of the road—bright yellow petrol from Romania, green from the Ukraine, orange from Bulgaria, light yellow (the poorest quality) from Yugoslavia, and red Shell Oil (the best) from Hungary. Because of the international embargo, regular gas stations were closed. Petrol prices changed daily, depending on the smugglers' private formula for determining them. The average rate was 3.50 dinars per liter—about $8.83 per gallon.

Slavica met me where her dirt road intersects the main highway, and we walked back to her house.

"Two days ago I traveled with much hardship to see my old childhood friend Ana in Ruma," she told me. "Only the day before, she had returned from seeing her grandson at his military camp."

"You mean she drove into the war zone?" I asked. It had never occurred to me that one could visit a relative engaged in fighting.

"Oh, yes, one can go," she explained wearily. "When the soldiers take their final oath, the family is invited. While Ana stood there watching her grandson's pledge, she could feel the earth rumbling under her feet from the bombing. These young soldiers have had no training. One of the young men told her that they wept with despair because they did not know how to use their guns. And yet they are forced to use huge, complicated weapons on the spur of the moment."

Slavica seemed tired and stopped to lean against the fence. She began to push a smooth stone around with her foot. "Here, now, in the twentieth century, Ana's grandson and his fellow soldiers are sleeping on straw, the way our ancestors did when they were fighting the Turks. I really could not believe what she was telling me." She began to walk again and I silently followed.

"Then, after privately visiting with her grandson," Slavica continued, "Ana walked over to the dining tent, where she was introduced to some of his friends. When Ana turned to say good-bye, she saw ten men sitting at a table, but under the table, there were only ten legs." Slavica opened the gate and held it for me as I walked through then let it gently swing shut.

"Yes, I have noticed," I said, turning to her. "There are dozens of young men begging all over Belgrade. Ninety percent of them have only one leg—the other ten percent have none."

"Land mines," Slavica said. "Only God can protect Ana's grandson now."

✧

I needed to locate a grandchild of Milana Bota Stefanović, Mileva's Zurich school friend. Milana's letters home to her parents often spoke of Mileva; maybe her family knew the story of Lieserl. After two telephone calls, Slavica had found Ivana Stefanović, Milana's granddaughter, living in Belgrade and made an appointment to see her, which meant getting back on the dreary bus.

Some historians think that Ivana's aunt Milica Stefanović, the daughter of Milana and the doctor-poet Svetislav, could have been Lieserl. Indeed, she did fit one of the prerequisites—she had a lifelong relationship with Mileva. But I soon learned that she was born in 1906, too late to weave into Lieserl's chronology.

Slavica and I arrived, exhausted, at the door of Ivana's fifth-floor walk-up. She greeted us graciously. A lovely woman of medium height, with a finely chiseled face, smooth alabaster skin, and short, gray-peppered hair, Ivana is a well-known contemporary composer and an accomplished violinist. She was locked out of her office at Radio Belgrade in January 1993 and placed on an indefinite leave when she took a position publicly opposing the government.

We walked down a long hallway hung with sophisticated avant-garde art. The main room of the apartment housed a harpsichord, various musical instruments, and shelves of books and musical scores. She invited us to sit around her coffee table for Turkish coffee and homemade *makovnjača,* poppyseed cake.

Socializing in the Balkans requires a unique form of etiquette. A visit can take hours. The conversation starts with a litany of family dates, then episodes, and finally, if you are deemed trustworthy, private family stories. Everyone is patient and polite, content to take their time. As we chatted, I noticed next to the cake some old letters written on light blue paper, sticking out of their envelopes.

Ivana made no sign of acknowledging the letters, so I began with a provocative question in an attempt to get things moving.

"Ivana," I asked, "did you know that Mileva and Albert had a daughter before they were married?"

"Of course," she responded knowingly, "but only recently. I read about the love letters, and I was not surprised. In my family, there had always been a veil of secrecy surrounding Mileva, almost as if they had taken a communal vow of silence. When I found out about Lieserl, I understood why.

"In fact, it encouraged me to go through some of our family letters. You see, my family has kept a voluminous collection of correspondence for the past hundred years. In the times when my grandmother Milana and then my Aunt Milica were in Zurich, they wrote to their family in Belgrade every day, sometimes twice a day.

"Here," Ivana said, putting on her reading glasses and reaching for the letters. "I found eight letters from my grandmother Milana, which she wrote to her parents when she was living in the same boarding house as Mileva."

The letters were chatty, somewhat obligatory, written home to anxious parents: "I have a good appetite," Milana wrote, "and I enjoy eating. Every morning at ten I eat two boiled eggs and then again for lunch I eat all kinds of food." She continued, teasing, "In the evening both I and Ružica drink beer. We have bought thirty bottles."

"But this is the most interesting," Ivana said, and slipped out another brittle piece of blue paper. "Milana writes a little about Mileva and Albert and then asks her mother, 'God only knows why the couple doesn't get married.' The answer should come on the next page, but that page is missing."

"Has anyone else seen these letters?" I asked.

"Yes, just a few months ago, I loaned a bunch of letters to Dr. Milan Popović for research."

"Popović!" I exclaimed. "How do you know Popović?"

"My dear," Ivana answered calmly, "everyone knows everyone here in Belgrade. We are a small community."

"I saw Popović just a few days ago," I said. "He told me he had some letters in German but he would not say who they were from. Did Milana write home in German?"

"Yes," Ivana said, "her parents encouraged her to write in German. Learning German was part of her education in Zurich."

"He must have been referring to your letters," I said, "He is claiming exclusivity, and he will not let me see them until after he has published his essay. I assume he has your permission?"

"I always give permission to researchers," Ivana responded. "But I will continue to look for you. I know there is a suitcase somewhere with more letters."

"By any chance," I asked, "are there photographs?"

"I think so," she replied. "Let me look further. I promise I will pull out anything having to do with Mileva or her family."

Ivana was leaving soon to join her husband abroad. Her time was limited, but we made plans to speak again.

"Not to worry," she soothed me. "I will do as I promised."

✧

After we left Ivana's, I suggested to Slavica that we walk down the Bulevar Revolucije to the Hotel Metropol for dinner. Slavica was reluctant.

"Let's just get a loaf of bread and some cheese and eat it on the bus," she said.

I persuaded her to go to the hotel. At the table next to us was a group of men from the Milošević regime. Like figures in a George Grosz drawing, they were dressed in black suits with white shirts and dark ties. They were fat and drunk and boisterous, eating caviar and spending more money on one dinner than Slavica and her husband together earn in a month.

✧

As Ivana Stepanović describes it, in 1994, Popović had borrowed at least a dozen letters, written in German by her great-grandmother Milana, but when he returned them in 1995, he didn't tell her that he had kept three original letters and at least two pages from other letters for himself—conveniently out of sight from other researchers—and Ivana had never bothered to count them. It was not until July 1998, when his book *One Friendship—Letters Between Mileva and Albert Einstein and Helene Savić* was published in Montenegro that Popović gave back the remaining material.

Several of the Stefanović letters, including the three that he had kept for himself and one of the missing pages, were reprinted in Popović's book. But one of the missing pages I had expected to find was not there. It was from the 1901 letter in which Milana wrote, "God only knows why the couple doesn't get married."

Finally, Popović cites from one of the letters sequestered with the Einstein Papers Project, an exchange between Mileva and Helene in December 1901, written from Novi Sad.

"Because of circumstances," Mileva writes, "I did not have time to congratulate you on your daughter. You must be more than happy. You have reached the highest happiness. How is your girl's health, what is her name? You must have a lot of work because of her, since babies are capricious."

The letter appeared to settle the question that the child named Julka indeed was Helene's daughter. But that opened up another possibility. In yet another of the Stefanović letters that Popović had kept (and that I could not read until his book was published), dated February 17, 1902, Milana wrote to her mother that the baby [Julka] is "3.5 months old." She describes the infant as looking "almost dead and so dry, that I could not have imagined such a child. Something horrible! Two specialists said that there is no hope. . . . The doctor said there is a problem with the intestines." If Julka had died soon after this letter was written (and as Slavica and I had come to find out, the death of infants often went unrecorded), it would have been the perfect time to adopt Lieserl, who was just less than two months old, into the Savić family—an event that would perhaps explain the delayed christening.

As for Julka's missing death certificate, it arrived in the mail—from Popović himself—*after* his book was published. Apparently, Julka died in 1985 and was buried at the Novo Groblje, the New Cemetery, in Belgrade. But when Slavica had gone there, she had not found a listing. She had walked up and down the rows of gravestones. She had carefully explored the area around the Savić family graves. She never found Julka's gravestone. In the end, Popović never made the claim that Julka was Lieserl.

✧

I learned the most about Julka's life not from Mileva's letters or from Popović, but from Mileva's biographer, Desanka Gjurić Trbuhović, a Serbian mathematician and physicist whose book *U Senci Alberta Ajnštajna,* In the Shadow of Albert Einstein, was first published in Serbia in 1969. Fourteen years later, it was translated into German and published in Bern.

Gjurić Trbuhović, a Serbian mathematician, physicist, and professor from Belgrade, decided to write Mileva's biography when she retired from teaching. She interviewed many of Mileva's friends, including Julka, some acquaintances such as her nurse and doctor, and a number of remaining family members. Gjurić Trbuhović must have seen many of the letters from Mileva to Helene, because she quotes them throughout her book. Since Helene was dead by then, it must have been Julka who showed her the letters. Mileva would never grant an interview—and it was not until 1968 that anyone wrote more than a short article about her.

"Was there any mention of Lieserl?" I asked Professor Ljubomir Trbuhović, Desanka's son, in a letter.

"Not a word," he replied. "Not a single word."

Evelyn Einstein had shown me a photograph of Zorka Marić sitting on a balcony with an ornately filigreed wrought-iron railing, holding an infant on her lap. This was the photo I had shown Slavica and her family to help determine the sex of the baby. The child, who appears to be a girl without earrings, was about one year old and very engaged with the teddy bear she was holding. All along, I had hoped that this was a photograph of Lieserl. I sent the photograph to Trbuhović, who lives in Zurich, and he took it to Mileva's various addresses in Zurich to see if he could locate the balcony. He did. He found it at her Gloriastrasse address. Mileva had lived at that address from 1914 to 1924, many years after the birth of Lieserl. The child in the photo remains unidentified.

✧

That Julka was not Lieserl was becoming more certain. The final piece of evidence that brought me to this conclusion was the 1939 letter Helene wrote to Albert in which she asked him to help save her aunt and cousin from the concentration camps. Would Helene have signed such a plaintive letter so formally, as "Helene Savić née Kaufler," if Albert were Julka's biological father? In such a dire situation, Helene would have been more familiar, emotional—especially if she had done Albert the favor of adopting his unwanted child so many years before.

PART
FOUR

Jovan Ružić, Mileva's second cousin, has assumed the role of family patriarch. When Slavica and I drove to visit him in Novi Sad in the fall of 1995, it was raining so hard that the windshield wipers could barely keep up with the deluge, and it was dark at two-thirty in the afternoon.

Ten days earlier, we had visited the cemetery in Titel, where we discovered the Ružić family gravestone lying on its face, which prevented us from reading the names on it. I had considered paying the gravediggers to bring in a tractor and set the stone upright, but I decided to try to get Jovan's permission first.

Jovan lives on the outskirts of Novi Sad in an enormous apartment complex. After stopping many times to ask directions, we finally found his building. We were pleasantly if somewhat coolly welcomed.

I offered my gifts, but Jovan seemed embarrassed by them, quickly taking a twenty-dollar bill for each of his two children and tucking them away on a shelf. Then, sitting down, he opened an elegant brown leather-bound notebook and read the birth and death dates of every male Ružić family member, going back three hundred years. There was no new information here. Each time I asked Jovan a question outside the bounds of the ledger in front of him, he would raise his hands, palms up, and shrug. If he knew anything, he was not about to reveal it to me. He closed the book and his wife, Dušanka, brought out a platter of delicious meat pastries, small slices of local sausage, soft Serbian cheese, coffee, and *šljivovica*, plum brandy.

Exasperated, I asked him, "If you were writing this book, what would you say happened to Lieserl?"

A smile stretched across Jovan's face. "First, I will ask you a question," he said. "What do you think about the situation in Serbia?" We were beginning a Balkan barter.

Slavica stared at her hands and kept crossing and uncrossing her ankles. The wrong answer could end any chance of his cooperation. Jovan was looking at me straight on, dead serious. I knew that if I gave him a polite visitor's response, he would see through it. *What the hell,* I thought, *here goes.* I told Jovan I thought the war in Yugoslavia was senseless, a war of ego and economics—a war cunningly encouraged by the West, a war crafted by killers. I told him that I thought Slobodan Milošević was making his government into a corporate conglomerate with himself as the CEO and that, together with his secret police and army, Franjo Tudjman and his Croatian army, Alija Izetbegović and the Bosnian government, he was out to become a new Ceausescu. I took a breath, looked around the room, and said, "I am sorry to say this out loud, but I feel they are all murderers."

Everyone was quiet. Jovan was now looking down at the floor. I could not tell if he agreed with me. Then he looked up, his face expressionless, and as if dropping a pearl into the Turkish coffee, he said, "Lieserl was indeed part of the family until she was about eighteen months old—this was a shameful story. I have never told anyone—it is hard for me to admit—but it has just slipped from my memory into my mouth. The family still lives with the shame of Lieserl being born out of wedlock. They take it personally—it is part of being from the Balkans. Because

Mileva made this mistake, we all feel the shame. One person's personality can be a reflection on your whole family."

At this point, everything relaxed—our voices, the way we sat in our chairs, the atmosphere.

"The gravestone in Titel is on its face," I said casually. "May I see what it says?"

"Impossible," Jovan replied. "Two days ago I sent it to be recut at the stone mason's."

"Was Lieserl's name etched into the stone?"

Again Jovan shrugged, turned his palms toward the ceiling, and smiled. Clearly, the conversation was over.

I took photographs of the family and did not mention Lieserl again. Jovan saw us out the door and walked us to Slavica's car. In genteel Serbian fashion, he kissed my hand as he said good-bye.

"Please remember," he said, "in Serbia you do not tell a child she is adopted, because you would spoil her happiness. I am convinced that Lieserl was not adopted. But if she was adopted, she would never have been told who she was.

"Another thing to know," he continued. "In 1918, soldiers bivouacked in our house in Titel. It was a cold winter, and many of our books and papers were burned to make heat and cook food. There is nothing left in our house from before. There is no sign of a child. None at all. Believe me, I have searched!"

✧

On one of my quick follow-up trips to Budapest I shared a roomy compartment on the train with a young Serbian couple. Although it was wartime in the Balkans, they were obviously well-to-do and had been visiting family in Paris. We chatted politely, and they asked me what I was doing in Serbia. When I told them about my search for the missing daughter of Einstein, they became very interested. The young woman told me this story: In her mother's family, there were seven children. One of her mother's sisters could not have children, so the young woman's grandfather asked another of his daughters to give one of her many children to the childless daughter. A girl-child was given by one sister to the other to raise. The child called her adoptive mother "Mother" and her actual mother "Auntie," but she always knew who was who and visited her biological mother throughout her childhood. There was never any question of maternity.

So now I had heard two conflicting renditions of Serbian practice—by some, I was informed that Lieserl would not have been told she was adopted; by this couple, I was told that Lieserl might well have been told she was adopted. Every eventuality had to be considered.

✧

"In my country we have a very big problem with signing our names to any piece of paper," Slavica said to me. We were sitting on a bench in her garden, enjoying a rare sunny day. She was trying to explain why I was having such difficulties with certain Marić family members I'd interviewed, who had insisted on anonymity.

"Our lives," she explained, "have been so scarred by a multitude of conquerors that our instinct is to be neither seen nor heard. I will tell you a story that I heard from a friend. Parts of it are true, some parts have been embellished over the years, some of the historical facts I question, but in the end it may help you to understand the terror of war and the psychology of the Balkans. It may even help you to see your way toward Lieserl."

✧

On August 6, 1917, a young woman named Vesna was walking down a boulevard in the center of Belgrade with her girlfriends. They were reminiscing, recalling their excitement when the first movie theater came to Belgrade. A Jewish family had erected a tent and hired a Romani orchestra to accompany an American cowboy movie. Later, they built a real theater for what they called "living pictures."

As the girls hurried along the avenue, they kept looking at each other and giggling. Because of the influenza epidemic, they wore white cotton masks over their mouths and were laughing at how silly they looked. They were, however, sufficiently nervous about the epidemic that had already killed thousands of people in the Balkans.

Suddenly, they heard the sound of approaching horses. *Dear God,* Vesna thought, *what is happening?*

The girls had been warned by their parents to stay off the main streets, but they had disobeyed—and now they were frightened. Rounding a corner, horses pulling carts with high wood-planked sides bore down on them, driving onto the sidewalks and blocking the road. Vesna could hear girls screaming from the carts. The girls ran in different directions—between the carts and around the panting, sweating horses. All Vesna could remember were hands—large, hairy hands—reaching for them, grabbing. Out of the corner of her eye, she saw one of her friends stumble on the uneven cobblestones. A man on horseback reached down and snatched her up as if she were a piece of cloth. She was gone forever. Vesna managed to escape.

A newspaper account of August 1917 reported the Serbian prime minister, Nikola Pašić, declaring in London that the Austro-Germans had deported eight thousand young Serbian girls, aged ten to fourteen years. Their whereabouts were unknown.

For four days, trains loaded with these girls passed through Serbia. Peasants along the way could hear their pleas for help. They could hear the girls being threatened and beaten and raped. Each time the trains stopped in a village, more young women were torn from their homes. (Since most of the men were away at war, the women had to fend for themselves.) Each time the train left a station, more young women leapt to their deaths.

That night, Vesna and her mother cut off all their hair and dressed in men's clothing. They packed a few belongings and some food, and set out for a relative's house in a town called Bajina Bašta, several days' journey away. Although this was still enemy territory, they thought they would be safer there than in the city. Staying off the main roads, they followed the Sava River to the Tamnava and then walked cross-country to Valjevo, a large town where they hoped to rest for a few days. They expected to find food in the orchards along the way. But nothing was left. When the Austrians and Germans captured the country, they cut down every fruit tree they could find. Now the hills where the trees once grew were bare of everything but graves and pigs and dogs.

When they reached a hillside on the outskirts of Valjevo, Vesna and her mother saw thousands of pigs dotting the fields. As they got closer, they realized that the pigs were eating the bodies of dead soldiers.

Covering their noses, Vesna and her mother hurried on to the town, away from the putrid wind. It took them four days to reach Valjevo, and although they had started the journey alone, by the time they arrived, hundreds of people were staggering silently alongside them, seeking sanctuary. Mother and daughter rested in the back of an ironmonger's shop for one day and one night. The town had no food. People were beginning to eat the carnivorous pigs; some were even eating their dogs.

Leaving Valjevo was a relief. Vesna and her mother were hungry but calmed by the beauty that lay before them. They walked along winding paths toward a misty greenish blue horizon. Here the trees had been left untouched because they did not bear fruit. On this part of the trek, they were alone. Most of the refugees had stayed in Valjevo or continued on to Užice. On the last evening of their exodus, they slept beneath an orange moon.

"Better a body in rags and a soul in silk than a soul in rags and a body in silk," goes a Serbian proverb. In rags, they rose early the next morning and drank from a stream. After walking for about an hour, they found themselves on another hilltop, overlooking a valley crossed by the Drina River. Bajina Bašta and the closest railroad were thirty-six kilometers away. They knew they would be safe now, since in those days, a war required a railroad.

✧

Slavica leaned back on the bench. "Our history is like a piece of gossamer—diaphanous, unstable—just like the story of Lieserl. You cannot find her in the traditional way, I promise you. You must embrace the Serbian customs. Allow the stories to unfurl, and think with your heart. And there you will find the answers."

✧

Through a labyrinthine path of Balkan sleuthing we had tracked down a woman who had written three letters from Novi Sad to Albert's son Hans

Albert Einstein in America, six years after Mileva's death. I will call the woman Ana Milić. When I found two of her letters in the Einstein Archives, it opened an investigation that led me to consider a woman I will call Nada Marić as a serious candidate for Lieserl.

In January 1955, Mrs. Milić wrote a polite letter to Hans Albert, claiming to be a member of the Marić family. Hans Albert wrote back, saying that he was having "some difficulty understanding exactly what our relationship is," but that he expected she was a cousin.

Mrs. Milić replied that they were actually second cousins, "bound with the blood of the Marićs."

The next communication to Hans Albert from Serbia was in April 1957—a letter written in English by Sofija Galić Golubović, a response to a letter that Hans Albert had written "quite a long time ago."

Sofija was the only daughter of Jelena Ružić Galić, Mileva's aunt. Around 1886, Jelena had married Tima Galić, a moderately wealthy businessman. Sofija was born in 1887. Her brother, also named Tima, was born on February 19, 1902—less than a month after Lieserl.

Sofija must have known about Lieserl. When Lieserl was born, Sofija was fifteen years old and living with her family in Vilovo, halfway between Kać and Titel and twenty-seven kilometers from Novi Sad. Interviews and photographs show that the Galić and Marić families spent much time together. Sofija's mother was not only Marija Marić's sister, but her best friend.

In 1905, Sofija's father, Tima Galić, had signed a letter of guaranty for a friend. The plan was for the friend to use a loan from Galić to pay off an outstanding debt. But Galić's friend did not pay off the debt, and the man who was owed the money murdered Sofija's father on the Vilovo village bridge. The murderer had mistaken him for the original borrower.

After Galić's death, his estate was sold "on the drums," at auction. All of the proceeds went to pay an assortment of personal and business debts. Jelena was widowed at the age of thirty-six and left without any means of financial support. Even if she had inherited enough money, she would still have had to live in a family member's home: No single women, not even widows, lived alone. So Mileva's parents took in Jelena and her children as, over the years, they had taken in other unfortunate female relatives. Jelena became a sort of family housekeeper, and her children, Sofija and Tima, were raised alongside their Marić cousins.

✧

In 1951, a correspondence regarding the Marić house in Novi Sad was struck up between Tima Galić and Hans Albert. Tima's first letter was written to Hans Albert in care of his father. Albert forwarded it to Hans Albert, who was traveling in Europe. He responded from the *Île de France,* en route to America. Tima's letter has been lost, but we can tell from Hans Albert's reply that it concerned the management of the house on Kisačka Street, which had been rented, with most of the Marić furnishings and Zorka's belongings still inside.

"I am definitely willing to help with the bureaucracy," Hans Albert wrote in reply.

Six weeks later, Tima responded, telling Hans Albert, "Your mother left the care of the house to Djoka Gajin, who died two to three years ago. After his death, his wife looked after the house and now wants to free herself of the care because of her age. . . . You and Eduard are the sole heirs. . . . As owners, you have total say over your property. I can help you in this matter, so let me know your intentions. As far as the entire inheritance is concerned, I will inquire of a local attorney about how to deal with this matter. . . . My sister, Sofija, lives in Belgrade and sends you her regards. Her husband died in Germany as a prisoner of war in a bomb attack. She has no children and lives alone, and supports herself on her [husband's army] pension and her dress-making."

Six years elapsed until the next piece of correspondence from the Galič family. On April 25, 1957, Sofija wrote to Hans Albert:

"Every time I go to Novi Sad I try to find out what things are [left] in the house. Several times I have asked the caretaker about the house and what are with the things in it. She told me that your mother had sold many of the things [but] to tell you the truth, I don't believe it. I have noticed that many things are missing. Perhaps some things are left. Please write and let me know what to do with the leftover things."

✧

Slavica and I walked through old double wooden doors onto the property of the Marić house in Novi Sad. The Marićs' rooms were on the left side of a courtyard, the servants' quarters on the right. They all have been converted into small flats. The buildings are painted a pale pink or a honey yellow. Their window frames are faded and peeling, blues and greens. In the courtyard is a small garden. Still visible were reminders of *perunika*, spring iris, and sticking up here and there, the yellow flowers sacred to the old Slavic god Perun, also called *Basilicum*. Tied with rough cordage to a rickety trellis against the wall were fading sunflowers whose seeds had already been harvested, and a jungle of drooping and withered, once-deep purple violas. It had rained that morning, and their scents lingered in the air. We made a sharp right, walked up three chipped, cracked steps, and knocked on Mrs. Kikić's front door.

Mrs. Vidosava Kikić (not her real name) lives in what is now called the Einstein House. She and her husband moved there in 1937, a year before Zorka's death.

Mrs. Kikić now lives alone. She is in her seventies and suffering from cancer. A tiny woman with a drawn face, she was clearly uncomfortable in our presence. She invited us into her small four-room flat, and we sat in the living room. On a table were stacked neat bundles of official-looking documents. For years, Mrs. Kikić has been trying to gain control of her flat as well as two others for her two daughters. The compound has nine flats altogether. When Tito became head of the new federal Yugoslav government, in 1945, five of the units were nationalized and four were left for Hans Albert and Eduard. There has been no landlord for many years; the maintenance has become the tenants' responsibility. Those paying rent stopped doing so, and the buildings began to deteriorate. In 1956, Mrs. Kikić's husband went to Zurich to talk to Eduard Einstein about the property. He found him at the Burghölzli Psychiatric Clinic, completely uninterested in it. Eduard only wanted to play a Mozart piece on the piano for him.

In 1956, Mr. Kikić asked the court to assign him ownership of the house. After a series of judicial proceedings, nothing was accomplished in his favor—in fact, nothing was accomplished at all. But in 1961, the people living in the nine flats were informed by the municipality that they could stay there indefinitely. Finally, in 1964, the Regional Cultural Association declared the house a cultural monument. Eleven years later, a plaque was placed on the wall to the left of the entrance. It reads:

IN THIS HOUSE LIVED IN 1905 AND 1907 ALBERT EINSTEIN, THE CREATOR OF THE RELATIVITY THEORY, AND HIS SCIENTIFIC ASSISTANT AND WIFE, MILEVA. THIS PLAQUE WAS PUT UP IN HONOR OF THE ONE-HUNDREDTH BIRTHDAY OF MILEVA EINSTEIN MARIĆ AND THE THIRTIETH ANNIVERSARY OF THE PEOPLE'S TECHNICS.

Albert visited the house in 1905 and 1913.

Now, more than twenty-four years after installing the plaque, the Cultural Association would like to retrieve Mileva's body from Zurich and bury her alongside her relatives in the local cemetery. They would like to make the house on Kisačka Street into a cultural center in her honor.

Early on in my research, Hans Albert's daughter, Evelyn Einstein, and I had become friends. I had hoped to instigate the resolution of the property matter on her and her brother Bernard's behalf. Slavica had done the legal work to clear the titles, but Evelyn would have to hire an attorney in Novi Sad to sell the four flats remaining in the family's possession. Perhaps it would not be worth the effort. Slavica figured that after all the legal proceedings which Evelyn would have to go through, there would be no profit to be made from the sale. Furthermore, Mrs. Kikić and the other tenants had done an admirable job tending the property all these years and felt they had a moral claim to it.

"Mrs. Kikić," I asked as we sat at her table, "where are Zorka's belongings? We understand from a 1951 letter written to Hans Albert by Tima Galić that most of the furniture and belongings of the Marić family were still in this house."

"What are you talking about?" Mrs. Kikić said. "There is nothing here that does not belong to me!"

"But the letter states that the house contained all the furniture Miloš and Marija left after their deaths," I insisted.

"Mrs. Kikić," Slavica said soothingly, "we understand that the furniture and belongings were never claimed and that you may be holding them for the family."

Mrs. Kikić pressed her lips shut and waved her hand across the table. *"Ne, ne,"* she hissed. "You need to talk to the Gajin family; they lived here before we did. We talk about *my* family now. Not *that* family."

✦

Desanka Gjurić Trbuhović, Mileva's first biographer, wrote that Mileva had kept some of Albert's letters and they were "found yellowed and wrinkled among her papers. She showed her letters to her sons." These were the only letters found after she died. They eventually became the body of *The Love Letters* (the photocopies are housed in the Einstein Archives), which revealed for the first time the existence of Lieserl. But it is doubtful that Hans Albert saw them while his mother was still alive, given his reaction in a letter of May 1, 1957, to his cousin Sofija Galić Golubović:

"We have recently read some old letters of my parents and found there to our astonishment that my mother had a daughter before me and that this girl was in Novi Sad or somewhere nearby. Do you know who that is and if she still lives?"

He continues: "Not very long ago I received a letter from a Mrs. Milić. Who is she? Is she this sister of mine or at least related to her? Does she know under these circumstances how we are related? She tried to explain something to me about our relationship, but it was not quite clear to me, what she tried to say."

Sofija wrote back on June 11 that Mrs. Milić "may be related to you on your grandfather's side, but Grandfather never cared for his family because they were a lazy and easy-going family and he despised people who were like that." Then she addressed the matter of Lieserl: "In regard to the sister that you mentioned, take that completely out of your mind because you never had one. You have been misinformed. If you think it might be true, do you think your parents would not trouble to find out anything about her concerning her welfare?"

The letter made complete sense to Slavica. The denial was a way of dealing with a serious shame in the family.

"You just pretend that it never happened," she explained. "If Lieserl died before Hans Albert was born, then she never existed as a sister for him."

"But if she died," I said, "isn't it the custom that Mileva would have told the boys a sentimental story about her? And the story would have been retold frequently in their home?"

"No, not really," Slavica answered. "Remember that Lieserl was illegitimate and Mileva would not have wanted her other children to know this. Even if Lieserl had lived and was adopted, Mileva's sense of shame would have stopped her from telling her sons the truth."

✧

We had to find Sofija Galić Golubović. Slavica and I drove to the graveyard office of the Almaška church in Novi Sad. The day was ice cold, made even colder by the wind. We found a gray, weather-beaten wooden shed with a rusty tin roof, patched with flattened Pepsi cans. The shed was surrounded, here and there, with old, cracked tombstones. Tufts of dead weeds poked through the rubble.

The elderly graveyard manager was sitting inside, next to a blazing wood-burning stove made out of a kerosene can. He was dressed in an odd assortment of layered garments—sweaters over shirts over sweaters. On his head was a faded Brooklyn Dodgers baseball cap. Over this was draped a moth-eaten army-issue blanket, the edges of which he held together under his chin with a gnarled hand.

Slavica, in her best singsong voice, asked for his help in locating the grave of Tima Galić.

"Pay the maintenance debts and taxes on the Marić and Galić family tombs," he told her "and you can see whatever you want to see."

We paid the debts and taxes, which amounted to around one hundred dollars. The graveyard manager then showed us the cemetery's record book. After turning many pages, Slavica found the death certificates for Tima Galić, buried June 13, 1980, and his second wife, Andjela, who died in 1985. On Tima's certificate it was noted that Andjela had arranged her husband's funeral; Svetozar Krajić of Belgrade had arranged Andjela's.

We walked to the back of the graveyard and found the Marić tombstone. According to the inscription, there were five people buried under this tombstone: Mileva's father, mother, sister Zorka, aunt Jelena, and a distant cousin, Dragica Galić. There was no mention of Lieserl.

✧

"I have tracked down Svetozar Krajić," Slavica said, hanging up the telephone. "He is a relative of Tima Galić's second wife. He told me that Tima had a daughter named Branka, who was Lieserl's second cousin. She lives in Belgrade, but Svetozar does not know her address. He promised to call the next time he goes there and give it to us."

"In the Balkans, that could mean next year," I groaned.

We began to think of other ways to locate Branka, but an hour later Svetozar Krajić called with her address and telephone number. Slavica was flabbergasted. She telephoned Branka immediately, and Branka agreed to an interview the next day.

The bus to Belgrade was crammed with soldiers and police. From the moment we boarded, loud Serbian music—a mixture of hard rock and Middle-Eastern folk—drowned out our conversation. About halfway there, the bus stopped at a military outpost. The music was turned off. Two soldiers, each armed with a rifle and a pistol, came aboard the hushed bus. They asked all the men for identification papers. Slavica gripped her hands together as if she were trying to restrain herself. At first, I was more curious than nervous.

Two seats in front of us, a soldier yanked a young man who looked like a student in his black sweater and beret from his seat and forced him off the bus without a sound. I was so furious that I began to get out of my seat, but Slavica firmly caught my arm and shook her head. Everyone was motionless. The bus started up. The music blared once more.

We were depressed and subdued as we took the number 11 tram to Branka Galić's apartment house, in a newer part of Belgrade, at the end of the line.

Slavica rang the bell, and Branka and a black long-haired dog emerged from the apartment. Branka introduced Zarko, the dog, as if it were human.

Then Branka and Slavica said in unison, *"Kad se pas raduje prijatelj je došao."* They laughed, and Slavica translated: "When the dog is barking happily, a friend has come."

Branka Galić was fifty-eight years old and had just retired from her job as an English teacher. Petite with steel gray hair cut short and large dark eyes, she exuded curiosity, excitement, and intelligence. She lived with her husband, a famous political cartoonist, Corax. A large piano, along with books and art, takes up a good part of her living room.

We began, of course, with coffee and cake and chatted about everyday matters. Finally, I broached the reason for our visit. "Did you know that Mileva and Albert Einstein had a daughter named Lieserl?" I asked.

"Absolutely not," Branka said, seeming genuinely startled. Slavica told her the story, then I showed her the June 11, 1957, letter from her Aunt Sofija to Hans Albert Einstein.

Branka read the letter, perplexed.

"I do not understand," she said. "By the time my aunt wrote this letter to Hans Albert, I had come to live with her. I was attending school in Belgrade. Indeed, I am the one who taught her English!"

Branka held the letter in her hands, shaking her head. "Why would Aunt Sofija say that he never had a sister? Why did I not hear whispers floating through her house while I lived there?" She thought some more.

"I know!" she said, suddenly. "My father's papers! He was very careful about keeping the family records and photographs. They are all in Novi Sad. I can get them for you to use in your research. And then, when you are finished, you can give them to Evelyn Einstein to be placed with her estate.

"There is only one problem," Branka continued. "My cousin, who is now in the mountains caring for his ailing mother, has the key. I will have to drive there to pick him up, and bring him back after we see what's in the baskets. And as you know, it is difficult to get petrol. I will have to figure this all out."

"Can we just go to him and borrow the key?" I asked.

"It is a complicated family matter," she answered. "Remember, this is a patriarchal country. My male cousin is in charge."

"Okay, but I will give you money for the petrol," I insisted.

"There is another problem," Branka said. "My cousin is always nervous that the fire in his mother's stove will go out. His mother is so old she cannot light it herself. So I will have to bring someone with me who will stay with his mother and watch the stove while I take him to Novi Sad, which is almost two hours away. It will take some planning to do all this. But I promise to do it for you."

We thanked Branka and said our good-byes. As we turned to go down the stairs, Branka said, "Remember, my dear, *sto oceva, ali jedna majka.*" Slavica and Branka laughed, and I was left wondering what they meant.

When it was dark we left Branka. During the long ride back to Novi Sad, Slavica and I sat in gloomy silence. We knew that getting her father's baskets could take many months. And we were right. Six months after I left Serbia, Branka had the opportunity to look through her father's papers—only to find no trace of Lieserl.

✧

Slavica took out her ebony combs and replaced them, trying to hold back her wiry, silver hair. We were listening to one of her favorite pieces of music, "Prayer" by Josif Marinković, on an old phonograph. It was October 31, St. Luke's Day, and the faithful, including Slavica, took it easy. St. Luke's Day draws the line between autumn and winter.

As the day grew older, the sun crossed behind Gornja Crkva Vavedenja, the deep yellow Serbian Orthodox church across the road. Its steeples reflected the sun, sending light through the windows and illuminating the windowsills.

"*Mrzne se,* it is freezing."

Slavica stepped through the front door onto the enclosed porch. Lining the walls were tiny pots of newly sprouted parsley and marigolds. Two pairs of shoes were sitting to the left of the door—an old pair of brown army-issue boots and a pair of run-down *sabots,* showing traces of the deep blood-red color they used to be. Slavica brought in the new plants and set them on the windowsills.

As she was watering the plants, she told me, "I found Mrs. Milić. She still lives at the same address that was on her letter to Hans Albert, forty-two years ago."

Slavica telephoned her. From listening to her often I had learned that her conversations begin with a singsong introduction and exchange

of pleasantries that always ends with her voice rising above her normal
range. I can tell when she is making arrangements because her voice
drops into a deeper register. Her voice dropped now.

"It is odd," Slavica said later. "She really did not sound very surprised
when I called. I think maybe she wants to help us."

I was practicing my Serbo-Croatian to prepare for the interview with
Mrs. Milić. *"Bili ste vrlo ljubazni što ste me pozvali,"* I was saying over and over
again. "It is very kind of you to invite me."

Slavica listened, smiled, and nodded, but it was obvious that she did
not understand a thing I was saying and was too polite to correct me.

The next day we drove to Mrs. Milić's house in Novi Sad and were graciously invited to come in and sit down. A grand lady in her seventies
with blondish curly hair, Mrs. Milić sat in an old chair, leaning against a
faded red antimacassar. Next to her was a small round table covered with
a white doily embroidered with red roses. Also on the table were her reading glasses and three framed photographs: one a stern-looking woman,
another of Hans Albert and his wife, Frieda, which appeared to have been
taken in the 1950s, and the third of a young, pretty woman, who had
dark marcelled hair and a left eyebrow that arched as if in suspicion.

The room was a rectangle with a table and piano at one end, a row of
windows along one side, and a wall of dark-brown cabinets at the other
end. Built in under the cabinets was a day-bed. As in many of the older
European homes I had visited, there was no such thing as a bedroom. In
these houses, a sleeping room was magically transformed into a living
room in the morning.

I had learned by now that in Serbia, a hostess does not even ask her
guests if they would like coffee. Guests assume they will be served at the
beginning of a visit.

"May I help you make the coffee?" I asked Mrs. Milić.

"Da, da," she said, and leaning on a wooden cane topped with an ornate carved bird, she slowly led me to the kitchen.

"You should never boil the water," she taught me. "You must let it
almost boil."

Mrs. Milić poured a small amount of almost-boiling water into a narrow-necked brass pot called a *džezva*. Then she poured finely ground coffee beans into the water. She set the *džezva* with the grounds on the fire and let it come almost to a boil again. The froth crept up to the top of the funnel each of the four times she passed it over the flames, and each time she blew on the froth to deflate it. She did not put sugar in the coffee ("This is not the Serbian way, it is the Bosnian way").

As we always did when we interviewed people, we showed Mrs. Milić photos from Evelyn Einstein's collection. She did not recognize a single person.

"I am sorry," she apologized. "I do not want to disappoint you. However, you might be interested to know that we had a nun in the family." She turned toward the side table.

"This one," she said, pointing to the photograph of the pretty woman. "At the convent, she was called Sister Teodora."

I looked at Slavica, who smiled at me across the cookies.

"Her name was Nada Marić," Mrs. Milić said. "She was born in Kać around 1902. Her father, Pavle Marić, was a relative of Milos Marić, Mileva's father. She had the Marić personality."

"What do you mean?" I asked.

"Nada always reminded me of Mileva. She was fierce about love. She became dark and brooding in later life, like Mileva. When she was a youngster, she often came to stay with Mileva's parents. Then, in 1914, Nada's father died of an infectious disease while he was serving in the army. He was thrown into the sea—known in Serbia as the Blue Graveyard. Her mother died that same year, of typhus. Nada was only twelve years old. After her parents' death, Mileva's father paid for her to be educated, though he refused to finance some of the other young women in the extended family, including my sister," Mrs. Milić said, pointing to the photograph of the stern-looking woman.

"A family member told me that he thought the school Nada attended may have been the Privat-Gymnasium der Schwestern Broch in Zagreb, which was owned by a Croatian woman named Ada Broch, a friend of Mileva's, but I really do not know for certain. I do know that when she completed gymnasium, Miloš offered to send her to university, but she declined. Nada just wanted to read on her own. Everyone told her that she would ruin her eyesight, but it was the only thing that seemed to make her happy."

After five years in Zagreb, Nada returned to Novi Sad on holiday, where she met Marko Lazić (a pseudonym), a high-ranking clerk in the Novi Sad Institution for Social Welfare. They were married in 1926. A dapper man with a well-trimmed mustache and oiled dark brown hair, Marko was fond of wearing fancy suits, bow ties, and roguish fedoras. He was outgoing, a flirt, and domineering.

Nada, on the other hand, suffered a shyness that was often mistaken for aloofness. She was highly intelligent—much more intelligent than her husband, but she loved him passionately.

In October 1936, after ten years of marriage, Nada discovered that Marko was having an affair. She was stunned. He was all she had. They had no children.

In a desperate rage, Nada poisoned their food and lay down beside Marko to die. The next morning, the couple was found by a neighbor and taken to the hospital where Marko died a few hours later.

Nada survived but was not charged with the crime. The medical examiner announced that Marko had died of salmonella poisoning.

After her husband's death, Nada grew even more remote. Often she left her house in Novi Sad, the one on Vojvode Mišića Street with the fifty red rosebushes, and wandered the Serbian monasteries—attending the liturgies, fasting, and confessing regularly—a pilgrimage that continued for forty years.

Throughout all those years, Nada's family watched her closely. She behaved normally, but they felt there was something amiss with her. When asked how she was feeling, she would answer, "Well, I live." She would appear perfectly fine for an entire afternoon's visit and then, without a moment's hesitation, she would accuse a family member of spying on her.

During the Second World War, Nada stayed with the Marić family in Kać. She seemed to shrink and shrivel, like a rag doll that has been laundered too often, remembered Mrs. Milić. After the war, she returned to the house in Novi Sad, where she lived a few years more. In 1951, officials from the Tito regime arrived, and, with no warning whatsoever, evicted her. They charged her with creating political unrest on the street by hanging on her front door the traditional *venac,* a wreath of small yellow flowers, a symbol of Serbian Orthodoxy protected a family from troubles.

At that point, Nada went to live with her childless cousin, Mrs. Milić, and her husband. She had only her pension, having given all her inheritance from her father and Miloš Marić to the church. The Milićs and Nada went to concerts, the opera, and sometimes the theater in Belgrade. Nada always insisted on paying her own way and then taking them out afterward for pastry and a glass of tea. But most of the year, she roamed the monasteries. When she came home, she worked in the garden and went to church. That was her whole life—until 1976, when she settled at the Krušedol Monastery.

✧

Thirty kilometers east of Sremski Karlovci, on the Irig Road, Slavica and I turned right onto a dirt lane and drove another six kilometers, winding through the Fruška Gora, a range of small mountains rising to 1,760 feet. These are the first hills of the Transylvanian Alps, where wildcats, deer, and wild boar still roam. The Serbian Orthodox Krušedol Monastery, founded in the fifteenth century, sits in a low, fertile valley where wine is produced. We arrived at the monastery's old wrought-iron gates. Directly in front of us was the chapel, its peeling, faded seventeenth-century frescoes providing a biblical tableau for a herd of sheep grazing on the front lawn. Dozens of refugees from the Krajina were wandering about the pristine grounds.

Sister Vera, a vivacious woman in her eighties with a round, pleasant face, came out to greet us. She was dressed in a monastic cassock, the traditional long, black clothing of nuns and monks. Her only ornament was a wedding ring on her right hand. (In the Orthodox tradition, nuns are not permitted to wear crosses.) She led us on a tiny path through white plum and apple orchards, up a hill to the monastery cemetery. Along the way, Sister Vera encouraged me to pick white plums and collect them in my pocket.

The cemetery was a small gathering of graves that looked out over the Fruška Gora. At the foot of each grave stood a three-foot-high white marble cross. One of these tombstones marked the grave of Sister Teodora, who died in 1991. Next to her, a blank slab of white marble covered another nun's grave, awaiting her death. We sat on the grass by the graves and ate the white plums, silently gazing across the valley.

We returned to the monastery and were shown into the visitor's parlor of Sister Apolinarija, the Mother Superior and Sister Vera's blood sister. We sat under twenty-foot ceilings, surrounded by numerous dim religious paintings. Like Sister Vera, Sister Apolinarija wore a monastic cassock, and she also wore a *kamilavka,* a stiff black hat that stood straight up twelve inches and resembled the headdresses of some of the saints depicted on icons.

Sister Vera told us slices of the monastery's history over Turkish coffee and freshly picked grapes from the monastery's vineyard. Whenever Slavica or I asked a particularly probing question, she would merely respond with facial expressions—smiling, grimacing, or raising her eyes to heaven. It is understood that you can talk about families and their wealth or intellectual success, but it is impolite to gossip.

Finally we asked for information about Sister Teodora. Sister Vera glanced at the Mother Superior, who nodded almost imperceptibly. Sister Vera folded her hands in her lap, crossed herself, and began to speak.

"You must understand," she said, looking at Slavica, "it is because of your father-in-law, the priest Dokmanović, that I am telling you this. We know and respect your family."

Slavica nodded and gave Sister Vera a thin smile.

"As you know, Sister Teodora died in 1991. She left us peacefully and without pain. I will show you her cell. Bring your coats, it is cold."

Sister Vera rose, and we followed her down worn stone stairs and around so many corners that I lost my sense of direction. She stopped in front of a small doorway set deep into a thick white-washed wall. I could detect the fusty smell of decay.

Although the doorway was taller than we were, the oppressiveness of the cell made us stoop. The cell was approximately ten feet square with a low ceiling and a stone floor. In the wall opposite the door was a tiny window almost entirely covered by ivy and smudged with smoke.

The light coming through it was greenish and dim. Sister Teodora's cell had been transformed from a simple, tidy room into a gloomy, smoke-filled dormitory for male refugees, with bunk beds stacked to the ceiling. After standing silently a moment, we were happy to leave.

We followed Sister Vera back to her office. On one of her shelves was a large book, which she took down and placed on a table. Opening it to a page near the end, she showed us the entry that said, "On the twenty-eighth of August 1987, at the age of seventy-nine, Nada Marić Lazić submitted a formal request to Sister Apolinarija to become a nun." The application required a commentary on why she wanted to join the convent. Sister Vera showed us the application: "I used to visit our Serbian monasteries often and I used to stay there quite long, for weeks and months, helping the nuns and the monks. As much as my financial situation allowed me, I made gifts to the monasteries; however, I never became a nun. . . . Since I have lived in this monastery and am very well introduced to the rules that exist, and also since my great wish is to become a nun, I would like to ask for a recommendation from you and also if you could ask the Bishop to organize the ceremony for me. Since I am very old I will not be able to serve myself or the others, and that is why I am asking for help from the other nuns in this monastery. I will need their help also if I get sick. In return, I promise to give two-thirds of my pension to the monastery. Hoping that you will transmit this request to the Bishop, Always grateful, Nada Lazić."

Sister Apolinarija gave her recommendation to the Bishop saying that "we are ready to accept her now. It is your decision." A few days later, Nada Marić Lazić became Sister Teodora.

Sister Vera told us, "Sister Teodora talked little but read a lot. She prayed to God as if she had committed sins in her previous life. She loved loneliness. She rarely talked about her husband, Marko. But she still loved him. His picture hung behind her bed."

Sister Teodora was very active in the preparations for the bishop's visits to this monastery. She did not care about ordinary people. She was very stubborn. In her last years, she fell often, because she had one leg that was considerably weaker than the other. For three years she was bound to her bed. She suffered a lot, but never complained."

Sister Vera invited us into the sitting room. "There is something else I want to tell you," she said. "I do not know what this all means, but it has puzzled me for a long time, and I am curious. Sister Teodora used to see the priest very often. When I asked her why she went to talk to him more than the rest of us did, she told me that it was in order to release her burden, her internal anger.

" 'You always seem so sad,' I would say to her. 'What did you do that has made you so sad? . . .' Sister Teodora would answer me, 'I had to do it because of my anger—but I have always regretted it. It has been a big burden on my soul.' "

Sister Vera sighed. "She never told me what the burden was. And, of course, since church law prohibits the priest from revealing others' confessions—he took her secret to his grave."

I glanced at Slavica with a maybe-we-should-tell-her look. Slavica pursed her lips and shook her head.

Sister Vera rose and said that she had to end our meeting because she was making plans for a funeral the next day. She held out her hand to me. I clasped her hand to shake it, but she placed her other hand on mine, closed her eyes, and mumbled something. I hoped it was a prayer.

On our way out of the monastery, I asked Slavica why we could not tell Sister Vera the truth about Nada.

"It would not be right," Slavica said. "She would believe that you had gone against the dictum of the priest. It would be a sinful burden for her to bear."

❖

Slavica and I drove back to Novi Sad. A storm had suddenly descended, with wailing wind and rain, and Slavica's little Zastava 101 was swaying in the gales. We drove over the Danube on the Old Bridge, and Slavica told me the story of a massacre by Hungarian troops of occupation that had taken place half a mile away, during the Second World War. It is called *Novosadska Racija,* the Novi Sad Raid.

"One January day in 1942," she said, "more than one thousand Jews and Serbs were rounded up and marched to the Štrand, the Novi Sad beach. There, standing in forced lines, they were systematically shot. The victims, sometimes still alive, were then thrown through a hole in the ice into the river."

Later, no matter whom I was with, whenever I traveled over the Old Bridge—which NATO bombs have since destroyed—I was reminded of the horror. This area also has another tragic history that people do not want to discuss. I was told by a number of women that in the nineteenth and early twentieth centuries countless illegitimate or unwanted female babies were tossed to their deaths from a bridge a few hundred yards away that has since been destroyed.

✧

Sister Teodora—Nada Marić Lazić—grew up within the extended Marić family. She displayed the same obsessive passion as Mileva for her husband. She was prone to profound and grim depressions. She was of exceptional intelligence. Her left leg was shorter than her right. But I could not confirm that Sister Teodora and Mileva had ever met.

When Albert divorced Mileva, she could have contacted Lieserl—there was nothing to stop her from doing so. But not one of the people we interviewed knew any anecdotes about a relationship between Mileva and Nada, (later Sister Teodora.) If Mileva had ever contacted Nada, someone in the area probably would have heard about it—especially Sister Vera, to whom Sister Teodora often spoke intimately. On the other hand, Sister Vera would not have disclosed such information if Sister Teodora had sworn her to secrecy.

Nada's birth certificate states that she was born in July 1904—more than two years after Lieserl. By now, though, we had learned how unreliable official documents in Serbia could be. When we tried to find her christening record in Kać, the village where her birth certificate said she was born, or in Titel, where Lieserl was born, it was nowhere to be found.

✧

We needed to find the family Gajin. When Mileva had appointed Sidonija and Djoka Gajin power of attorney, she had also arranged for them to live in the house on Kisačka Street. We knew that this family had been trustworthy in keeping the legal affairs of the Marić family in order, and we wanted to learn whether any papers they had might have related to Lieserl or perhaps to Nada Marić. We had also heard rumors that they had kept some of Mileva's belongings from the house on Kisačka Street.

Uncannily, throughout the day that we tried to telephone the records office in Novi Sad to make an appointment to obtain the most recent Gajin family death certificates, Slavica's phone rang constantly. We were being pursued by historians searching for Lieserl. Telephone calls came from Zurich, Belgrade, Titel, Kać, and America, pressuring us to divulge our sources. One historian was consistently six hours behind us in her requests to interview people who had just agreed to be interviewed exclusively by us. We were told that she was furious at "that woman from America." Through all of this we were polite but firm in our determination to persevere on our own.

"I feel as if I am in the middle of an hysterical-historical blitz!" Slavica said.

Finally, Slavica got through to the records office and made arrangements for a meeting. The next day we went to the Novi Sad office, only to find it scarcely functioning. Bare lightbulbs dotted the entrance, groups of twenty to thirty refugees stood in the dingy hallway, smoking, waiting, seemingly hopeless. We entered a small, bare room with one wall of worn leather-bound books that held all the birth and death records for the city. We told the clerk that we needed the Gajin death certificates, and she began leafing through the two-feet-tall ledgers. Within a few minutes, she found the death certificates for Sidonija and Djoka Gajin, which listed their address at the time of death as the Marić house on Kisačka Street. Also listed was their daughter's name, Mira Gajin—without an address.

"I will have to call Mrs. Kikić," Slavica said gloomily. "She will know what happened to Mira, because she originally rented the flat from her."

Slavica called Mrs. Kikić from the records office, and I watched her face light up during their exchange.

"She had the address," Slavica said. "But she did not know Mrs. Gajin's married name. It turns out that Mrs. Kikić has relatives living in the same building where Mrs. Gajin lives. She remembers a conversation about the coincidence." We hurried to Mrs. Gajin's street, where we were confronted by a maze of twelve-story apartment buildings. "Do you know a woman named Mira whose grandparents used to live on Kisačka Street and whose maiden name is Gajin?" Slavica asked anyone within earshot. Within an hour, she had found Mrs. Gajin's apartment. But in Serbia it would be terribly impolite to knock on a stranger's door without an invitation, especially given the heightened tension of wartime. We went home.

Slavica called one of her friends at the phone company, who was able to locate Mrs. Gajin's number using her address and her first name. Within a few minutes, Slavica had Mira Gajin on the phone. She explained the purpose of the call and emphasized our relationship with Evelyn Einstein. After many minutes, Mrs. Gajin told Slavica reluctantly, "Yes, I have some things that belonged to Mileva. I will talk to you, but I do not want you to use my married name. Use Gajin instead. No other journalists, no television people. I want to be left alone."

Slavica agreed, and she and Mrs. Gajin set a meeting time for the next day.

The next morning, Slavica and I drove to Matica Srpska, the oldest Serbian cultural institution, founded in 1826. Serbs used to meet there to discuss the latest in scientific and philosophical ideas. Today it is the primary archive and library in Novi Sad. In its holdings we found a rental agreement between Mileva and the Gajins, signed on July 1, 1940, stating that the Gajins could rent two rooms at the Kisačka Street house "for not one penny" and that the "lease will never expire."

Then we went on to visit Mrs. Gajin and her quiet daughter, Sanja, who was out of work. We exchanged pleasantries, and I gave Mira some coffee and chocolate. While we were having coffee, Slavica asked, "Did you know that Mileva had a daughter before marrying Albert Einstein?"

Mrs. Gajin put down her cup and said, "No, absolutely not. Such a thing to believe!" Her face was stormy. She sat still and did not ask any questions. Her daughter remained silent. Slavica sat quietly. I could tell that she was formulating a plan.

"Look, Mrs. Gajin," Slavica said finally. "Maybe we can help each other. I know it is hard to find a job nowadays, and I think I can help your daughter. I will try. In the meantime, if you could help us, my friend here from America would be most grateful."

Suddenly, the atmosphere changed. Sanja sat up straight, though she still did not utter a word. Mrs. Gajin smiled for the first time.

"In a basket on the ceiling, in the attic, I have papers, letters, and photographs. And right here," she said, pointing at the table, "I have some of Mileva's books and her drafting set. I will give these to you to take back to her granddaughter, Evelyn, in America. I also have letters proving that Mileva helped Einstein more than has been acknowledged. I promise that by Sunday I will go through everything else and give you whatever you want."

"*Krava se drži za rep a čovek za reč.* One holds cows by their tail and people by their word," Slavica said kindly to her.

"*Dajem vam časnu reč.* I give you my word of honor," Mrs. Gajin replied. And they shook hands.

A few days later, we returned to Mrs. Gajin's, but she was quite wary again, and visibly uncomfortable. Nevertheless, she did give us papers, including some pertaining to the Marić estates. We learned that in 1914 Mileva's father had lost one of his Bosnian estates in Banja Luka to a peasant, Karl Fhurneisen [sic], who claimed that since his family had been farming the land for forty-five years, it was his. The court ruled in the peasant's favor.

Also in "the basket on the ceiling" were uncashed National Bank Stock Company dividends amounting to only 2,800 kronen. And we found the song that Mileva had written after falling in love with Albert. Unfortunately, there was not a whisper about Lieserl—and nothing at all about Mileva helping Albert with his theories.

However, included in Mrs. Gajin's papers was a book, *Die Sexuelle Frage, The Sexual Question,* by Dr. August Forel. This same Dr. Forel had been director of the Burghölzli in Zurich—the psychiatric hospital to which Zorka Marić had been admitted during her disastrous visit to Mileva in 1917 and to which Eduard Einstein was later committed. Another of Forel's books, *Der Hypnotismus,* had been mentioned by Mileva in a 1901 letter she had written to Albert from Stein am Rhein: "Forel differs from a quack only in that he faces his patient with more self-confidence, read impertinence, because of his more extensive knowledge," she wrote. For years, historians have been looking for the copy of *Der Hypnotismus* that Mileva and Albert had in their library. It has never been found.

But no one knew about Mileva's copy of *The Sexual Question*. Later, as I was putting the book in my bag, I noticed an edge of paper protruding from it. A small pamphlet titled "Alkoholismus und Degeneration," "Alcoholism and Degeneration," by Dr. G. von Bunge, printed in old German script, fell out. It had been published in Bern in January 1904 and held a dusty-pink silk ribbon as a bookmark. Both the book and the pamphlet were extensively underlined and had notations in the margins.

"People underline because the words are telling them something they are interested in knowing," I said, running my finger along some of the sentences.

"Or," Slavica said, "because the underlining is affirming what they already know! Remember, Mileva was *mudra glava,* a wise head. She would not underline something unless it was very important to her."

The remaining books were *David Copperfield, Allgemeiner deutscher Muster-Briefsteller (The German Way to Write a Letter), Das allgemeine Strafgesetz (German Common Criminal Law),* Weiner's *Medizinal-Kalender,* and *Knjiga Za Paru: Silazak Sa Prestola (A Book for a Penny—Descending from the Throne)* by Kario Amurelli. The last was a Serbian history and biography of the Croatian king Mutimir. On one page describing Mutimir's life, Mileva had underlined the sentence "Love is not a sin."

I looked inside each book, page by page. In *David Copperfield,* I found a *Postai föladó-vevény,* a postal coupon that had probably been used as a bookmark. It was a receipt for money, although the amount was not specified—and also for a five-hundred-gram package. It had been sent to Mileva, in Bern, from her father in April 1905. In the margins of the postal coupon are Zorka's attempts to create her initials, "ZM," sixteen times—some in Cyrillic, some in Latin letters.

Finally, I opened Mileva's black leather drafting box with gold fleur-de-lis at the corners. Inside, neatly laid in reddish-purple velvet beds, were beautifully crafted brass tools.

✦

Because of the international sanctions, unemployment in Serbia was over fifty percent. Nonetheless, Slavica managed to find Mrs. Gajin's daughter a job as a clerk in the Clinic of Gynecology and Obstetrics.

Slavica and I had assumed that, in the old bartering tradition, Mrs. Gajin would look for more baskets in her attic. In fact, the day after Slavica found a position for Sanja, the phone rang and it was Mrs. Gajin.

"There are two more baskets on the ceiling," she said, "and I am feeling bad about not telling you."

We made another appointment and returned, only to be handed one useless piece of paper.

"I am tired," Mrs. Gajin complained. "I do not feel like working. Come back another time. There is nothing more today."

We later learned that Sanja had decided not to take the clinic job after all.

✧

The next evening, Ivana Stefanović, Milana Bota Stefanović's granddaughter, telephoned. "You must come back to Belgrade," she insisted. "I have found another bundle of things for you!"

On one of those blustery windy days with a driving rain racing around the corners of buildings, Slavica and I visited Ivana again.

After we had settled ourselves around her table, I noticed a pile of photographs and a few more letters next to the blue sugar bowl. Slavica had spotted them too. She tried not to look at me.

As soon as etiquette permitted, Slavica asked to see the photographs. Ivana fanned out the pile of photographs on the table. Incredibly, she had a copy of almost every photograph of interest to me in Evelyn's archive.

"This one is a picture of my aunt Milica as a young woman, in 1929," Ivana said, handing it to me.

Mileva, Eduard, and Milica are posing in front of a cluster of tall shrubs. The sun is casting lacy shadows upon their clothes. Milica, wearing a simple white summer blouse, her dark hair pulled away from her face, is looking in a begrudging way at the camera. Eduard, also dressed in white, is standing close behind her, holding a sheet of white paper. He is gazing down, away from the camera. Mileva is on their left. She is fifty-four years old, and is wearing a paisley-patterned long-sleeve dress that covers her from chin to ankle. She looks stout, matronly, and unhappy. She is also gazing down at her feet.

"Mileva was trying to make a match between my grandmother and Eduard," Ivana continued, "so Milica was often invited to Zurich." Indeed, in 1929, Milica wrote to her mother and father about one of these visits. Ivana read us the letter.

"I was asked by a circle of Mrs. Einstein's friends to read one of Papa's poems, so they could hear how Serbian sounded. I found Mrs. Einstein's copy of Papa's book *Verses and Rhythms*. Papa, Eduard asked me to translate one of your poems into German. Accidentally, I opened your book on the page where there is the poem "The Pain of the Unknown." I said that the poem was written, if my memory holds, at the time when Paja [Milica's brother] was seriously ill with scarlet fever. That observation seemed to Eduard very interesting. Eduard asked me to explain to him why Papa wrote the poem: Was it a pure coincidence or was it a premonition of illness?"

"Do you have the poem?" I asked Ivana.

She got up and slipped a slim volume out of a bookcase. "I will translate for you," she said.

"Tonight, I had a horrible vision in my dreams:
A lifeless head, in a scarlet mantle
A little child passed by me
The whole of my soul was covered by a dark cloud.

Where did it come from, what is its meaning?
What tragedy does it forecast to me?
What evil hope does it carry to me?
Why, with the emperor sign, death to combine?

Oh, I did not dream in vain,
I knew it and felt it innately,
Something bad, somewhere, happened to me.

Somewhere a star shivered,
Somewhere a soul shed tears,
Heaven, like a deluge, was darkness flooding."

"He was fearing for his son's life," Slavica interpreted. "Very few children survived scarlet fever in those days. His son was lucky."

Eduard was sliding toward madness. Pornographic pictures of women covered the walls of his bedroom. Mileva did not want Milica to see his room, but Eduard kept inviting her in.

One evening, speaking nonsense, Eduard tried to kiss and fondle Milica. The next day, she returned to Belgrade, and the yellow car came from the Burghölzli to fetch Eduard, shattering Mileva's last hope of a normal life for her son.

We went through the remaining photographs. Most of them were pictures of Ivana's family that had been sent to Mileva over the years. But one of them was nearly identical to the one of Milica, Mileva, and Eduard, except that Milica was replaced by a woman who bore a striking resemblance to Mileva. On the back is the date "Juli 1929," written in Mileva's hand.

Although this photograph was taken only minutes apart from the one with Milica, its tone is just the opposite. The shrubs are the same, even the light falling on them is the same, but everyone looks cheerful. In this photo, Mileva has combed her hair back and pinned it up loosely in a chignon. The hairdo becomes her. She is gazing dreamily up at the trees. Strangely, she looks twenty years younger. Eduard is staring directly into the camera. His illness had not yet become physically apparent. Later, he also became obese.

The unnamed woman is on the left in this photograph. Her dark hair is pulled back off her face, low eyebrows hover over her dark eyes. She has a small, turned-up nose and a pleasing mouth. She is the mirror image of Mileva.

"And here is another interesting letter I found, which I think explains who the woman is. It was written by my grandmother to her mother during a visit to Mileva in Zürich.

" 'Third July, 1929,' " Ivana read. " 'There is a student from Zemun living with Mitza [Mileva] and she is very nice.' That must be the mystery woman in the photograph. She was there during the same month as Milica. What do you think of that?"

✧

Slavica often said when we were frustrated about our research, "God sometimes shuts one door to open a hundred others." I had concluded that the young woman from Zemun was probably a student at the Polytechnikum. Over the years, Mileva had maintained a connection with the school.

I took the train to Zurich. At the Polytechnikum, now the Swiss Federal Institute of Technology, I requested biographical information from the 1929 student register, for an unidentified student living at Mileva's address.

An hour later, I was told by the clerk, "Your mystery woman is Anka Streim from Zemun. The address on her record confirms that she boarded with Mileva Einstein."

Anka Streim was born in the city of Zemun, which sits directly at the point where the Sava and the Danube Rivers converge. According to her student records, Anka's father, Hinko, was a pharmacist and her mother kept house. Zemun acted as a commercial outpost for its big sister, Belgrade. When Anka was growing up, the houses were cumbersome, timber-beamed structures that lumbered away from the river with its constant flow of water traffic and brightly colored boats. People used to say the river reminded them of a collection of floating water birds from the jungle.

Anka went to school in Zemun, but was so intelligent that when she was ten years old, she left home for a more rigorous education. From 1918 to 1926, Anka attended the girls' college in Zagreb. From there she went to Switzerland and the Polytechnikum, the mecca for Vojvodina students, where she received her diploma for mechanical engineering in 1930.

The school's records noted her birthdate as 1908, six years after Lieserl's. But, more important, if Anka was Lieserl then she certainly would have continued to be a part of Mileva's life in one way or another.

However, she moved out of Mileva's apartment building the next school
year, 1929–30, and there was no further mention of her. Perhaps she left
Mileva's home as Eduard's condition deteriorated.

Nevertheless, Slavica and I persisted. We tried to find Anka's family in
Zemun, but there was nothing—no birth records, no school records, no
pharmacy, no sign of Anka Streim whatsoever.

✧

After two days, I took the train back to Novi Sad. At the Serbia-Hungary
border my first-class compartment became classless and flooded with
women traveling to Sofia, Bulgaria, to buy goods to smuggle back into
Serbia. (Only women made that trip on the train. Men smuggled cigarettes, whiskey, petrol, and medicine in buses, by truck, and on foot.) The
women were experts at transforming their compartments into sleeping
dormitories. They placed all their luggage between the seats, threw their
coats over it, and one by one lay down to sleep, feet to head, head to feet.
I counted twenty-one women in a compartment that was intended to seat
six people. Up and down the aisle snaked a man selling packaged food out
of a rusty shopping basket. The smells of apples and oils permeated the already stuffy train. Passengers had loud debates about opening and closing
the windows. It was a relief to arrive at the Novi Sad train station, and
then to return to Slavica's home.

The next morning, I walked down the road to the Gutenberg Book-
store, where there were a few titles in English, primarily translations from
Serbo-Croatian. Tacked on one wall was an old blue-and-white enameled
street sign that read ТРГ БРАНКА РАДИЧЕВИЂА, *Branko Radičević Square,*
named for the great Serbian Romantic poet who lived from 1824 to 1853.
Before Tito's Communist regime took power, Sremski Karlovci was under
the Fascists, the Croatian Ustaša movement. It was during that time that
the street sign was removed. Now there seemed to be a reluctance to put
it back. Maybe the present regime wanted to name the street after one of
its own heroes?

I asked the proprietor if the street sign was for sale.

"No," he said. "In fact, I am trying to donate it to *Gradski Muzej,* the
Town Museum, where the poet's works are displayed. But the authorities

do not know how or where they are going to place our history—in public, or in the catacombs!"

Later, in the afternoon, the proprietor telephoned me at Slavica's house. The museum had rejected his offer, saying it was an act of political defiance. When I told him the sign was a piece of art with historical value, he tried to give it to me. I refused. We settled on a price of twenty dollars. That night, Slavica recited one of Radičević's poems that reminded her of Lieserl.

"If you are a star my dear,
You should be among the stars,
Among stars, my dear,
Which are your closest sisters."

PART
FIVE

In 1922, Mileva's father, Miloš Marić, died of apoplectic *insultus,* a type of stroke generally induced by severe stress. He was seventy-six years old. According to family members, at the end of his life he considered himself a failure. He believed that in spite of all his dreams and struggles, nothing had worked out for him. He felt that his children had dishonored him. In his later years he had become a recluse, rarely leaving the house on Kisačka Street in Novi Sad. Mileva returned to Serbia to bury him. Around this time, her sister, Zorka, suffered another psychotic episode. Mileva went to court a few days after her father's funeral to have Zorka declared mentally ill.

✧

That same year, Albert Einstein won the Nobel Prize for his work on theoretical physics and the discovery of the law of the photoelectric effect.

Although the awards had been suspended during the First World War, Albert was so confident that he would eventually be a Nobel Laureate that he offered the cash prize as a financial settlement to Mileva as part of their 1919 divorce agreement. In the end, however, the money came with strings attached. Although she received income from the interest on the money, she could not access the principal without Albert's permission. In 1923, Albert told her that he had transferred 45,000 francs to her bank account for the purpose of buying property. He ordered that the remaining cash be deposited in her name in a New York bank, in Argentinean, Swedish, and Danish currency.

Mileva decided that it would be wise to own property. Over the next four years, she purchased, with Albert's permission, three apartment houses in Zürich. When she sent him photographs of one of the properties, Albert wrote back that he was happy she was again "pregnant with a house." He wished her luck and told her that he hoped the tenants would "pay their rent, and not annoy you, or you them. I look forward to seeing the house, the more so as its purchase came about as a result of my sacrifices." Although Mileva and her sons were to live off the rental income from the three houses, it did not sufficiently cover their expenses. Even so, she was still not permitted to draw additional funds without Albert's agreement.

✧

In 1923, fully recovered from her years of debilitating illnesses, Mileva received an amazing gift. Out of nowhere, a card from her brother, Miloš, arrived in Novi Sad, addressed to her mother. He was alive, in Russia, and on his way home. Mileva rushed to the Vojvodina to greet him. But at the last minute, mysteriously, Miloš chose to remain in Russia.

A few weeks later, he wrote a postcard to his French wife, Marta, who was living with the Marićs in Novi Sad, awaiting his return. She was free to do as she pleased, he wrote, since he was never coming home. Miloš went on to become a professor of histology in Saratov, where he was admired by his colleagues for "his very good scientific knowledge, his being enormously well read, his phenomenal memory, and his ability to explain complicated matters shortly and simply," though they noted, "toward others Marić was a little closed off and not very talkative."

The Russian life of Miloš Marić has since disappeared into the government's sealed Saratov archives. But in his home country, he was privately branded an *otpadnik*, a deserter, another disgrace to the Marić family. His wife, Marta, left the Marić home in Novi Sad and she was never heard from again.

✧

By 1923, Albert was prosperous. He had a new violin made for himself; "[I]t sounds wonderful," he wrote to Hans Albert and Eduard. He allowed Mileva an unlimited amount of time to repay the money she had borrowed from him without interest. He boasted to her, "You will notice that there can scarcely be such an accommodating divorced husband as I am. I have indeed been true, in a sense different from the one the young girl dreamed of, but true."

In June, Albert came to Zurich to discuss Hans Albert's plans for further study. He had considered staying in Mileva's flat but was afraid of the "public scandal it would cause. Even without this, I am already too much the subject of talk."

At this time, European travel carried with it some danger for public figures. Anti-Semitic reactionaries were pejoratively calling Einstein the "Jewish Saint" in their pamphlets. Just a year earlier, Albert's friend, the newly appointed German Foreign Minister, Walter Rathenau, was assassinated while driving in an open car through a park in Berlin. Since 1918, there had been more than three hundred political murders, and so it was that Albert canceled all his lectures and public appearances in 1922.

Elsa keenly felt impending disaster. She was convinced that Albert's life was in danger and begged him to leave early for a planned trip to work at Leiden University, in Holland. He agreed, although he felt Elsa was overreacting. He did not know that she had arranged for police protection. At the railroad station, on the day of his departure, a number of policemen watched for suspicious-looking people. And in Albert's compartment were two armed plainclothes men, who were assigned the task of escorting him safely to his destination.

✧

Day by day, life in Germany was becoming ever more difficult. There were interminable strikes and riots due to the failing economy. In November 1923, Hitler's attempted coup d'état in Munich failed, and he fled to a friend's house outside the city. Two days later the police found him cowering in a wardrobe, behind the clothes of the woman who owned the house. He was arrested and imprisoned at Landsberg, where he wrote *Mein Kampf.*

Albert informed Hans Albert and Eduard that "here [in Berlin], things are again rather crazy. God knows what will come of it all. For a week we were without light or gas and sometimes without water. The university was closed." According to a family friend, he believed "Nazism was born on an empty stomach."

To Mileva, he wrote that since she had "ceased speaking ill" of him, he "would like to resume our old friendly relationship, and I am even thinking of coming to stay with you if I come back to Zurich." As usual, however, their rapprochement did not last long.

Albert had brought some gifts back from his trip to Brazil in the spring of 1925, and sent them to Zurich, most likely as a peace offering. However, Mileva did not respond in a way he thought appropriate. He complained, "Nothing I do is appreciated. All I get from you is dissatisfaction and distrust. I don't take it badly anymore because I believe that I am dealing with someone abnormal."

In 1925 Mileva wrote to Albert that she was considering writing her memoirs in order to make money. Albert replied that she made him "laugh with your threat of your memoirs. Doesn't it ever occur to you that not even a cat would give a damn for such scribblings if the man with whom you were involved had not happened to have accomplished something important? If a person is a cipher, there is nothing you can reproach him with. However, one should be nice and modest and keep one's mouth shut, that is my advice to you."

With the rental income and the small amount she earned from giving piano lessons and tutelage in mathematics, Mileva struggled to make ends meet. Eduard needed more and more rest cures, sometimes in the mountains, sometimes at a lake, always expensive. Nevertheless, Mileva continued to assert that whatever was wrong with him was merely "a nervous disturbance."

At the same time, the Einsteins' mutual friends Michele Besso and Heinrich Zangger were trying to mediate the couple's prolonged dispute. In a letter to Zangger, Besso suggested that Mileva inform Albert that in light of mounting debts, she was being forced to consider declaring bankruptcy, giving Eduard into guardianship, and going on welfare. Eventually, she had to sell two of the apartment buildings in order to pay for Eduard's care. Albert refused to provide her with any additional help.

✧

In February 1928, two months before the Nazis won ten seats in the Reichstag, Albert suffered a mild heart attack. He had been delivering a free lecture on physics in Davos, a resort town in eastern Switzerland—the same town that provided the setting for Thomas Mann's *Magic Mountain.* (His lecture was part of a series intended to promote a better understanding between the French and the Germans and to offer intellectual stimulation for tubercular patients in the town's sanatoriums.) A few days later, Elsa brought him back to Berlin, where he was ordered to bed for four months.

During this time, Albert and Mileva became friendlier once again. Indeed, he wrote to Mileva apologizing for not coming to visit her the previous summer. But, he said, "It was only because I was afraid to disturb. I thought you would be more comfortable with the young visitor without me." Who was the "young visitor"? Could it have been a young woman from Serbia? Could it have been a boarder? Could Lieserl have been one of the female visitors whom Mileva entertained in 1928 and 1929?

✧

Despite all her financial difficulties, 1929 was a good year for Mileva, primarily because Eduard was experiencing a blessed calm. He was now nine-

teen years old and had just begun medical studies at Zurich University.
Like his mother, who avidly read papers written by noted physicians on
psychiatric conditions, he was fascinated by psychology. He wanted to
become a Freudian analyst. Einstein biographers would later contend
that Eduard was so well educated in the Freudian methods of psychoanalysis that he was impossible to analyze—he either knew more than his
analysts or he outsmarted them.

Albert, though he knew Freud personally—having met him in Berlin
in 1926—was not a believer in Freud's theories, and had refused to submit
to psychoanalysis. In February 1932, he wrote to Mileva, "I have no faith
at all in psychoanalysis." Eight months later, in a letter to Eduard, Albert
wrote, "When you come to visit, you must teach me about psychoanalysis; I'll try to keep a straight face."

There is no detailed clinical material about Eduard's illness. Right-
fully, his psychiatric records are sealed. One can only deduce from the
small amount of non-medical information available to biographers from
friends of the Einstein family that his condition was diagnosed as schizo-
phrenia.

In 1930, when Eduard was twenty, he began sending hysterical, ac-
cusatory letters to his father. He blamed Albert for casting a shadow over
his life, for siring him then deserting him. In letter after letter, he told his
father that he hated him.

On November 29, 1930, Mileva traveled to Berlin. She arrived in time
to stand among a crowd of Einstein fans and the usual battalions of newspaper reporters and watch Margot Löwenthal Einstein, Albert's stepdaughter, leave the marriage registry in the Schöneberg district with her
new husband. The husband, Dimitri Marianoff, later said that he "would
not have noticed [Mileva], except that she looked at us with such an intense burning gaze that it impressed me. Margot said under her breath,
'It is Mileva.' We never knew then or afterward why she was there." She
was there to discuss Eduard's condition with Albert.

Eduard had an intelligent understanding of his own psychological
condition and could carry on an informed conversation with his father
when he was feeling well. Albert maintained that nothing was really
wrong with his son. "Men are like bicycles," Albert lectured him. "Only

when one is going forward can one keep one's balance. As long as you are working well, all is well."

Eduard could not work well; indeed, he could not work at all. His acute sense of rejection by his father and the accompanying self-loathing paralyzed him. Mileva begged Albert for help. Although Albert discounted psychiatry, he finally consented to send Eduard for therapy.

When Albert went to Zürich in 1930 to judge Eduard for himself, Eduard basically ignored him. Two days after he left, Eduard tried to throw himself out of a third-floor window—but was held back by his diminutive mother. Mileva was able to soothe him enough to prevent a hospitalization.

The following year, 1931, when Eduard was twenty-one, he suffered his first acute episode, plunging into an intense spell of melancholia. It was apparently brought on by a failed love affair with an older woman who was a medical student and who may have been married. Albert was blasé about the affair and told Eduard to get himself a "plaything" rather than a "cunning female."

By the autumn of 1932, Eduard had begun his final descent into madness. He obsessively banged on the piano, creating a cacophony. He physically threatened and sometimes attacked Mileva. On occasion, when she had company or was giving a piano lesson, Eduard sidled into the living room stark naked. Mileva would have to hustle her guests out the door, horrified, embarrassed, yet still protective of her son. After a particularly violent episode in which he tried to strangle her, Eduard was committed to the Burghölzli Psychiatric Clinic, where he remained for a number of months. Once again, Mileva was desperate.

"You have here a dear, seriously ill child," she wrote Albert. "Often he asks if his father will come, and with each postponement, he becomes more morose. He is terribly wounded."

Albert refused to come back to Zürich to see Eduard. And he refused to acknowledge the financial and psychological battles that Mileva had to wage over his care. "I am not in favor of psychoanalytic treatments," Albert wrote to her in 1932. "Nothing good ever comes from it. If a man cannot find the strength to stand on his own feet, then in God's name, he ought to remain tied to the apron strings."

Over time, Eduard was treated in a variety of ways—rest cures, sleep deprivation, forced baths, drugs, insulin therapy, shock treatments. Hans Albert felt strongly that the shock treatments "ruined my brother." In the end, Eduard, like his aunt Zorka, was considered "a hopeless mental case."

After years of denial of his son's deteriorating mental health and the merits of psychiatric treatment, Albert finally capitulated. In a letter to Eduard in 1936 he confessed, "I have come to realize that Freud's main thesis is correct." But by then it was too late.

✧

Further compounding Mileva's troubles with their sons, Albert stated his intention to draw up his will and disinherit his former family. "I gave you the Nobel Prize money to secure your future and that of the children," he wrote Mileva. "It should have been clear that this sum, the only money I possessed at the time, should at my death become the inheritance of the children.

"It is up to you to restore the trust between us," he challenged her, "by making a legal agreement that the Nobel Prize will be counted as the children's inheritance, or that you will not contest my will."

There was little left of the prize money after paying for Eduard's care. Albert's declaration caused a huge uproar among his family and friends. Albert backed off, telling Hans Albert to "do what you think is right, after consulting with [Mileva], and if possible, with Eduard. Our future relations depend on your answer."

Mileva had known Albert for thirty-four years, and he was still an enigma to her. One day he could be generous and emotionally responsive—the next, distant, severe, and cold.

✧

Eduard's older brother Hans Albert, whom he adored, was now a hydraulic engineer. Five years earlier, in 1927, he had married Frieda Knecht, whose family lived in the same apartment house as Mileva on Gloriastrasse in Zurich from 1914 through 1924. As Mileva was to Albert, Frieda was older (in this case, nine years) and an intellectual peer of her mate.

In spite of the objections of his parents, Hans Albert was determined to marry her.

"There is a difference of age," Albert complained to his son, "even worse than it was in my case. How I suffered from this and how difficult it will be for you! . . . In ten years . . . she will no longer satisfy you; you will find the marriage an unbearable fetter: she will be insanely jealous. . . . I must alert you and do all I can to hold you back." He sounded like his own mother, twenty-five years earlier, when she had warned him that if he married Mileva, she would be an old hag by the time he was thirty. Hans Albert was not deterred.

Albert was unyielding in his position. He, who had suffered his mother's censure when she did not approve of his marriage to Mileva, was now behaving with the same discrimination. He told Mileva that the "business with [Hans] Albert concerns me greatly. I believe that the girl has him by the neck, but he is too naive to judge the situation correctly. . . . In any case, we must do all we can to prevent this disaster."

Albert blamed Mileva. "If you had let Hans Albert go to Munich to study, he would have had more experience with women and would not have fallen into the clutches of an elderly, sly virgin. If only he [does] not have any wretched children. But *she* will take care of that!"

Albert had been advised by an expert that it might be catastrophic for them to bear a child since there was evidence of "such significant faults of heredity in both families." Albert and Mileva apparently believed that Frieda's mother's family had a history of mental illness.

In a February letter he wrote, "If they would never have children, I could rest easy. But the heredity of our own children is not without blemish."

This was the first time since 1903 that he may have been referring to Lieserl in writing to Mileva. Only one child—Eduard—had demonstrated blemished genes. Hans Albert was perfectly healthy. By referring to children in the plural, he was ostensibly including Lieserl.

Even after they had been married for almost one year, Albert continued to complain about the couple. He told Mileva that "[Hans Albert] will visit in July, but unfortunately with his hanger-on." And yet, when the couple did arrive and Albert finally met Frieda for the first time, he was "pleasantly surprised with them both. [Hans Albert] is happy, more relaxed and open. Her influence is without question a positive one. She is not as bad for him as I expected. She is a bit egotistic and self-centered and not very tactful, but it could be much worse. In short, if they remain childless, I will be reconciled to fate."

Within a year, Frieda was pregnant. "I am sorry to hear," Albert wrote Mileva, "that the couple are to have a child. This disaster must run its course." In the end, it turned out that there was no mental illness in Frieda's family—her mother merely had an "overactive thyroid disorder." Frieda and Hans Albert went on to have three sons and adopted a daughter, Evelyn. All of them were healthy.

Evelyn Einstein told me that her father's decision was a wise one. "Frieda was a wonderful human being, absolutely. She had a crush on [Hans Albert] like a teenager until the day she died."

✧

In 1929, Virginia Woolf published *A Room of One's Own,* articulating every woman's need for privacy and independence. Concurrently, Mileva was beginning to experience a sense of individuality and appreciation for her new life. Albert was relieved that Mileva was now "content. I myself want to bury the hatchet." So he decided to attend the 1929 Zionist Congress in Zurich—and to stay in Mileva's house "as if in his own home."

Albert and Elsa still lived together in Berlin, but Albert led his own life, and Elsa made certain to stay out of the way. After ten years of marriage, Albert's relationship with Elsa had become a replica of his marital relations with Mileva: He was aloof, cold, and demanded privacy. (Hans Albert was later to describe his father as capable of "turning off his emotions like a tap.")

Mileva was thrilled to have Albert back, if only for a week. The atmosphere in the flat was merry, better than it had been during their marriage. Milica Stefanović, who was also visiting Mileva at the time, said that Albert would get up in the morning, "roll up his sleeves, and improvise on the piano." In her excitement, Milica continued, Mileva was

Miloš Marić, Mileva's father. This picture was part of his 1919 identity papers.

Mileva's mother, Marija Ružić Marić, with the family of her sister, Jelena Ružić Galić, in Titel, circa 1905. *(Seated, left to right)* Jelena's husband, Tima Galić, holding his son, Tima Galić the younger; Marija Ružić Marić; Anika Matic, Jelena's niece; and Jelena Ružić Galić; *(standing)* Sofija Galić Golubović and Lazar Golubović.

Mileva's brother,
Miloš Marić, in
uniform, circa 1917.

The Marić family in Novi
Sad, circa 1883. (*Left to
right*) Marija, holding
Zorka, Mileva's sister;
Jelena Ružić Galić;
Mileva's father, Miloš;
and Mileva, age eight.

The family house
in Titel, one of the
largest ranches in
the area. Shown is
a back wing of the
main house.

he Novi Sad
railway station,
circa 1902.

The Novi Sad
Theater and the
Queen Elizabeth
Café, circa 1900,
where Albert
Einstein enjoyed
coffee and
conversation while
in Novi Sad.

The Marić family
house in Novi Sad.

Dr. Laza Marković, the Marić family physician, around 1920. Marković was named godfather to Einstein's sons when they were christened in Novi Sad in 1913.

Pauline Einstein, Albert's mother, in the mid-1800s.

Albert Einstein and Mileva Einstein-Marić with their first son, Hans Albert, who was born in 1904. This family portrait was taken in Bern probably around 1906, when Albert worked at the Swiss patent office.

A previously unpublished photograph of a pensive Mileva in 1906.

The 1900 wedding photo of Helene Kaufler, Mileva's closest friend and confidante, and Milivoj Savić.

Mileva *(seated left, with, left to right),* her brother Miloš, Hans Albert, her cousin Sofija Galić Golubović, and her aunt Jelena Ružić Galić, circa 1907, Novi Sad.

Eduard and Hans Albert Einstein,
circa 1911, Prague.

Mileva's sister, Zorka Marić, on the
balcony of the Gloriastrasse
apartment where the Einstein-
Marić family lived from 1914 to
1924. The identity of the child on
her lap, a little girl, is unknown,
but the speculated date of the
photograph excludes the possibility
that she is Lieserl.

Eduard and Hans Albert in Zurich,
1919. By this time, Albert was living
with his cousin Elsa Einstein
Löwenthal in Berlin.

A previously unpublished photograph of Mileva at home in Zurich, circa 1927.

Helene Kaufler Savić's daughters, Julka *(left)* and Zora, circa 1912. Julka's German birth certificate lists her date of birth as October 28, 1901, three months before that of Lieserl.

Julka Savić Popović in Belgrade, circa 1928. Six years earlier, she had married Novak Popović.

Nada Marić Lazić (a pseudonym), circa 1926. A second cousin to Mileva, she joined a convent near Novi Sad and took the name Sister Teodora.

Anka Streim, Zurich, 1929.

Sister Vera, a Serbian Orthodox nun who knew Nada Marić Lazić in the final years of her life at the Krušedol monastery.

Anka Streim, Eduard Einstein, and Mileva Einstein-Marić, 1929. Streim, a student at the Polytechnikum in Zurich, was one of several boarders Mileva took in over the years.

Elsa and Albert Einstein at a party in New York in the early 1930s. By this time, he was an international celebrity and a sought-after guest.

The actress Grete Markstein in costume in a publicity photograph taken in Berlin in 1922.

Paul Rückelt, circa 1932, Berlin. Markstein and Rückelt parted ways in 1933, when Markstein fled to London after Hitler was named chancellor.

Grete Markstein in London, circa 1935. In March of that year, she approached Einstein's associates in Oxford with the claim that she was Lieserl Marić Einstein.

Albert Einstein with János Plesch, his personal physician and longtime confidant, in Berlin, 1932.

Markstein's son Gustav Georg, circa 1936.

Branko Miškov, Mileva's cousin.

Marie Grendelmeier, Mileva's neighbor at her last Zurich residence.

Milan Popović, Julka Savić Popović's son.

Dragiša Marić, a second cousin of
Mileva's, and his mother, Ljubica
Marić.

Jovan Ružić, a second
cousin of Mileva's.

Milenko Damjanov, a relative of Mileva's
girlhood friend Milana Stefanović.

Slavica Dokmanović, the
author's Serbian colleague.

Slavica Dokmanović at the Kacko graveyard in Kać,
looking for Lieserl's grave.

Mileva's last home, on Huttenstrasse in Zurich, where she lived
with Eduard from 1924 until her death, in 1948.

Hans Albert's daughter Evelyn Einstein, in Berkeley, California, circa 1953.

Mileva with Hans Albert's son Bernhard Einstein, circa 1931, Zurich.

Albert, Mileva, and Eduard on the balcony of the Huttenstrasse apartment on what was possibly Albert's last visit. In 1929, before his mental condition deteriorated, Eduard had begun his medical studies at Zurich University. In March 1933, Einstein emigrated to America; he never saw Eduard or Mileva again.

Scholars have contended that the child in this photograph is Lieserl, although Evelyn Einstein, from whose collection it was taken, disputes this. It is likely that it is a picture of Hans Albert.

The Spire, the Marić summer residence in Kać, in the early twentieth century. At the bottom of the photograph are the figures of an adult, a toddler, and a dog. This may be the only existing image of Lieserl. The original print was in the possession of the Galić family for decades until it was loaned to a Swiss publisher in the 1980s, during which time it was lost.

"filled with a spiritual charm." She told jokes. She "glowed with an inner fire and was as beautiful as a flower which only opens under a sunbeam." Perhaps they resumed intimate relations in some form or another.

✧

Marie Grendelmeier lived in the same four-story apartment building as Mileva, at Huttenstrasse 62 in Zurich, for fifty-three years. By the mid-1990's she was a poised, gentle woman in her eighties, with shocking white hair, startling blue eyes, and a deep tan. Her English was halting, but her words emerged clearly. When I visited her, I brought her a gift of American chocolates, having been told that in the affluent country of Switzerland there is absolutely everything except American chocolates.

I asked my fail-safe first question. "Did you know that Mileva and Albert had a daughter?"

Marie Grendelmeier smiled politely. "Not until the book of love letters came out," she replied, folding her hands in her lap. "Nothing was ever said about a daughter—by Mileva, or by anyone else here in Zurich. I never even heard rumors. And you have to remember that Zurich is a small city, especially the academic community. Everyone knows everyone's business.

"Once a month—beginning in 1942, when we moved into this apartment, until 1948, when Mileva died—I would walk up the one flight of stairs to give Mileva her rent check. I would pet the Siamese cat, who to my amazement was allowed on the table, and admire her new blossoms. Mileva collected cactus plants, and when there was a new blossom it was very exciting to her.

"She was alone—very, very lonely. There was something in her heart that made her sad. Maybe it was her lost little girl, maybe it was her ill son, Eduard, maybe it was her lost love for Albert. I do not know. I never saw her cry, but she looked sad all the time. She never opened up."

Marie stopped for a minute and looked out the window. "Eduard was so much in her heart," she continued. "All her attention was centered on that son. She had to fight for him by herself. I remember he did not like the Föhn, the warm wind that descends from the north side of the Alps.

It made him very nervous, and he would throw things out the window to stop its howling. Mileva always warned me when he began to do this. She was afraid he would hurt me accidentally.

"Albert was not nice to Mileva concerning money. She was very badly dressed. She wore long, black dresses to cover her feet. Perhaps she was ashamed to be seen in a dress shop. The last few years, she did not bathe very much; she seemed unclean. I remember that her hands were very thin and she wore her wedding band on her right ring finger. She often wore an oval brooch but never wore earrings. At the end of her life, she had very little hair. What she had left, she wore in a small knot. Whenever she went out of her flat she wore a black kerchief over her head and tied it in the back. She was such an obviously poor woman that I always made it my business to deliver her check exactly on time."

In 1939, Mileva had asked Albert for help since she could no longer afford to pay for both Eduard's care and the upkeep of the apartment house. Albert agreed to assume ownership of the building to prevent foreclosure. But despite Mileva's pleas, he turned around and sold the apartment house on Huttenstrasse—the one she had been living in for almost twenty-four years—to a private party for 85,000 Swiss francs. He told Mileva that he had arranged for her to live in her own apartment rent-free for the rest of her life. Months later, however, on December 31, she received a notice from the Zurich Housing Department: the lease on her apartment was terminated. She would have to move despite Albert's promise. Fortunately, a friend of Mileva's went to the appropriate authorities and arranged for an extension. Meanwhile, the 85,000 Swiss francs had accidentally been paid directly to Mileva. Albert was furious.

"Perhaps she has hidden the cash, or it has been stolen," Albert wrote to Hans Albert. "Given her withdrawn, distrustful nature, anything is possible." He demanded that the money be sent to him in Princeton and threatened to write Eduard out of his will if she did not comply.

✧

In 1998, Slavica and I drove the seventy-two kilometers east from Sremski Karlovci to Titel, the village and the house where Mileva was born and where Lieserl was probably born, too. Once a huge ranch, it is now broken up into several properties. But you can track the perimeter of the original estate by locating the unusual wrought-iron pineapple ornaments atop the gates and following them to similarly ornate crosses at the corners of the property. A first cousin of Mileva's, Emil Ružić—Jovan Ružić's father—who is well into his nineties, still lives on the original property. Slavica had tried to make an appointment to meet him, but she said that he was "always busy with excuses." It turned out that he was very ill. We had decided to go to Titel anyway, if only to take photographs. Maybe we would even have the luck of finding Emil Ružić at home. Once we arrived, though, he was nowhere to be found, and the gates were locked.

Slavica began to chat with neighbors on the street, asking them if they knew where the remaining family members lived today. She quickly learned that some relatives named Miškov were living directly across the street.

"Wait outside," she instructed me and entered the walled garden full of faded pink late-blooming rosebushes. Ten minutes later, she emerged, beaming.

"Follow me," she said, "we have been invited in."

Inside the kitchen, sitting in front of us on a narrow bed, next to which rested a cracked white enameled spittoon, was a thin, elderly man. Slavica introduced him to me as Branko Miškov. At first he was tense and wary.

"These walls are beautiful," I complimented him, looking around at the elaborately patterned walls. "I have never seen walls painted like this. How is it done?"

A smile crept across his face as he unfolded himself from the bed to stand and shake my hand. Tall and gaunt with thin, gray hair, he was dressed in black and wore a black knitted cap that he nervously slid around his head while talking.

"It is called *moleraj,*" he explained. "A long strip of paper with designs cut out, like a stencil, is held against the wall. Then we take a roller and paint the stencil. After a few moments we lift off the stencil and the wall is decorated. Some of these walls were painted more than one hundred years ago," he continued, spreading his arms wide, "and they still look new!"

Miškov's middle-aged wife came into the room and introduced her-self. She was dressed in a mixture of colors and patterns, with a sweater tied around her waist and a kerchief covering her hair. Her arms were bare and muscular; her hands were obviously familiar with the soil. She smelled earthy and had a fearless laugh. Their shy daughter, who barely nodded when introduced, sat on an old blue milking stool in the corner of the kitchen, while a garrulous distant cousin leaned against the tin sink, a cigarette hanging from her mouth. Her wrinkled face was a mask of suspicion.

We all sat down for coffee. I asked the old man if he knew of Lieserl.

"I remember nothing," he said.

"But I gather you have lived in this house all your life. Do you not re-member family stories about Lieserl?"

"I remember nothing," he repeated. "But"—he laughed with a con-spiratorial tone—"I do remember that Mileva was a very sane woman and that her sister, Zorka, and Albert Einstein were a little off."

When I asked him to explain, he simply shrugged and smiled at me. Then he said, "If Lieserl lived, which I doubt, you must remember that she was born with a stigma—she was born into shame. You must look for an unhappy woman. Then you will find Lieserl."

❖

Until Zorka Marić died, in 1938, she lived in her mother's home. Al-though she had become chronically morose and contrary, she managed to look after herself, adhering to a simple routine. But if anyone were to ask her for something, or a plan were to change, she would tumble into fury. And yet she always managed to catch a branch on her way down, saving herself from being institutionalized.

Since 1829, Novi Sad had had its own mental institution—in the form of one dreary room "for demented minds" tucked away at the rear of the city hospital. Its records have been lost or destroyed, but it is doubtful that Zorka was ever committed there—at least while Miloš was alive—be-cause of the embarrassment it would have caused the family.

On New Year's Day, 1935, Mileva's beloved mother died at home on

Kisačka Street. She was eighty-nine years old. Because Mileva was caring for Eduard and could not leave Zurich, it was left to Zorka to arrange the funeral.

I was told by family members that Zorka went to the undertaker and paid for the most expensive hearse and casket available, in cash. She wanted to bury her mother alone, but the priest took it upon himself to inform family friends.

On the day of the funeral, Zorka rose before dawn to meet the priest, the funeral driver, and, apparently to her chagrin, her mother's friends. They placed Marija in a coffin lined with white satin and carried her outside to the funeral carriage. A man carried the *barjak,* a black banner with a cross on it, in front of the pallbearers and the driver as they moved down Kisačka Street, and the priest began the *opelo,* a prayer for the peace of the soul: "Everything is but a shadow, like a dream, fickle. In a moment the life on earth ceases and the kingdom of death takes over. Oh, Jesus Christ, give this soul peace and let it see the light of your face."

The procession had to travel only eight hundred meters from the Marić home before turning left into the graveyard, Almaško Groblje and another fifty meters to the family gravesite. Marija Marić was buried in the family tomb, above her husband. In three years' time she would be sandwiched between her husband and her daughter Zorka.

Soon after the funeral, in February, Mileva was able to come to Novi Sad to settle her mother's estate. She arranged for Zorka to move out of the main part of the house into one of the smaller wings facing the courtyard. Zorka did not mind. She adored Mileva and did whatever her older sister asked her to do. After their mother's death, each time Mileva visited, Zorka made an effort to pull herself together. This probably meant she would stop drinking. Then she would place her multitude of cats with various people around the city so Mileva would not see how many she had, and thoroughly clean the house. However, as soon as Mileva left, Zorka would lapse back into her usual ways and her condition would once again deteriorate.

After her mother died, Zorka's well-being became the responsibility of the Gajins. The Gajins most likely preferred to keep her away from the local hospital in Novi Sad, which would only provide a gloomy room with six beds, tucked into the dingiest wing. By then, because both of Zorka's parents were dead, she may have spent some time at the Kovin Lunatic Asylum, on the other side of Belgrade, or at a monastery in Zemun, or at a monastery for cloistered nuns in Rakovica.

Finally, on January 26, 1938, after Zorka's neighbors had not seen her for three days, they broke into her house. Zorka was found dead on a pile of straw. Her forty-three cats had left her body alone because mounds of food and buckets of water had been put out for them. She was fifty-five years old.

✧

Three years later, in the spring of 1941, on a Saturday afternoon, Dr. Mihovil Tomandl, the director of the city library of Pančevo, was sitting in Velfert's brewery, ninety-seven kilometers from Novi Sad. The brewery maintained a small bar in the front for men only. Patrons sat at wide-planked, rough-sawn wooden tables under an old shade tree. While he was enjoying a beer, Tomandl overheard a conversation between two German administrative officers sitting at the next table. On the following Monday, seven train cars would transport materials from the state archive in Petrovaradin, directly across the Danube from Novi Sad, to the Archive of the Military Ministry in Vienna. He also overheard that anything in the archives written in German had already been transported out of Vojvodina. At that point, the Germans' conversation came to an end and they stood up, paid their bill, and left the brewery.

The Nazis were interested in accumulating every German language record, book, and manuscript in the archives of occupied Europe. Before the Second World War, there had been a large German population in Kać, so the village's German records were confiscated—and the Orthodox Church records were mistakenly taken as well. The only archives recovered after the war concerned livestock, not human beings. Hence, if Lieserl had been baptized in Kać, her records could no longer be traced.

Dr. Pavle Stanojević, the current director of the Archives of Vojvodina in Novi Sad, says that even today the German government has in its museums and archives church icons and artifacts stolen from Vojvodina, which they refuse to return. The German government claims that the Serbs cannot prove ownership.

But there is more to the story. A German man from Berlin came to Novi Sad in 1928 and ingratiated himself with the Serbian community—all the while working as an informer for the Nazis. Three years after the first theft of records, he arranged for the removal of thirty more full train cars. He ordered that those records be stored in the salt mines of Czechoslovakia and then left Novi Sad, taking the inventory with him. When the archives arrived in Czechoslovakia, the Germans assembled a team of sixty scientists to review the material in an attempt to prove that the Kingdom of Serbia had been the aggressor that had instigated the First World War. At the end of the war, only one of these train cars of material was returned, and as of 1997, their contents had still not been inventoried.

In 1944, a year before the end of the Second World War, Hofrat Doktor Peter Broucek, the director of the *Kriegsarchiv*, the War Archive, in Vienna, began negotiating the transfer of some of these archives back to Yugoslavia. He told me in a 1998 telephone interview that some of the material had been returned to the Archive of War in Belgrade. But those archives dealing with the German-speaking population of Vojvodina were lost somewhere between Vienna and Berlin.

"Was there an inventory of the archive?" I asked.

"As far as I know there was no inventory from this archive in Vienna. Remember, during the war, this was a Nazi archive. And although the Third Reich was well known for its record-keeping, these records seemed not to have been inventoried or the inventory has been lost."

✧

Great chunks of the past have been destroyed in the chaos of war. In my search for Lieserl, I would find random birth documents in a village record office only to learn that the death documents kept in the adjoining room had been destroyed by bombs, or that the enemy had tossed a hand grenade into a municipal office, or that people had been forced to burn the papers to keep from freezing to death, or that a government official had had the documents destroyed. Slavica and I sat down one evening and made a list of thirty-two archives in Serbia, Hungary, and Austria that were important to the search for Lieserl. It was plain that the Novi Sad Hospital Archive was one that still remained unexplored, and we hoped it was still intact.

At the Novi Sad Hospital archive, we were met by Dr. Grozdana Čonak, a petite woman with long black hair and dark eye makeup who is writing a history of medicine in Novi Sad. We walked past old, empty run-down wooden buildings. The hospital grounds, once lush with well-tended gardens and pebbled paths, were desperately in need of care. Dr. Čonak apologized for the disrepair.

"You must understand," she said, "I am paid an equivalent of your one hundred dollars a month. I cannot afford to subscribe to medical journals. I cannot even afford to photocopy articles I need for my work. I have to copy them out by hand. The hospital is broke. The people of Novi Sad are broke. Whatever money we receive is a meager handout from the government."

We stopped in front of a building that looked like an army barracks. There, a man, nattily dressed in an old and worn British tweed suit, bowed and kissed my hand. He introduced himself as Mr. Aleksandar Roslavljev, the hospital's archivist. In halting English, he invited us in.

First I smelled mildew. Row upon row of bowed shelves were stacked with wet, moldy papers. The ceiling showed vast damp areas from the previous day's rains—and from the rains of the past fifty years. Papers were stacked on the floors, some actually in puddles of water. Slavica and I were speechless. The doctor and the archivist could only shrug their shoulders in resignation.

"We are trying to save our archive," Roslavljev said. "Come, I will show you our new room for restoration."

We walked to another barracks-like building, about a hundred meters away. The archive restoration room here was clean and dry—too dry. Heat was being blasted into the room in an attempt to dry out the paper. Two bookbinding machines were screwed down to long tables constructed from pieces of recycled wood. One bookcase held a few lonely restored and labeled archival boxes.

"Have you seen any records from around 1903?" I asked Mr. Roslavljev.

He shook his head. "It will be years before they are found. If they do exist, they will be at the bottom of the piles. Because everything is so wet, we cannot move the papers. Otherwise they will blur further and fall apart—the year 1903 would probably melt in your hands."

"Our country has been in turmoil for a very long time," Dr. Čonak said. "These records have lived under many regimes. I know for a fact that at the end of the Second World War, the Communists recycled many of our old records into new paper. Most likely, Lieserl's records are not even here."

Dr. Čonak specializes in infectious diseases—and we were interested in what she had to say about scarlet fever.

"Very few children survived scarlet fever in the years that you are researching," she informed us. "There was no cure. You had to be plain lucky to live through an epidemic such as the one in 1903. Who knows," she continued with a wry look, "maybe Lieserl died of the fever and was buried under the threshold of the Marić house. It was known to be done, you know. If I were you, I would write her dead."

✧

Milenko Damjanov, an elderly relative of Ivana Stefanović's, lives in Novi Sad. His housekeeper showed us into a large room where there was a long table covered with an embroidered linen tablecloth, two empty crystal candlesticks, and a crystal ashtray. After we were seated, the dapper Mr. Damjanov walked in and we rose to be introduced. It is still customary in Vojvodina to kiss a male elder's hand. Slavica hesitated, then put out her hand to shake.

Damjanov was born in 1909 and had turned eighty-nine shortly before the time of our meeting. He has the classic Balkan-shaped head, a broad forehead, thick gray hair, and a jaunty moustache.

"Of course, I remember Mileva," he said. "Each time she came to Novi Sad I saw her. I remember seeing her first in 1916, when I was almost six years old. I remember the stories about her, because her husband was the most famous man in the world—and of course my family took great pride in her company. We also understood that she helped the professor with his theory. Did you know," he questioned us, "that Mileva was better in mathematics than her husband? No one can stand to give Mileva her due. This is a worldwide shame. Everyone is protecting the great man, the Einstein!"

Mr. Damjanov went on, "In my family, it was considered liberal, actually avant-garde, for Mileva and Albert to live together before they were married. My family did not judge them. On the other hand, I know that Mileva's parents had a hard time with the situation. They had never expected her to marry. And, of course, I know about their daughter, Lieserl. You must understand, no one was surprised when Mileva became pregnant—even though it created a bit of a *scandale!* But her baby—she was called Ljubica in our family—was not one-hundred-percent right. Mileva had tried to hide her pregnancy by wearing tight corsets. This cut off some of the oxygen to her unborn daughter. Her baby did not live a long time. This I can assure you. This I know."

"Mr. Damjanov," I asked, "before Lieserl died, do you think Mileva and Albert placed her in an institution?"

"Never!" he said emphatically. "Never would the Marićs do something like that! If the child had lived, Mileva would have taken her to Switzerland after she married Albert, where the child would have been made legal. I would give my head to prove that she was not adopted. She was probably not even christened. When a child died early in those years, you just put them in a wooden box and took them to the graveyard.

"In those days, unchristened children were buried at the edges of the cemeteries. No record was made of the child's death. Gravestones for children did not become part of our tradition until after the First World War. If any sign was left of a dead child, it was a wooden cross—probably without even a name carved on it. And such a cross would have disintegrated within ten years."

According to the *Collected Papers from the First Congress of Doctors in the Federative People's Republic of Yugoslavia,* there were approximately one thousand children living in the Novi Sad area in 1903 before the scarlet fever epidemic. Before the end of the year, approximately forty percent of them died, which meant nearly four hundred unmarked children's graves from that year alone. It would have been impossible, even in 1903, to find Lieserl.

✧

By the time Slavica and I left Mr. Damjanov's, evening had descended with a thick fog. As we drove over the Stari Most, the Old Bridge, we had to slow down, creeping along with our amber headlights barely lighting the way. It was my last night in Serbia, and Slavica wanted to prepare a full Vojvodina dinner for me, including fish from the Danube.

"I will find the turnoff," she promised. *"Dobro.* Here it is!"

Slavica turned onto a dirt road running along the banks of the Danube. A few hundred feet ahead was a dim porch lamp, guiding us to the fishmonger's house and shop. The water came up to the wall. Two small wooden boats were tied to a dock in front of the house.

We left the car and walked down a path. The cool night fog carried on it the unique odor of the Danube—the smell of freshly turned soil and a tinge of fish. A dog announced our arrival with sharp barks. The door of the house opened, and an elderly woman let us in. Inside was one big room with a wooden table, caned chairs, and a long work counter made of thick slabs of wood. Cooking on an open fire was an old cast-iron kettle of *kotlić,* a delicious-smelling thick fish soup. A few men stood around drinking beer and smoking, while two women set the table and another stirred the pot.

Slavica told them I was from America, and they immediately offered me a *rakija.* "To freedom. To America," one of the men toasted, and we drank.

After Slavica completed her singsong bargaining, we left with the *jesetra,* Danube sturgeon, wrapped in old newspaper tied with used string. Slowly, we made our way home.

Slavica immediately went to work in her kitchen, insisting that I sit with her family and have another *rakija.*

"Živeli! Cheers!" her husband, Nikola, said. Marija, Miloš, Nikola, and I raised our glasses. *"Sve najbolje!* Good luck!" they said in unison.

Four beeswax candles burned in the center of the table. In the background, a Mozart concerto played softly on the radio. The Dokmanović's gray cat, who was never allowed in the house, had somehow slipped inside and was curled up in front of the radiator.

It is Serbian custom for a visitor to be served a special meal on his first and last evenings. This dinner was a feast. The dark silver baked fish with its glassy eyes intact was placed in front of me. It was decorated with sprigs of parsley and tiny mounds of bright red paprika, circled by onion rings, and punctuated with tiny sweet pickles. Then Slavica brought in *sarma*, stuffed cabbage, along with browned potatoes and green beans. After a moment of quiet, we began to eat.

When I had come to Serbia, I was keenly aware of the country's reputation in the world. I was worried about the war. I was worried about the people I would meet and our political differences. But in the time I had spent there, I had found decency and honor, and in Slavica, a lifelong friend.

After dinner, we sat around the table and drank more of Nikola's home-brewed apricot *rakija*.

"I am going to have nightmares about Lieserl," I joked.

"No, you must not," Slavica soothed me. "You are almost to the answer. Not to worry. Anyway," she said laughing, "in my country, it is easy to prevent nightmares. We are taught that all we have to do is place a broom upside down against the bedroom door. When the nightmare sees the broom at eye's-height, it rushes away into the night."

None of us wanted to go to bed. We decided that since we had to leave at five in the morning for the airport in Belgrade, we would not go to sleep. So into the early hours of the morning, we went through all the material we had collected, translated some of the final interviews, dated everything, and put each piece in its appropriate file.

"All these possibilities!" I exclaimed. "All these possible scenarios. All these possible Lieserls."

"Remember what Branka Galic said? *Sto očeva, ali jedna majka,*" Slavica reminded me.

"Okay, Slavica," I said with mock weariness. "What does that mean?"

She laughed. "There can be one hundred fathers, but only one mother! Do not forget—you need to understand Mileva in order to find Lieserl."

Slavica does not like to say good-bye at airports, so we prepared to leave without her. I was so upset to leave her that I did not know what to say. We embraced and kissed three times on the cheeks. Then she took my hand in hers and whispered, *"Srećna i zdrava bila.* May you be fortunate and healthy."

PART
SIX

In early November 1935, when autumn was turning its back and winter was beginning to embrace the English countryside, Grete Markstein boarded a London train to Oxford. She was on her way to meet Frederick Lindemann, the director of the Clarendon Laboratory and a friend of Albert Einstein's. Her purpose was to stake the claim that she was Einstein's daughter.

To arrive at that November day, I began my research in Berlin because I had discovered that Grete was an actress and had worked in a theater there. A journalist, Stefan Elfenbein, agreed to be my interpreter and guide. On my behalf, he had approached the *Geheimes Staatsarchiv Preußischer Kulturbesitz,* the Secret Archives of the State of Prussia, a repository for state records and documents from the time of the Holy Roman Empire in Germany through the dissolution of the state of Prussia, in March 1947. Also archived there are the records of state employees who were classified as *Unruhestifter,* troublemakers. Since Grete Markstein had worked for the German state theater, it seemed possible that she would have a file of her own there. The actual records are stored in concrete bunkers in Potsdam, nearly thirty kilometers outside Berlin. After three days of searching, a file was found: Identification, *Lit. M, Nr. 220, 1920–1924, 1928.*

Entering the grounds of the archives in Berlin is a surreal visual experience. Surrounding the imposing two-story building is a curiously out-of-place white picket fence. We unlatched the small gate and walked up a long gravel path. Once inside, we established our credentials as researchers and were given keys to two lockers in which to store our belongings, save for one pad and one pencil. No pens or cameras were allowed in the reading room. Wide granite steps led to a lofty wooden door that opened into a cavernous room. In front of us, and on either side, sat approximately sixty historians typing quietly into their laptop computers from yellowed papers and books dating back to the seventeenth century. In a musty side room, a man behind a desk handed us a folder. "Fräulein Grete Maria Markstein" was written on the tab in elaborate cursive. When we opened the folder, forty-five documents brought her to life.

✦

Grete Markstein was born in Vienna and grew up on Währingerstrasse, just around the corner from the home of Sigmund Freud, near the university, in the ninth district, a few blocks from the Danube Canal.

Nearly half the Jewish population of Vienna lived in Leopoldstadt, between the ninth and second districts, many in poverty. But Grete's father, Samuel, was an agent for the shipping company of German Lloyd and a respected member of the Jewish middle class. He was born in 1854, in Szeged, Hungary. Five years afterward, Jews were granted greater civil rights under the law, and by the time Samuel entered young adulthood, he was able to move freely to Vienna. In 1883, he married Helene Neumann Markstein, a Jewish woman born in Vienna in 1863.

In 1884, their first child, Katharina Lili, was born, and two years later, Leopold, their only son. Their third and final child was Grete. Although a Viennese birth certificate places her birth in 1894, Grete insisted in later life that she was born in 1902.

In 1914, when Austria declared war on Serbia, the Markstein family moved to Baden, the spa town fourteen miles south of Vienna. At the time, Grete and her two siblings were registered with the synagogue in Baden and, as required by law, with the police.

As a young woman, Grete was short and a bit stocky, with dark brown curls that would never stay in place. She had high cheekbones, a stubborn chin, and dark eyes. She was the family extrovert, the spoiled last child. She was a somewhat petulant adolescent, prone to dramatic outbursts, and displayed an unusual talent for acting and singing, which her parents encouraged with lessons.

Grete's family remained in Baden for the duration of the war, but as soon as she was deemed old enough, she returned alone to Vienna, where she became an actress.

✧

Besides food and music, one of Vienna's specialties at the turn of the century was anti-Semitism. Indeed, one of the first questions asked of a person was, *Ist er ein Jud?* An insidious, yet certain, bigotry wove itself through the arts. By the time Grete was performing, Jews wanted to be free of the culturally imposed *jüdische Eigenschaften,* Jewish characteristics, and be accepted for their talents without prejudice. As a result, there was a serious movement to assimilate, to be an *Überläufer*—a deserter of one's Jewish ancestry. Hannah Arendt called it the "renunciation of characteristics," a radical individuation that left one without a heritage and supposedly free of the past.

In Vienna, Grete succeeded in slipping herself into the persona of actress, rather than Jewish actress. As with many other Viennese Jewish artists, she is not listed in the archives of the *Israelitische Kultusgemeinde,* which holds most of the genealogical registers dating back to 1860—and none of her later work ever identified her with Jewish roles.

It was probably in Vienna that Grete met the famous theatrical director Max Reinhardt. Reinhardt, whose family name was originally

Goldmann and who was Jewish, brought his work to Vienna from Berlin after the First World War. The *Theater in der Josefstadt* was restored specifically for him to mount his grand expressionistic productions, known for their spectacular color and bursts of pageantry.

❖

In 1918, the Central Powers lost the war. Precipitated by this defeat, Austria's war bonds collapsed. Many middle-class Jewish investors, including Grete's father and brother, lost all their money. And in the same year, within two months of each other, both men died—probably in the devastating flu epidemic.

A year later, Grete moved to Brüx, in Bohemia (now Most in the Czech Republic), aged either seventeen or twenty-five. Apparently, through Reinhardt's connections, she had been hired to act with a troupe at the *Stadttheater,* the City Theater, where she performed before an audience of seven hundred lignite coal-miners.

It was in Brüx that Grete met and worked with Lola Stein, who at thirty-four was an established actor with a union number and an address. Grete had neither. But like Grete, Lola was Jewish and a long way from home, having been born and raised in Hamburg. In late 1919, she and Grete left Brüx and moved to Berlin together. They remained friends for the next twenty-four years.

❖

"It was just before the end of the year [1919] that I arrived in Berlin," Grete wrote to Leopold Jessner in 1920, "after having been invited by Herr Professor Reinhardt." Most actors new to Berlin claimed to know someone important in the theater. It was a joke that "all actors, if they were lying, said they worked with Max Reinhardt." But, of course, Grete actually did know Reinhardt from her work in Vienna.

In 1919, Berlin was cold, bleak, and trying to revive itself after the war of "filth, lice, idiocy, disease, and deformity." The flu epidemic was finally over, and refugees from the east and exhausted ex-soldiers were flocking to the city. Grete herself had very little money, but she must have sensed optimism in the air. It was the eve of The Golden Twenties, and the arts were enriched by the multitude of artists who had come to Berlin to find aesthetic freedom from repressive governments. There were 245 cinemas and thirty-five major theaters, usually filled to capacity for every performance.

Nevertheless, it took Grete six months to find work because there were an abundance of young actresses in Berlin. While waiting for their big break, they were often compelled to perform in one of the many glamorous nude revues. By June 1920, Fräulein Grete Maria Markstein had signed a contract with the *Staatliches Schauspielhaus,* the National Theater, the most prestigious theater in Berlin, under the directorship of Leopold Jessner.

Jessner, known for his daring interpretations of classical literature, had opened his first season as director of the *Staatliches Schauspielhaus* with an expressionistic version of Schiller's *William Tell.* He designed an avant-garde stage set with large gray landings jutting out at odd angles. In the play, the tyrant Gessler, cheeks rouged bright red, was costumed in a military uniform with flashing gold medals, personifying a Prussian Junker, an aristocratic and haughty landholder. The audience went berserk and the first great art riot of the 1920s erupted—with fistfights, horns blowing, and screaming matches. Everyone had a marvelous time.

In this vibrant company, Grete found a place for herself. Jessner's repertoire included such playwrights as Brecht and Wedekind, and his list of primary actors read like a Who's Who of the German thespian élite. For Grete to have been hired meant that she was a fine actor, and she became a member of the Co-operative German Theater Artists. On her contract, she stated her specialty as a "young female lover," but her age was not mentioned.

Without delay, Grete asked the National Theater to "transfer an advance of twenty-five hundred marks into my bank account." Although her request seems reasonable enough, advance payment was not common at the time. Theaters paid their actors *after* a production, not before, not during. That way they could dock them for unexplained absences, too many days of illness, even poor behavior. According to the contract, an advance of 2,000 to 2,500 marks was to be deducted from Grete's salary at the rate of 200 to 250 marks a month at four percent interest.

✧

Grete had been acting in Berlin for less than a year when the Austrian National Assembly took up the problem of Eastern Jewish refugees. Senators demanded to "know why the expulsion of the refugees was not being expedited." The rage at Jews struck close to home when Grete heard on March 14 that a childhood friend in Vienna, the actress Sári Fedák, was assaulted in an anti-Jewish demonstration. The police had guarded the bridges, thwarting the crowds from attacking the Jewish ghetto. But some of the rioters had unleashed their wrath on the windows of a Jewish restaurant, devastating the place and beating the diners.

As the crowd screamed *"Juden raus,"* Grete's friend was dragged from an automobile and whipped. Most of her clothes were torn from her body. The leaders of the riot said that the movement was directed against "foreign profiteering Jews, not residents of Vienna." They claimed they were only "reducing the Jewish Peril."

Meanwhile, Grete had signed another contract with the *Schauspielhaus,* with a raise to thirty-three hundred marks, still contractually obligated to play the roles of a young lover. One of her major parts was Camilla Palpiti in *Lumpazi Vagabundus.* On the first of January 1922, according to Alfred Klaan, the critic for *Vossische Zeitung,* "The evil spirit Lumpazi Vagabundus moved into the theater yesterday, at the advent of the new year, and justified his being on this new ground through an honest success. He came led by the good spirits of righteous mirth, snappy wit and optimistical faith (. . .) The other cast members spiced up the more minor roles through small bits of humor, specifically . . . the Signora and her obliging daughter, Grete Markstein."

Out of thirty-five actors, only eight were mentioned by name in the rave review. Grete was singled out, and also was the only actor photographed for the *Abendprogramm,* the playbill. She was costumed in a long, white elaborate *décolleté* dress, her dark hair arranged in ringlets. A camellia was pinned above each ear, and she held a third in her hand. She wore a coy, slightly naughty expression, and looked as if she were about to break into song.

Taking advantage of her situation, she wrote Jessner at the end of the year on new pink engraved stationery, requesting a few days off because of "very important personal matters." Jessner allowed her the days off, without comment.

Life was beginning to go well for Grete. She had money, a successful career, a promising future, and so she began to live more extravagantly.

"I take the liberty of your kindness," Herr Steinhardt, owner of a fine clothing establishment wrote to the theater on January 30, 1922, "to inquire about the credit-worthiness and financial situation of Fräulein Grete Maria Markstein. I am asking you to graciously send me one sentence because I highly regard the lady as a customer and would like to open an account for her regular expenses."

But the theater's management turned down Herr Steinhardt's request on the reverse side of his letter: "On principle we do not give out any information about the personal situation of the employees of the state theaters."

But by the end of the year, Grete began to complain about her position in the company. She told Jessner after trying, and failing, to see him in person that "because I had a feeling that I came at an inconvenient time during my last visit with you, I wanted to present my concerns in writing. Mrs. [Grete] Sandheim," Grete complained, "played the role of Recha last time, not me. At the same time, a regular switching of actress was firmly promised me. You, Mister Theatre Manager, will understand what it means to a young actress to perform for the first time in front of the press. I am asking you not to do an injustice to me and to designate me this time for the part of Nathan."

"My dear Fräulein Markstein," Jessner answered, "you indeed were right having a feeling that during your last 'visit' you came at an 'inconvenient time.' After it was told to you that I was in the offices of the administration on the first floor, you unexpectedly entered my room *through the back door* just at a moment when I had returned to look through some documents. You will understand that this 'visit' was not suitable for an explanation on your part.

"Concerning the matter itself, I comment that in general and under the right circumstances I had *no objection* to alternating the role of Recha.

"It is true that Mrs. Sandheim appeared in the last performance of

Nathan, but before that you played the role of Recha *three times in a row.* Moreover, because of the current artistic constellation, Mrs. Sandheim had few appearances on stage while you acted in every *Peer Gynt* performance. This was reason enough to appoint Mrs. Sandheim to play the role of Recha on December 28, long before you interfered."

On December 29, Grete checked into the Cecilien Sanatorium. A psychological pattern had emerged in which Grete would dive into hypochondria whenever she suffered a setback. A note was sent to the theater.

"Fräulein Grete Maria Markstein is being treated in my clinic and will probably not be able to take up her work within the next ten days. Signed, Dr. Herzberg."

The Cecilien Sanatorium in the Schöneberg district was a private clinic that catered primarily to artists, single mothers, and women who needed abortions. The clinic also specialized in pulmonary disorders, which would plague Grete later in life.

She had been out of the clinic for two weeks when she again requested money. "After my period of illness," she wrote to the theater manager, "I am very weak now and the doctor told me to eat well, so I need more money."

Grete requested 50,000 marks, a sum which at that time of galloping inflation was worth almost nothing. Because she was on a fixed salary, it must have been difficult for Grete to cover the basic necessities.

In January 1923, Grete went back to work and signed a new contract with the *Schauspielhaus* for another year—from September 1, 1923 until August 13, 1924, at 5,500 marks. Within three weeks of the commencement of the contract, Grete wrote to Jessner. Her other letters to him had been written in *perfektem Hochdeutsche*, proper German. It would not have been unusual for a person with her education to ask someone else to write her professional letters. This time her language was informal and unsophisticated—her own.

"Dear Mister Theatre Manager Jessner," Grete wrote, "I take the liberty to remind you about our conversation from the evening of the twenty-seventh. Since years, I am now alternating with Frau Sandheim in the roles of Recha in *Nathan der Weise* and Ingrid in *Peer Gynt.* Now Frau Sandheim is leaving and I would like to play these roles alone—only if this would be in accordance with your wishes, Mr. Theatre Manager. Moreover, I would like to play the Sohey in *Peer Gynt.* Maybe it might be a good opportunity for me right now. I apologize for approaching you with my wishes just in these days where you Mr. Theatre Manager are so busy anyway. But I really would love to perform more often and I am sure that you will understand me. In admiration and devotion, yours faithfully. Grete Maria Markstein."

Grete was taking a risk. By now, she was listed sixth in a cast of thirty-six. A week later, Jessner's secretary replied that "at this time Herr Jessner is not able to make any decisions about your wishes."

✧

One month after Jessner's brush-off, Grete left for New York on the S.S. *George Washington.* She had reported to the theater that she was going to America for two months to make a movie, but there is no evidence of her ever having worked in the American film industry.

On the ship's manifest, she stated that she would be staying for three months. Also on the manifest, Grete claimed that she was joining her friend "President Rückelt," who was "President of the German Consulate" in New York City. She declared that she was twenty-six years old and born in 1897, the first of her many mysterious birthdate declarations. She named as her closest living relative her mother, Helene Markstein, in Vienna.

There was no President Rückelt at the German Consulate in New York—the consul was Dr. Karl Lang. Grete was joining her friend Paul Rückelt, who had been an apprentice shoemaker in Alt-Buchhorst, a suburb of Berlin, where his father ran a small hotel and restaurant. There is no record of what Paul did for a living once he moved to Berlin. A relative, Margaret Rückelt, remembers that he transformed himself into a theatrical agent and thus must have become acquainted with Grete. By the time they met, he was married and had a son.

A month after Grete's arrival in New York, she apologized to Jessner for being out of touch. In a letter dated February 6, 1924, she explained, "I was in such a hurly-burly with all the new developments in my job and personal life. These days coming from Germany, New York is like a fairy tale and a wonder. To crown it all, jobwise, I did pretty well. Coming from Germany, however, one unfortunately still has to struggle with great mistrust from the American people. Anyhow, there are only Americans because even the Germans who live here mostly consider themselves Americans."

Grete was showing very bad form; her letter was too familiar. "There will be much to talk about," she wheedles, then asks for her holiday to be extended two more weeks and continues, "If everything goes well, then you, Mr. Theatre Manager Jessner, will be here for awhile as well—wielding your artistic scepter.

"Rückelt is very busy with organizing the financing up until the very last cent. Rückelt will not write before everything will be signed and sealed. He hopes to be back in Berlin at the beginning or the middle of March at the latest. With best wishes—in admiration, your thankful Grete Maria Markstein."

Grete had transformed Rückelt from president of the German Consulate to theatrical producer. Her "offer" to Jessner was either wishful thinking or outright fantasy; there is no record of Jessner ever having worked with Grete or Rückelt in New York.

Grete returned to Berlin at the end of March—one month later than agreed upon with Jessner—and immediately took to her bed. A physician wrote to Jessner's office, "due to a heavy state of exhaustion, Grete is bound to her bed and still requires looking after for two more weeks." Two weeks later, the doctor wrote again, confirming "in writing that Fräulein Grete Markstein is still suffering and for the time being, unable to work until May 15."

Grete stayed on with the *Schauspielhaus* for another year and a half. But at the end of 1924—the very day Hitler was released from prison—her contract was not renewed. Dark times were descending on Germany, and on Grete, too. She was without work and living with Rückelt, but there is no information about what they were doing or where they were.

The known thread continued in August 1925, when Grete traveled to

Vienna to attend her mother's funeral. She and her older sister tended to their mother's affairs, but within a few days, Grete was back in Berlin.

By the end of 1925, Grete was pregnant. Their timing was poor. Along with most other lower- and middle-class Berliners, they were struggling to make ends meet, even as Weimar decadence thrived in the city's cafés, nightclubs, and dance halls.

Gustav Georg Markstein was born on August 26, 1926, at the Cecilien Sanatorium, the clinic where Grete had gone to recover from various physical and psychological episodes, with the same attending physician, Dr. Herzberg, supervising her care. She gave her home address in Berlin as Keitzstrasse 11, but that was the address for the Actor's Union—there were no apartments in the building. By now, she was no longer living with Rückelt. She and her new son moved into the Hotel Kaiserhof, a cheap boarding house on Potsdamer-Chaussee, the noisy thoroughfare to Potsdam.

✧

In 1926, the German government was spending more and more money on its military as economic hardship slowly turned Berlin into a depressed and ghostlike metropolis. Grete could no longer pay her rent. On December 27, 1927, the actress Grete Maria Markstein was sent a warning by the District Court of Charlottenburg.

"The creditor is entitled to receive the amount of two hundred marks, plus seven percent interest starting from October eighth, 1927 from the debtor. Because of this claim, including the cost of one mark and fifty-five pfennig for the delivery of the warrant and four marks, eighty pfenning for the application of this warrant, the creditor will seize two-thirds of the debtor's weekly salary determined by the contract between the debtor and the management of the State Theater, Berlin, which exceeds an amount of thirty marks. Accordingly, the theater must not pay the salary to the debtor. The debtor has no right to raise any objection to this procedure." The Distress and Transfer Warrant was served on February 15, 1928.

On March 7, 1928, the theater wrote to the attorney Max Goldstücker "regarding the Distress Warrant against the actress Grete Maria Markstein. The general management informs you that the debtor does not belong to the staff of the State Theater. Therefore, the seizure is ineffective."

Straightaway after this letter, Grete pulled herself together. She moved to a flat at 39 Emserstrasse in the Schöneberg district, a wealthy Jewish section, ten long blocks away from the Einsteins. The letter from attorney Max Goldstücker was the last document in Grete's folder. Since she no longer worked for the state, her file was closed.

✧

In 1991, Herr Berthold Leimbach published *Tondokumente der Kleinkunst und ihre Interpreten, 1889–1945, Sound Documents from Cabarets and Their Interpreters,* a book about minor artists, primarily Jewish, who had worked in Berlin until the end of the Second World War. Leimbach claimed that Grete had belonged to a cabaret group called *der Blaue Vogel,* the Blue Bird, and that she was a Russian Jewish immigrant who died in the Holocaust. None of the information is correct, except for the fact of her Jewishness. Later, Herr Leimbach corrected this section.

However, in 1929, she did make a gramophone recording for the Ultraphon Society—a collection of folk tales from around the world—and Herr Leimbach sent me a tape recording of it. It included a fable written by Grete called *"Jim Bibo."* When I inserted the cassette into my tape recorder, out floated Grete's melodic voice from sixty-eight years before.

"One summer, Jim Bibo, a Negro boy, loved a girl. Her name was White Cloud. Because he loved her so much, he tattooed her name into his arm. When the summer was over, White Cloud took another lover from the hostile tribe, Akibin. When Jim Bibo discovered this, he bit out her name from his arm. He put the piece of flesh in the sun because only the sun is so understanding. The sun is pure because she understands all the suffering of the world. Afterward, he stole to White Cloud's tent and—while she was sleeping—wove the little piece of flesh into her cape. When White Cloud wore her cape, she could not feel the sun at the spot where he had woven his skin. This is what Jim Bibo told me."

Like other artists of the time, Grete probably sent copies of her recording to contacts in the upper echelons of Berlin society. It was customary among the elite to have vocal or musical entertainment at dinner parties. Grete seemed to be making a portion of her living by giving recitals. There is no other information about how she survived financially—no school records for Georg, no forwarding addresses for the family.

✧

In the May 1928 election, the National Socialist German Workers Party won ten seats in the Reichstag. Hitler's Nazi party abhorred Berlin, condemning it as a "melting pot of everything that is evil—prostitutes, drinking houses, cinemas, Marxism, Jews, strippers, Negroes dancing, and all the vile offshoots of so-called modern art."

Albert Einstein, in addition to being a Jew, was a liberal, an internationalist, a pacifist, a skeptic, and a freethinker. He was denounced by the Nationalists, some of whom threatened his life. They would gather outside his apartment and shout slogans, or hand-deliver hate mail to his door.

"The yellow press and other half-wits are at my heels to the point where I can scarcely draw breath," he complained to a colleague, "let alone do any really decent work."

In January 1929, Einstein published a six-page paper on the Unified Field Theory which caused a media frenzy. The *New York Herald Tribune* cabled the entire text to New York, where a team of scientists from Columbia University attempted, without success, to decipher it. Einstein's new theory was deemed unprovable and incomprehensible. There was a quiet and confused response from fellow scientists.

"Many of us regard this as a tragedy," said the eminent scientist Max Born, "both for him as he gropes his way in loneliness, and for us, who miss our leader and standard-bearer."

Nevertheless, Albert was as famous as ever. Invitations to international academic and social events piled up on his clumsy Biedermeier hall table.

"Why do you want me to go there?" he complained to Elsa in front of Antonina Vallentin, a friend and writer. "These people don't interest me."

"His celebrity," Antonina wrote, "allowed him a great margin of indulgence, and his reputation as a crank protected him to a certain degree."

The only events Albert and Elsa faithfully attended were the lavish dinner parties given by Dr. János Plesch and his wife, Melanie. From simple beginnings, Plesch went on to own a palatial villa.

The Plesch villa was designed by a friend, the architect Bruno Paul. Grandly baroque, some of the rooms had flamboyant panels handpainted by Max Slevogt, a fashionable painter of the time, while others had Louis XV paneling with intricately carved cherubs and crowns. Especially impressive was an embroidered silk bed curtain in royal blue, yellow, and Chinese red from the Imperial Palace at Peking. Extravagant Chinoiserie paneling in another bedroom featured painted lattices of oak trees and exotic birds from a Parma palazzo that dated from the fourteenth century. The family lived in the main part of the villa and Plesch had his surgery in one wing.

According to a series of "Party Books" which the couple kept, the dinners were always elaborate. From veal with truffles, to salmon with oyster sauce, to *foie gras,* so special that it was served in individual crystal bowls, the Plesches were luxurious hosts. Indeed, one evening Plesch treated his guests to his prize wine, the 1884 *Johannisberger Schlossberg* that had been given to him by his friend Princess Metternich.

Plesch was also known for his opulent stag parties, whose guests included men such as the diplomat Count Rantzau, Nobel Prize winner Fritz Haber, musicians Fritz Kreisler and Arthur Schnabel, and painters Max Slevogt and Emil Orlik. Plesch maintained that these parties were an opportunity for men to discuss lofty and important ideas—and to enjoy the entertainment provided by female cabaret performers.

"All my guests," Plesch said, "were known to each other and were on friendly and even familiar terms, so that the talk was frank and informal." He always offered his guests the best liquor and the most expensive cigars. At such events, Einstein was his most precious trophy.

✧

In Germany, the stock market crash of 1929 made an already critical economic situation even more so. Companies were laying off more than one million workers a month; many were closing down completely. In Berlin, a city of four million, there were 750,000 unemployed people. On her assigned day, Grete would stand in a long line to receive a small stamp that authorized her to receive a monthly allotment of the equivalent of seventeen dollars. In October 1930, Hitler claimed one million members in his National Socialist party.

✧

On November 28, 1930, Elsa Einstein wrote a letter to Grete Markstein, presumably in response to a copy of Grete's recording she had received.

"Because the endorsement of the Ultraphon Records that was sent to you has been lost, I want to write you personally about the recording," Elsa wrote. "The recording has given great joy to my husband and me. It is the first time a harmony has been created between fairy lands and exotic lands in this artistic and popular form. I also consider it creatively and artistically first-rate and I am convinced that the recording will bring pleasure to many people, great and small. With friendly greetings, yours, E.E."

Two years later, in 1932, Albert arranged for eighty marks to be sent to Grete Markstein, the "female storyteller." The money paid to Grete came from Einstein's *Der Physikalische Fond,* the Physical Fund. This fund was actually a bank account of 10,000 marks that had been established anonymously by friends of Einstein's. The money in this discretionary fund was to be used in whatever way Albert saw fit. After every withdrawal, Albert's anonymous benefactors quietly replenished the funds.

✧

Once the romance with Elsa was over, Albert moved to a separate bedroom at the far end of the apartment. As he had with Mileva, Albert recast their relationship as one of mere convenience.

Illness had aged Elsa prematurely. Her body had become stout, her face haggard. Her gray hair, like Albert's, had become eccentrically disheveled. Elsa's prettiest feature was her vivid blue eyes, and though she was both far- and near-sighted she refused to wear glasses. It is said that once at a banquet she tried to eat the decorative orchids on her plate.

Albert, meanwhile, had become a middle-aged Lothario. His long silver hair swept dramatically upward, accentuating his dark eyes, and his body remained strong and muscular. At the age of forty, he was considered ruggedly attractive. And women never seemed to leave him alone—they left flowers at the door and love notes under the mat, and provided limousines for his private use. He tended to have a few romances going at once, but after Mileva, he was known to prefer simpler women. Chaim Weizmann's wife, Vera, said that she did not mind Albert's flirtations, "since intellectual women did not seriously attract him."

One of Albert's liaisons may have produced a boy child born on April 14, 1932. In 1995, Ludek Zakel, living in Prague, claimed to be the child of Albert and Elsa Einstein. Though many summarily dismissed his claim, Ludek's story may have more truth to it than has been acknowledged.

Ludek contends that his mother, Elsa Einstein, was in Prague having a tumor examined at St. Apollinarus Hospital, where the director was a friend of Albert's. She had been reluctant to seek medical attention in Berlin because of Einstein's prominence. When she was examined, Ludek said, instead of a tumor, they discovered a full-term pregnancy! But this contradicts Elsa's medical history. In 1913, a year after Elsa had begun her affair with Albert, she complained to him of an enlarged heart. He advised her to rest for a few months. At the time, she was thirty-seven years old and had already given birth to three children by her first husband, Max Löwenthal—the last, a son born in 1903, died shortly after birth.

In 1932, the year Ludek was born, Elsa was fifty-six years old. She was already suffering from the heart and kidney disease that would kill her four years later. It would have been a medical phenomenon if she had given birth to a child at age fifty-six, twenty-nine years after her last pregnancy.

However, at the time Ludek was conceived, in July 1931, Einstein was having an affair with a Viennese woman named Margarete Lebach. Margarete visited Einstein every week at his country home, traveling from Berlin by train to Potsdam and then by mail bus to Caputh.

Caputh is a small village just a few kilometers south of Potsdam, where the lakes of Templin and Schweilow flow into each other. In 1929, the Einsteins had a wooden summer house built there. "I love living in the new little house enormously," Albert wrote his sister, Maja, "even though I am broke as a result. The sailing boat, the distant view, the solitary walks, the relative quiet; it is paradise."

Margarete was Elsa's opposite—beautiful, blond, full of life, and radiating sexuality. The couple sailed together on Albert's beloved boat, the *Tummler,* and picnicked in the woods surrounding the lake. The liaison continued throughout the summer, forcing Elsa out of her own home during Margarete's visits. Albert did not offer Elsa a choice—either she keep out of his private life or there would be a divorce. Elsa chose to go shopping in Berlin. "She left the field clear, so to speak," their maid, Herta Waldow reported.

Ludek bears a strong resemblance to Albert, and both his behavior and his intellect are reminiscent of Hans Albert. He even became a physicist. His adoptive mother, Eva Zakel, has sworn that he was Elsa Einstein's son. Ludek was told that because Albert did not want more children, and because it was apparent that they would soon have to leave Europe, Elsa decided to give up the child. Mrs. Zakel testified that she gave birth to a son who died a day later in the St. Apollinarus Hospital in Prague. Her husband so desired a child that within hours an adoption was negotiated for Elsa's child Ludek. Indeed, the name of Mrs. Zakel's biological son, Jindrich, was scratched from the medical log and replaced by the name Ludek.

There is no proof that Elsa was in Prague at the time. She was probably at Caputh with Albert. On the other hand, Margot Einstein, Albert's stepdaughter, gave a "solemn vow" that Ludek was Elsa's son. The answer probably lies in Margot's correspondence, which is under seal at the Hebrew University until 2006.

Margarete Lebach could be Ludek's mother and her original plan could have been to put the child up for adoption. The circumstances of Mrs. Zakel's sad situation happened at just the right time to make this possible. Margarete may have used the name Elsa to ensure that her baby would be given his rightful heritage in the Einstein family.

A mitochondrial DNA test would be necessary to prove Zakel's claim, but this is not possible. There is no stable genetic material available from Albert or Elsa, nor Margarete, who died in 1938 after the Nazi regime denied her medical attention for cancer.

✧

At the stroke of noon on Monday, January 30, 1933, Hitler became chancellor of Germany. Within minutes, the streets of Berlin filled with Nazi supporters. More than eighty percent of the city's liberal population, who did not support the Nazi regime, locked their doors and closed their windows. Thousands of party members converged to celebrate only twelve blocks from where the Einsteins lived and six blocks from where Grete was living with her seven-year-old son. Hitler's supporters gathered under the trees of the Tiergarten and formed into columns. Sixteen fervent believers stood, shoulder to shoulder, in each row. They marched in unison triumphantly onto the Charlottenburger Chaussee, turning eastward toward the Brandenburg Gate amidst the thunderous whirling of drums and bellowing of brassy military bands. En masse, the worshippers sang the "Horst Wessel Song"—and the words rolled over the country once and for all. Five weeks later, the exodus of the Jewish intelligentsia began in earnest. The first group of Jews was purged by the director of the newly formed Ministry of Propaganda and Public Enlightenment, Joseph Goebbels.

✧

Grete and Rückelt had separated shortly after Georg was born. Nevertheless, he plagued her with surprise visits in the night, which terrorized her son. Sometime in 1933, Rückelt appeared at Grete's door, she refused him, and he left in a fury. Hours later a group of men reappeared, dressed in the brown uniforms of storm troopers. They forced their way into Grete's flat and assaulted her. Meanwhile, Georg, in horror, had burrowed into a clothes closet in another room. She later told him that she was attacked because she was Jewish and had recited the work of the German poet Goethe. When Georg recalled the event in later years, he felt that Rückelt was responsible.

Grete prepared to leave the country. She cleaned the flat, washed the dishes, and left a full glass of water on the kitchen table. She later told Georg this was a ruse to make it appear that they were still living there, so their rapid disappearance would go unnoticed for a few days.

Grete and her son left Berlin in a panic. She had no passport, no visa, no permits, no letters of recommendation—because she was Jewish, she had probably been forced to surrender her passport and her identity papers to the authorities. The only documentation she carried was a congratulatory telegram from Hermann Goering concerning the performance she had given reading Goethe, while living in Berlin.

With whatever she could scrape together, Grete and Georg—along with 37,000 other terrified Jews—fled to Paris, crowding into trains leaving daily for the west from Anhalter Bahnhof, moving through the billowing steam and flying cinders of the railroad platform, loaded down with suitcases and bundles.

But Grete knew they would not be safe in Paris for long. During the massive demonstration of January 30, the brown-shirted marching bands had passed before the French embassy on Pariser Platz. Each band stopped in front of the embassy, and with a preliminary roll of the drums, struck up the challenging old war song, *"Siegreich wollen wir Frankreich schlagen!"* Victorious, we are going to defeat France!

✧

When Hitler became chancellor, Albert and Elsa were living in Pasadena, where Albert was researching and lecturing at the California Institute of Technology. Elsa, always torn between her devotion to her daughters and her loyalty to Albert, was frantic. Margot and Ilse and their husbands were still in Germany!

Albert wrote his former mistress Margarete Lebach in Berlin, "In view of Hitler I don't dare step on German soil." The day after he wrote these words, the Reichstag was burned and Hitler suspended the freedom of speech for the country, including the press.

On March 10, Einstein announced publicly that he could "only live in a country where civil liberty, tolerance, and equality of all citizens before the law prevail. . . . These conditions do not exist in Germany at the present time."

The following day he and Elsa boarded a train for New York and, by the last week of March, they were sailing toward Antwerp on the S.S. *Belgenland.* Albert felt obliged to return to Europe to fulfill his lecturing

obligations. It was aboard the ship that they heard about the "purifica-
tion" measures in Germany. As Albert had earlier foreseen, they would
never return to Germany.

On March 28, they arrived in Belgium and Albert was driven to Brus-
sels. He walked into the office of the German legation, handed them his
passport, and renounced his German citizenship.

"Good News of Einstein—He Is Not Coming Back!" screamed the
headlines in the *Berliner Lokalanzeiger.* A reward equivalent to 50,000 dollars
was offered for his capture as an enemy of the state.

"I did not know that I was worth so much," he reportedly replied.

The Einsteins went into exile at the Villa Savoyarde on Le Coq sur
Mer, a resort on the Belgian coast. Albert, King of Belgium, ordered that
their house be guarded and that Einstein be escorted by two plainclothes
policemen at all times.

In fact, they could have gone to Zurich. Mileva had invited both of
them to live with her until they could obtain safe passage back to America.

"You made me really happy and surprised me enormously," Albert
wrote in April 1933. "It was not so much the friendly invitation as your
recognition [of our plight] that made me happy." In the end, however, he
declined her offer: "Switzerland is flooded by doubtful German elements
and I thought it would not be safe."

On March 29, Albert and Elsa's apartment on Haberlandstrasse was
ransacked by Brown Shirts, and some of their belongings were plundered.
Two days later, their bank accounts were confiscated. The final blow came
when they were informed that the Nazis had pillaged their beloved home
in Caputh and even had dug up the garden. They were looking for
weapons but found only a kitchen knife. Albert's papers were saved by his
stepdaughters and their husbands and shipped to the Quai d'Orsay by
diplomatic post. Except for a few rugs, some paintings, and other unidentified valuables, most of their furniture was rescued and dispatched to
Princeton.

In May, Eduard was admitted to the Burghölzli, and Albert made a
quick trip to Zurich. While he was there, he had a disagreement with

Hans Albert about an undisclosed issue and wrote him when he returned to Belgium, complaining that his "life [was] more burdened with obligations and duties than that of an average man. Therefore, I cannot be subject to the same claims and demands as an ordinary person."

✧

Since 1928, Helen Dukas had been employed as Einstein's secretary. She had obtained the position through one of her older sisters, Rosa, who was the executive secretary for *Jüdische Waisenhilfe,* an organization that helped Jewish orphans. Elsa Einstein was the organization's honorary president.

Born in 1896 in Freiburg im Breisgau, at the foot of the Black Forest in western Germany, Helen was the fifth of seven children. Her mother, Hännchen, died of tuberculosis and exhaustion when Helen was thirteen years old. From then on, she was raised by her father, Leopold, a wine merchant who had a distillery behind the house, and her older sister Celine. When Celine left home to marry, it became Helen's task to care for the family. She was forced to leave school before completing her studies.

Finally, in 1921, when Helen was twenty-six years old, she took a position as a kindergarten teacher and then as a governess in Munich. In 1924, she became a secretary in a small publishing house in Berlin. She held this position until 1928, when the company went bankrupt and she was out of work.

When Rosa suggested that she apply for the job as Albert Einstein's secretary, Helen exclaimed, "You have gone mad, I can never do something like that!" But she was persuaded to try. Helen began working for Albert on Friday, April 13, 1928, and remained in his employ for the next twenty-seven years.

✧

In October 1933, Albert, Elsa, Helen Dukas, and Albert's assistant Walther Mayer sailed for America aboard the S.S. *Westerland.* Albert left it to Elsa to write Mileva, Hans Albert, and Eduard from the ship to let them know that he was en route. She was also instructed to inform Mileva that all of the money that had been destined for his sons had been confiscated by the Nazis. But this was not true. Over the years, Albert had stashed his earnings from abroad in accounts in the Netherlands and the United States.

"I have been careful and made provision," he wrote the physicist Max Planck in April 1933. He also assured his best friend, Michele Besso, that "personally, I was not caught out."

Once Albert left the shores of Europe in March 1933, he never saw Eduard or Mileva again.

Elsa perceived family obligations differently. She tried to convince her daughters and their husbands to emigrate with them, but they refused, intending to join them later. Margot was in Paris at the time, and Ilse moved there a year later when she became gravely ill with tuberculosis of the stomach. Until then Ilse had insisted that her illness was psychosomatic. Physicians were finally beckoned, including an unnamed doctor from Berlin. But it was not János Plesch—his passport does not show a trip to France in 1934.

Elsa was not summoned from Princeton until Ilse's condition had become critical. She pleaded with Albert to sail with her, but he refused. In mid-May, Elsa sailed alone on the *Belgenland.* By the time she arrived, there was nothing she could do but comfort her daughter as she watched her die. Elsa felt that she had betrayed her.

"Both children have undergone terrible trials and they must have needed me," she told Antonina Vallentin. "Why, oh, why did I not go earlier?"

Elsa departed Europe for the last time with her daughter's ashes hidden in a feather cushion upon which she rested her head during the long journey to America.

✧

Grete and Georg disembarked from the Berlin train at the Gare du Nord to find utter bedlam in Paris. The platforms were jammed with German Jewish refugees, thousands of whom had fled to Paris only to be harassed by members of the French Fascist movements and ordinary citizens alike. The Jewish refugee committees were ill prepared to handle the deluge. Indeed, before these ad hoc committees were even fully organized, twelve

hundred Jewish children were starving at any one time. Some of the arriving Jews were so stunned by the state of affairs in the city that they
boarded trains back to Berlin.

By June 1934, some private citizens and assistance organizations were
beginning to provide meal tickets and a sum of money equal to about
twenty-five francs for each refugee. But many refugees were too terrified
to leave their lodgings to claim the assistance. As soon as they left, their
personal belongings were routinely stolen. The culprits covered their
tracks by denouncing the Jewish victims, who were then expelled from
France. According to reports from refugee groups, the misery was fright-
ful and the despair of the people unutterable. The cases of suicide multi-
plied. Some refugees, driven into the streets by hunger and poverty,
resorted to begging. Many were taken to the Shelter on rue Lamarck
which was desperately overcrowded and infested with vermin.

The French records of Jewish emigrants that survived the Nazi occupation were eventually turned over to The Jewish World Relief. If Grete
had applied for assistance, she would have been listed among them. But
neither Grete nor Georg is mentioned in any of the existing records. Nor
is Grete listed in any hotel archives. Presumably, she had some other
source of income. Although Jewish émigré employment was almost
nonexistent, she may have found work that went unrecorded, or a private
individual may have helped to support her. A document found in the Einstein archive reported that Grete's aunt in Vienna, Melanie Neumann, believed that she had found refuge in a Parisian Jewish family's home on the
Place d'Odéon in the sixth *arrondissement.*

✦

While Einstein had emigrated to America, János Plesch and his family left
Berlin for Frinton in southeast England, bringing with them a number of
automobiles, a Busch-Zeiss telescope, and a multitude of traveling trunks.
Everything else that the family owned was appropriated by the Nazis, including their elegant home on Budapesterstrasse. Plesch rented an old
mansion at Thorpe-le-Soken in Essex.

In order to practice medicine in the United Kingdom, Plesch had to
return to school for two years, which he did, passing his exams with ease.

His reputation as an excellent physician was so well established in Europe that it did not take long for his practice to flourish.

"I trust," he wrote in his memoir, *János, the Story of a Doctor,* "that I shall not be thought immodest when I say that, in fact, my opening of a practice in London was something of an event. From the really sick people to the 'lion-hunters' who spend their lives collecting specialists, they all streamed into my consulting rooms. . . .

"One day, a woman with a child came to me and informed me that she was Einstein's illegitimate daughter and that her child was therefore his grandchild. I was surprised, but the thing was not impossible and the woman was extremely persuasive. I even began to see family resemblances between Einstein and the child, an intelligent, wide-awake, and attractive little lad. Well, she convinced me. . . . Then I wrote a tactful letter to Einstein explaining the situation and giving him news of his daughter and grandchild. To my great mystification Einstein showed no proper interest, and so in order to move his paternal and grandfatherly heart I sent him one or two really clever and delightful little coloured sketches that the boy had made and a photo. There! I thought the features of the boy would move him. I then received a letter telling me that the whole thing was a swindle. It amused Einstein and made me blush for months."

A collection of twenty-one small brown leather appointment diaries belonging to Dr. János Plesch are in his archive at the Jüdisches Museum in Berlin. Each book is three and three-quarter inches by two inches, with gilt-edged pages and the year embossed in gold on its cover. Two are from the time when he lived in Budapest and the rest from his years in England. There are none recording his life in Berlin.

On March 15, 1934, Plesch had an appointment in London with "Einstein." There was another appointment with "Einstein" on Thursday, April 19, and an appointment with "Kaiser" just before. "Kaiser" may have been Elsa's daughter Ilse or, more likely, her son-in-law, Rudolf Kayser. Though Albert had mentioned to Mileva the possibility of his making a trip to Paris in 1934, ultimately he did not, and therefore these "Einsteins" are not Albert. Albert's correspondence during this time situates him firmly in Princeton.

"I fear," Albert wrote to his friend Frederick Lindemann at Oxford in

January 1935, "that I shall not be able to come to Europe again so soon because if I come to Oxford I must also go to Paris and Madrid and I lack the courage to undertake all this. And so I am going to remain here [in Princeton]."

Plesch continued to see the mysterious "Einstein." On January 9, 1935, he had "Lunch at 1:30 with Einstein." On the tenth, he had an appointment with "Einstein" at five o'clock that lasted one hour. On Friday the eighteenth, he had an appointment with "Einstein" and then noted after the name, "make up more beds." In fact, Plesch noted "Einstein" on an almost daily basis thirty-five times between January 9 and March 17 of that year. And then "Einstein" appeared no more.

Albert never returned to London after 1933. There are no mysterious gaps in his chronology, no sightings, no stories. Who was this Einstein? There were six Einsteins listed in the real estate records and telephone book as living in London from 1933 to 1937: A. Einstein, Mrs. Edna Einstein, Mrs. Helene Einstein, two M. Einsteins, and Norbert Einstein.

Mrs. Edna Einstein and Mrs. Helene Einstein were widows who had married into a different Einstein family. One M. Einstein was a tobacconist on Grafton Street; the other was a tailor who rented space from Mrs. Fanny Ginsberg, a milliner. Norbert Einstein was a banker's agent in a building on Old Broad Street. None of the men were related to Albert. This left A. Einstein, who rented a room at 119 Highbury New Park, next door to the Salvation Army Officer's Nursing Home.

At first, I thought this Einstein might be Alfred Einstein, Albert's cousin, a well-known musicologist and reviewer for the *Berliner Tageblatt*. In 1933, Alfred fled Berlin for London, where he lived until he emigrated to America, in 1938. But he never lived at that address. In addition, János Plesch, who was prone to name-dropping, never mentioned Alfred in his memoir, nor does Plesch appear in the Alfred Einstein archive. It is possible, then, that Plesch's Einstein was Grete.

At this juncture, the whereabouts of Grete Markstein forks into two possible routes. She might have arrived in London with Georg sometime before August of 1935 and found refuge with a friend. Or, as her registration with the Jewish Refugees Committee in London states, she might have arrived on August 20, 1935, with Georg and her future husband,

Zygmunt Herschdoerfer. The problem is that the Jewish Refugee Committee notes that Grete did not register with them until 1943, the year of her death.

Herschdoerfer was born on August 19, 1906, in Drogobych, Poland. He had studied in Vienna and become a research chemist; by 1935, he was living in Paris with his older sisters, Maria and Stephania. Somewhere in the sixth *arrondissement* he appears to have met Grete and fallen in love. It is certain that he emigrated to the United Kingdom, leaving his sisters behind to be deported by the Nazis on convoy number twenty-two on August 21, 1942. They perished at Auschwitz.

✧

In 1923, a no-pass excursion ticket system between France and Britain was established for the weekend tourist traffic. Until it was discontinued in June 1933, thousands of Jewish refugees took advantage of this and entered the country without papers. During this time, displaced Jews were encouraged to register with the Jewish Refugees Committee after they entered the United Kingdom, giving a short but detailed history of their family and pertinent facts about their education, professional status, and financial situation. In addition to helping financially, the Committee assisted these refugees in finding housing and employment. One of their missions was to create a list of all Jews who entered the country, so that family and friends could locate one another. When Grete registered herself, she gave 1902 as her birthdate—the same as Lieserl's. She would have had to prove that date by producing her passport or refugee papers to show the date-stamp of her arrival. Because many of the refugee files were fire-bombed during the war, her detailed personal file no longer exists, though the Committee still retains an index generated from the original registration slips that states the name, year of birth, place of birth, occupation, and destination address for all registered applicants.

Clearly, the information Grete provided is suspect. She claimed that she first came to the United Kingdom on August 20, 1935. But on that date, only two ships arrived from France—the *Quaker City* and the *Jamaica Progress*—and neither a Markstein nor a Herschdoerfer was listed on the manifests, nor were they listed as entering on a no-pass excursion ticket.

She also claimed that she was Polish and a psychologist by profession. She gave her address as 99 Addison Road, London W14, but this address does not appear on any of the Land Registry nor voter's rolls as being hers for that time period.

Nine days later, on August 29, Zygmunt Herschdoerfer, aged twenty-nine, profession chemist, and living at the Waldorf Hotel in Aldwych, married Grete Maria Markstein, aged thirty-three, profession spinster, also living at the Waldorf. The Waldorf Hotel was certainly not a hotel for refugees. It was, and still is, an upscale establishment in the center of London. Their marriage was solemnized at the registry office in the district of the City of Westminster. So Grete Markstein, born in 1902, became Mrs. Zygmunt Herschdoerfer.

It is doubtful that Herschdoerfer married Grete thinking she was from Poland, since he was from Poland himself and probably would not have fallen for such a claim. But if they had entered the country together, then they could have collaborated on a story to facilitate her entry, presenting her as a professional rather than an out-of-work actress.

✧

Three months after Grete and Zygmunt were married, on November 23, 1935, Albert's friend the German mathematician and physicist Hermann Weyl received a telegram at his home in Princeton. It was from Frederick Lindemann.

MRS. HERSCHDOERFFER [SIC] PRETENDING TO BE EINSTEIN'S DAUGHTER TRIED TO FIND SUPPORT IN HIGH CIRCLES NOT BEING ABLE TO ASK FOR HIS HELP ON ACCOUNT OF STEPMOTHER STOP FEEL SUSPICIOUS PLEASE ASK EINSTEIN PERSONALLY AND CABLE IMMEDIATELY = LINDEMANN CHRISTCHURCH.

"High circles" referred to a group of elite physicists who taught and lived in Oxford. Lindemann claimed that Grete had come to Oxford to reveal her true identity to him and claimed she was unable to ask Albert directly for help because her stepmother, Elsa Einstein, was somehow in the way.

"Do not contact us. Get lost. You are not anything to us," Elsa re-

portedly wrote in one of several letters she sent to Grete. Grete had kept
these letters along with photographs of herself, but they were destroyed
by Zygmunt Herschdoerfer's second wife, Aurelia, after his death, in 1993.

Clearly, sometime between 1932, when Albert paid Grete eighty
marks, and November 1935, when Grete claimed to be Lieserl, Elsa and
Grete had a falling out. "You are not anything to us" could only mean that
Grete had tried to establish some kind of position in Albert and Elsa's lives.

When I interviewed Aurelia Herschdoerfer in 1996, she told me that
she had married Zygmunt in 1953, ten years after Grete's death, and that
he never talked about the past. "And I never asked him about his past either," she said. "It was understood that we would not discuss it. When he
died, I found letters, but I was not interested in them. I destroyed all of
them."

✦

Elsa, Albert, Helen Dukas, and Walther Mayer arrived in New York on October 17, 1933. They were met by Abraham Flexner, the founding director of the Institute for Advanced Study in Princeton who had offered
Einstein a position and organized his arrival. Flexner arranged for the
Einstein entourage to be met in the harbor and taken by launch to the
Battery, in downtown Manhattan, to avoid the press and the crowd of
fans. From there they were driven to the Peacock Inn in Princeton; a few
days later, they were moved into a house at 2 Library Place, near the university campus. They celebrated their first night in this new home with
a musical evening; Albert played Mozart, Haydn, and Beethoven with a
string quartet.

Two years later, they moved to their permanent residence at 112
Mercer Street. In all the activity of the move, Elsa's left eye had become
badly swollen with an edema on the retina—the precursor of deadly kidney and heart disease. She was sent to bed and ordered to remain immo-
bile. By November 23, when Lindemann sent the telegram, Elsa was
gravely ill and incapable of blocking anyone's access to Albert, as Grete
had claimed.

It could be that Grete was only using Elsa as an excuse for her inability to get in touch with Albert directly. There is neither a telegram nor a

letter of reply to Lindemann from Einstein in Lindemann's archive at
Nuffield College, Oxford. But some sort of communication—perhaps a
telephone conversation—must have been received by Lindemann within
seven days, because Grete was informed posthaste of Albert's response by
Lindemann himself. On December 1, 1935, another Einstein friend, the
physicist Max von Laue, wrote to Albert from Oxford, saying that "the
matter of your pseudo-daughter has amused me, the only thing that
galls me is how credulous these British are. When the lady had heard
about our enquiry to you and your response she asked Lindemann by
telephone for discretion!!!! There is such a thing as naive impertinence
that seems extraordinarily funny."

It appears that Einstein "disavowed all knowledge of the woman,"
Lindemann wrote a friend, Bertha Bracey. But when I tried to find the
Bracey letter because I needed to examine what else Albert had to say, I
found that it had disappeared. Two Einstein biographers, Roger Highfield and Paul Carter, reported in their book, *The Private Lives of Albert Einstein,* that the letter which they quoted from seems to have "been lost or
removed from the Nuffield Archives [at Oxford University]."

✧

Zygmunt Markstein Herschdoerfer loved Grete enough to take her name
as his middle name. He clearly knew about his wife Grete's claim to be
Einstein's daughter, since he saved Elsa's letters to Grete. He was a
chemist, respected professionally, and the editor of a three-volume work,
Quality Control in the Food Industry, still in print. Money was not a problem, as
he was employed by Unilever, the chemical corporation, from the moment he arrived in the British Isles, and was appointed a Fellow of the
Royal Institute of Chemists. When he died, he left behind an estate of
more than 24,000 pounds. He also left jewelry that had once belonged to
Grete to relatives and friends. In reporting Grete's claim to be Lieserl,
none of Einstein's associates (Weyl, Lindemann, or Plesch) mentions that
Grete was asking for money. The object of her claim, then, if it was not
extortion, is mysterious.

Einstein may have convinced his friends that Grete was an impostor,
but János Plesch had other ideas. On Saturday afternoon, February 1, 1936,

a little more than two months *after* Lindemann's telegram was sent, Grete visited Plesch for one hour at four-thirty in the afternoon. From then on, Plesch—with the "assistance of other friends" (whose names he fails to mention)—was convinced of her claim and set out to help Grete, despite Einstein's rejection of her. They found her a job, the exact nature of which is unknown, and placed Georg, now called George, in school.

From February until August, Grete saw Plesch twice a month, for fifteen sessions in all. She may have been seeking treatment for pulmonary tuberculosis, the disease that would soon kill her. Her husband, "Dr. Herschdoerfer," himself had three appointments with Plesch.

✧

Ten months after Grete made her initial overture to the Einsteins through Lindemann, Albert asked his secretary, Helen Dukas, to hire a detective to find out more about her. In August of 1936, Dukas retained a German male "Jewish detective" named F. Biel. The tone of the correspondence between Dukas and Biel suggests that she and Einstein knew him personally. He was probably a relative of a Dr. Herbert Biehle (Biel being a transliteration). Dr. Biehle's name and address were listed in Plesch's 1934 telephone book. Coincidentally, Dr. Herbert Biehle had lived only ten doors away from Grete on Momenstrasse in the Schöneberg district of Berlin and may have been acquainted with her. Dr. Biehle also may have been friendly with Albert, which led to the hiring of F. Biel.

"With a bit of luck," Biel was able to report to Albert on August 19, that he had determined that Grete Markstein was born in Vienna, in the ninth district, on August 31, 1894. Her father, Samuel, had been born in Srezny, Hungary, and had died in Berlin. Her mother's birthplace was not mentioned, but Biel reported that she also had died in Berlin. Biel found an aunt, Melanie Neumann, in Vienna's ninth district, who said that Grete was an actress with the Berlin *Schauspielhaus* but that "during the upheavals in Germany, she left the country." Grete's Paris address, according to Neumann, was VI Paris, "Place de Lodión."

"There can be no more doubt that my account concerns the person sought after," he said, "and I hope that with this, I have been of service to my most honored employer."

There are a number of errors in the detective's report. According to the Israelitische Kultusgemeinde and the Magistrat der Stadt in Vienna, Grete's parents did not die in Berlin; her mother died in Vienna and her father in Baden. Melanie Neumann was not the sister of Grete's father, as Biel claimed, but the sister of Grete's mother. And the street in Paris he names as the Place de Lodión is in fact the Place de l'Odéon.

Furthermore, the detective stated that Grete's "bad reputation was described to me by a gentleman in Baden who still knew her personally," insinuating that Grete bestowed sexual favors. There was no such accusation in her records at the *Geheimes Staatsarchiv,* the Prussian Secret Archive in Berlin, nor in any other available material. Nor was there any innuendo of the kind in Plesch's records of her.

✧

In 1936, presumably after Biel presented his findings, Albert sent the following poem to Plesch:

> All my friends are hoaxing me
> —Help me stop the family!
> Reality's enough for me,
> I've borne it long and faithfully.
> And yet it would be nice to find
> That I'd possessed the strength of mind
> To lay eggs on the side—so long
> As others didn't take it wrong.

Plesch replied with a poem of his own, posting it to Albert on September 9, one month after Grete's last appointment with him.

> Joyful may be children's chatter,
> But often they're no laughing matter,
> And suddenly to have one more
> Without the fun that goes before—
> That's a bore!

An evil tongue can spatter mind
Presenting a genius as a stud,
But no-one should be too upset
Nor be ashamed of such a fate.

In view of General Relativity
Be not ashamed of your fertility.

Fools only will resent a slur
Knowing how easily such occur.
And if your seed world-wide you scatter,
This world thereafter may be better.

Amen. Signed J. Plesch, Stepuncle.

Einstein and Plesch began a twenty-two-year correspondence as soon
as they both left Berlin, but only twenty-two letters from János to Einstein
are in the Einstein Archive; there are only thirteen letters from Einstein
to Plesch in the Plesch archive. There is a notable gap in the archived letters during the Grete Markstein era. All of these letters are missing—
probably destroyed at Einstein's request by Helen Dukas and Plesch
himself.

✧

But the real question in all of this remains: *How did Grete know that Albert Einstein ever had a daughter?* Lieserl was an amazingly well-kept secret. Grete
never claimed to be Lieserl by name, only by birthdate. But how did she
know the date of Lieserl's birth? No one knew about Lieserl—not Albert's
friends, not his doctor, maybe not even his second wife. Moreover, how
did Grete convince Oxford scholars that she might be Einstein's daughter? And by what means did she continue her association with Plesch *after*
the Oxford group had rejected her? If she was a scoundrel, why didn't she
take the story to the press, why was there no whiff of extortion? None of
her theater records suggest that she was larcenous, merely ambitious and

manipulative. If Grete was a fraud, she was surprisingly elegant in her charade.

After her last appointment with Plesch, there are no further entries about Grete. Seven years later, on September 7, 1943, in the county of Chester, the registration district of Wirral, Grete Maria Markstein Herschdoerfer died of pulmonary tuberculosis, as certified by J. W. Cowen MB, P.M., with Zygmunt and George by her side.

Until George Markstein was twenty-one, he maintained contact with Grete's friend from the theater, Lola Stein. Lola knew about Grete's claim to be Einstein's daughter.

In 1947, four years after Grete's death, Lola wrote to Albert Einstein from London in *Schriftsprache,* proper German, saying that "Georg G. Markstein, the son of your daughter Mrs. G. M. Markstein-Herschdörfer (formerly of Vienna and Berlin) until her death [in London], owes me £35.16.0. I am enclosing a photocopy of the promissory note and hope that you, most esteemed Professor, will pay this debt of your relative to me, because as a Jewish refugee, alone in the world, I can hardly provide for my livelihood and am very much in need of this money.

"As a friend of your late daughter, true to her memory [Lola continued], I looked after the young man when he was seventeen years old."

Most likely, when Grete passed away, Lola, then living in London, had offered her assistance. George was not an easy adolescent. He hated his stepfather. He thought he was too strict, too pedantic, and that he had forced Grete into becoming a traditional *Hausfrau.* After his mother died, he left home and ignored Zygmunt's pleas for reconciliation.

"I summoned Georg G. Markstein by registered post after he came of age for payment of his debt and received the message 'Gone Away,'" Lola wrote to Albert. "The original promissory note 'I owe Miss Stein the sum of £35.16.0' is in my possession. Please forgive [me] that I turn to you personally, most esteemed Professor Einstein. I do not know of any other alternative."

Lola was sixty-two years old when she wrote this letter. She had left Berlin eight years before. In 1947, thirty-five pounds would have paid a year's rent on a flat, even a small cottage—it was probably her life savings.

Albert replied that he had already "had very funny experiences because of the now deceased Frau Markstein, who had claimed to be my natural daughter with marked success and with this invention was even believed by close friends. I have been able to prove the falsity of the story since it was determined that according to official birth records of Baden near Vienna, Frau Markstein is only thirteen years younger than I. The story thus comes to have little credibility, even to those who otherwise have little confidence in my creativity and productivity."

Biel's report had stated that Grete was born in 1894—fifteen years after Einstein, not thirteen.

"As far as the young Markstein is concerned," Albert wrote, "it appears that this little apple has not fallen far from the tree, provided that your pronouncement of his guilt is more solidly based than his mother's claim of being my daughter."

Although a troubled and perplexing man, George Markstein went on to become a famous writer of seven espionage novels and four television series, the most well-known being *The Prisoner.* He died in 1987.

Lola persevered, corresponding again in a handwritten letter in poor German that she considered it "a special honor to have received such an interesting answer from you. Even though it was a negative result with respect to Markstein—a loss which I must now accept—there exists nothing bad which does not lead to something good." She then proceeded to ask him to help her obtain an affidavit to emigrate to America. Albert never answered the letter.

✧

János Plesch began writing his memoirs in 1942. In January 1944, he sent Einstein a copy of his manuscript, asking him to read it, particularly the sections involving him, and to make any corrections he desired.

Albert replied, "I am looking forward to receiving your biographical book. Having read the first excerpts, I am now expecting a whole host of truths which is created out of a mosaic of inaccurate details. Of course, I always get annoyed about the things written about me because I do not like it at all to have light shed on the individual. I rather prefer to keep it in the fog or the twilight. The beast is so full of contradictions that everything told which seems coherent is somehow untrue. I feel this to be the most true when the writing deals with me . . . Do you know that even professors in Oxford fell into Markstein's trap?"

Albert made comments and corrections in a five-page, single-spaced typed letter to Plesch on February 3, 1944. "Even though my first marriage was very painful," he wrote Plesch, "it lasted from 1902 to 1914. I did not marry Elsa in Prague, but around 1917 in Berlin." He himself was incorrect in at least two of his statements. He married Mileva in 1903, not 1902, and left her in 1914. They were not divorced until 1919. He married Elsa the same year, not 1917. Nonetheless, Plesch incorporated Albert's corrections.

"You are so right that the kind of reminiscences which I am attempting to write are a mosaic of inappropriate details," Plesch wrote Albert on May 10, 1944. "In order to enlarge the lie that they live, people will place themselves on a pedestal in high-heeled boots and dress themselves in a toga. One is not entitled to describe them undressed and not as they wanted to appear, but as they are seen sometimes, especially by a doctor. That is why I had the intention to entitle the book *Lies from A to Z.*"

Plesch continues, saying, "You can believe me that while I was writing these seven hundred pages, I was laughing a lot about how marvelously we are all trained to lie and how little human beings are allowed to state the truth. Our good Ibsen hit the nail on the head when he said, 'Take somebody's life's lie away and you will take away his whole life.' The whole book is written with this compromise."

Plesch's manuscript eventually landed on the desk of an editor and translator, Edward Fitzgerald, at the London publisher Victor Gollancz. Fitzgerald was interested in publishing it, and he was especially interested in the chapter concerning Einstein, since Einstein "himself has vetted the chapter, we are told."

The original "vetted" manuscript is not in Plesch's archives at the Royal Society in London. Because I was looking for marginal notations and edits that could help my research, I asked Peter Plesch, János Plesch's son, what had become of it.

"The manuscript has been destroyed," he wrote me. "There was no reason for keeping a vast, messy stack of papers."

✧

Four months after Biel's investigation of Grete, on a snowy day in December 1936, Elsa Einstein, Albert's wife of seventeen years, died of kidney and heart disease. It had been a year and a half since her daughter Ilse passed away, and Elsa had never recovered from the trauma. To Antonina Vallentin, Elsa's friend and now a foreign correspondent for the *Manchester Guardian,* it seemed as if she had simply given up.

"If my Ilse walked into the room now, I would recover at once," Elsa wrote in her last letter to Antonina. And Antonina, in her book *The Drama of Albert Einstein,* wrote, "I know that she died from the cruel conflict between her passionate motherhood and her love for her husband."

In her last letter to Antonina, written a few days before she died, Elsa wrote, "[Albert] wanders around like a lost soul. I never thought he loved me so much. And that comforts me." And yet, a few years after he married her, Albert told Plesch, when they were still in Germany, that "marriage was surely invented by an unimaginative pig."

On the day Elsa died, Albert is reported to have said calmly, "Bury her." In a January 1937 letter to Hans Albert, he wrote, "Two weeks ago my wife died after a long illness. Everything conspires to make my existence a hard one."

✧

Meanwhile, nothing had changed for Mileva. Her financial state was in chaos, and Eduard was now irretrievably lost to mental illness.

Many years before, during a hopeful period in her life, Mileva had planted blackberry bushes at the edge of her lawn and a *Rotbuche,* a copper beech tree. On May 23, 1948, they had just begun to flower when Eduard suffered another debilitating episode. He had become obsessed with something he had lost and was raging through the apartment, overturning furniture, throwing objects from the shelves.

The next day, Mrs. Kerekes, the woman who helped Mileva keep house, came running to the downstairs neighbor, Marie Grendelmeier, for help.

Marie ran upstairs and found Mileva motionless on her bed. When she looked closely, she could see that Mileva's eyes were moving, though she lay speechless.

Marie called for an ambulance, then sat by Mileva's side and held her hand. Marie remembers comforting Mileva, telling her not to worry about Eduard, that she would make sure that he was well cared for. After Mileva was taken away, Marie and Mrs. Kerekes tried to tidy the flat. Marie found the pantry stuffed with hoarded kilos of rancid butter and moldy chunks of bread.

Mileva was taken to a private clinic on Karamenstrasse, where it was determined that she had suffered her second stroke in two years and that it had paralyzed her left side. For almost three months, she lay in the hospital next to a window that opened onto a garden. She cried most of the time, *"Ne, ne, ne,"* frantic about what would become of Eduard. But Eduard was right there beside her, holding her hand, having mustered the clarity of mind to offer his mother comfort and compassion.

Mileva wanted to see Hans Albert, to be reassured that he would take care of his brother. But Hans Albert and his family were living in America. His last visit to his mother had been almost two years earlier, in 1946. Albert offered to pay Hans Albert's fare, but at the same time, he discouraged him from making the trip. "If you see your mother again, in these circumstances," Albert warned, "it will be a shock and a farewell."

Hans Albert never came.

On August 4, 1948, a steamy summer day in Zurich, when the vapors rising from the lake were captured by the mountains and held hostage in the city, Mileva died. One moment she was aware of her surroundings and able to speak clearly, the next moment she was dead.

Helen Dukas and Frieda Einstein, Hans Albert's wife, flew to Zurich to dispose of Mileva's belongings. They looked high and low for the missing 85,000 francs that had been accidentally paid to Mileva two months before, when Albert sold her house. At last, they found it under the mattress. Like her father, who hid his money in the stove, Mileva hid her money at home. The Serbian expression is *Pare iz slamarice,* money from the mattress.

Helen and Frieda retrieved the money, the love letters between Mileva and Albert, and other valuable objects. They gave Marie, the neighbor, an old skein of pink angora wool, which she knitted it into a sweater, and wore until it was in tatters.

✧

Eduard was bereft and utterly alone. Instead of bringing him to America, Albert arranged for a guardian in Zurich, Dr. Heinrich Meili, to make arrangements for his care. At first Eduard was placed with a pastor, Hans Freimüller—who had a background in psychoanalysis and experience with disturbed young men—in the Swiss village of Uitikon. Eduard happily stayed there for a year. Then, for an unknown reason, Meili moved him to Höngg, a suburb of Zurich, where Eduard lived with a lawyer's widow who cared for him.

While Eduard was in Höngg, Carl Seelig, one of Albert's biographers, developed a trusting relationship with him and took him under his wing. Seelig must have learned a great deal about the Einstein family during this time, but out of his respect for, and friendship with, Eduard, very little of it went into his book. In fact, at Eduard's behest, Seelig offered to take over Eduard's guardianship but was rejected by Albert, who stated simply that the post was already filled. Eduard was sent to reside permanently at Burghölzli Psychiatric Clinic.

The last letter Eduard received from his father was written in 1944, four years before Mileva died. Ten years later, Albert wrote Seelig to explain why he had severed his relationship with his son.

"You have probably wondered," he wrote, "about the fact that I do not exchange letters with Teddy. It is based on an inhibition that I am not fully capable of analyzing. But it has to do with my belief that I would awaken painful feelings of various kinds if I entered into his vision in any way."

Eduard continued to disintegrate. He no longer played his beloved piano because the hospital personnel told him that he disturbed the other patients. Most of his time was spent working on the grounds of the hospital as a gardener, dressed in faded blue overalls and *sabots*. His large, dark eyes looked far away; he was rarely able to focus on the person to whom he was speaking. The only feature that reminded people of his father was his moustache.

Eduard died on October 25, 1965. He was fifty-five years old. Newspapers announced the death of Eduard Einstein, son of the late Professor Einstein. Mileva was not mentioned.

✧

Toward the end of Albert's life, he wrote his memoir, *The World as I See It*. In it, there are no mentions of his family—no Mileva, no Lieserl, no Hans Albert, no Eduard, no Elsa. Indeed, he proudly proclaimed that he had tried all his life to liberate himself from the "chains of the merely personal."

"I always get by best," he once wrote to a friend, "with my naiveté, which is twenty percent deliberate, you know. This is done simply if you are indifferent enough to your dear fellow men; all the same, you can never be as indifferent as they deserve."

Albert's secretary, Helen Dukas, was his accomplice in this endeavor. She was also his fiercest protector. A plain, thin woman, who favored sensible shoes and buttoned-up cardigans, she chose to be invisible, all the while maintaining an iron hand over Albert's affairs. Hans Albert suspected they were lovers. His allegation was fortified by the proximity of her room in Princeton—just off Albert's study and down the hall from Elsa's. In addition, Einstein left Dukas more money in his will than any other member of his blood family, as well as the net income from his royalties and copyright fees and all his books and personal effects.

Peter A. Bucky, the son of Einstein's friend Dr. Gustav Bucky, proposed in his book *The Private Albert Einstein* that Helen Dukas could have been Lieserl. The Einstein and Bucky families first met in Berlin and were quite close by the time they all emigrated to America, where Gustav Bucky replaced Plesch as Albert's doctor and confidant.

After Gustav died, in 1963, Peter began assembling material for the book. He suggests that Helen had been adopted by the Dukas family and in some mysterious way found herself on Albert's doorstep. Consider, he submits, how Helen was "perfectly suited to deal with the technical requirements of organizing Einstein's work. In her genetic makeup are, after all, the seeds of science, having sprung from the greatest physicist of the twentieth century and his physicist girlfriend." And he asks rhetorically, "Who could understand both Albert's soul and his scientific mind better than someone of his own blood?"

Indeed, Dukas was so fused to Albert that when she died, Otto Nathan, the second trustee of Albert's estate, declared that "Einstein died a second death." But Helen was born in 1896, when Albert was seventeen years old, six years before Lieserl.

✧

On April 18, 1955, at 1:20 in the morning, Albert died, without family or friends present, at the Princeton Hospital.

János Plesch was having his morning coffee and listening to the radio in a New York hotel room when he heard the news that his friend had died of a massive aneurysm of the aorta. Although Plesch thought that Albert was a "noble soul," he also knew that he had "a rather weak vascular system" and was not surprised. In fact, Albert's pulmonary problems were very similar to those of Plesch's now deceased patient Grete Markstein.

Gustav Bucky and János Plesch had had a long-standing date to meet that night. They had known each other in Berlin and had maintained their friendship over the years. Bucky telephoned Plesch and informed him that Einstein had already been cremated and that they should continue with their original plan in New York.

"You can imagine how I feel," Plesch began in a long, rambling letter to his son. He reported that the doctor had settled Einstein in for the night and that he had slept until about one in the morning.

"Then he murmured a few German words, which the nurse could not understand and very soon thereafter took two deep breaths and died in his sleep without agony."

Plesch next wrote about Albert's "strongly sexual person, as clearly indicated by his full lips and his well-formed but large nose." He also insisted that Albert had syphilis, the "gentlemen's disease."

"[In] my long medical practice I have found, almost without exception, that abdominal aneurysms which Einstein suffered from are of syphilitic origin. It might, of course, be that Einstein was exceptional in that respect too and that his aneurysm was nonspecific. However, an earlier syphilitic infection is also indicated by the fact that he suffered from extensive secondary anaemia attacks."

Because both his "sons from his first marriage came from healthy parents. . . . I think that the infection was acquired during the interval [between his marriages]. . . . Even though many may shake their heads about this, I am adhering to my thesis."

A day later, Plesch was still writing his letter, now focusing on Albert's smoking. Albert had always been a heavy smoker, especially addicted to cigars—"the longest, fattest, blackest ones he could find," wrote one of his biographers, Peter Michelmore. "He smoked one after the other so that, even as a young man, his teeth were stained brown and his throat was raw." When Albert was in Japan in 1922, he was asked by the cartoonist Ippei Okamoto whether he smoked for pleasure or in order to keep busy while unclogging and refilling his pipe.

"My aim lies in smoking," he replied, "but as a result things tend to get clogged up, I'm afraid. Life too, is like smoking, especially marriage."

Since Albert's arrival in America, he had been warned that his smoking carried the risk of provoking an aneurysm. Albert responded, "Well then, let it burst." Strangely, he found an ally in Plesch, his long-time physician, who did not believe that smoking was bad for one's health and thought that Albert should smoke as much as he wished. In fact, Plesch was outraged when he heard that Albert had been picking up cigar and cigarette butts off the street on his way to the Institute in a surreptitious attempt to fill his pipe. Plesch, "resolv[ing] that this kind of subterfuge should never be necessary again," took it upon himself to supply Albert with tobacco and cigars. Nevertheless, he was puzzled by Albert's attitude toward his own well-being. It was, Plesch wrote, "as if it really had nothing much to do with him personally. He did not want to be dependent even on his own body in order to live entirely for his work. What a remarkable example," he diagnosed, "of an extensive splitting of a personality."

Plesch concluded his letter to his son with what he perceived to be the consequences of Albert's personal life. He said that Albert and Mileva's "marriage was dissolved in an amicable manner," and that his second marriage "was absolutely harmonious and peaceful because Elsa, who knew him like no one else, let him live his life as her little Albert thought it right."

Plesch's revisionism, like that of Einstein's many mythologizers (which included Albert himself), allowed for the mysteries in his friend's life to remain undisturbed, and unsolved, for decades to come.

PART
SEVEN

Dr. John Phillips is almost eighty years old and was a psychoanalyst by profession. In his long career, he often worked with schizophrenics. A great friend of his was the late Erick von Kahler, author of *The Tower and the Abyss: An Inquiry into the Transformation of the Individual.* Von Kahler had been a neighbor and a friend of Einstein's in Princeton. In 1951, Phillips and von Kahler were having dinner and talking about Einstein's children. Phillips was particularly interested because he knew that Eduard Einstein had been diagnosed as a schizophrenic. He remembers von Kahler saying, "Professor Einstein told me that his first child was a Mongoloid idiot." At first he thought von Kahler was talking about Eduard; then he remembered that Eduard was the younger of Einstein's two sons.

"Von Kahler was not talking about Eduard," Phillips said to me dur-

ing our 1996 interview. "Believe me, I know the difference between a schizophrenic and a Mongoloid idiot. And so did Einstein."

✧

In February 1912, Albert became acquainted with Paul Ehrenfest, a brilliant physicist and a master teacher. Whenever possible, the two men
spent time together, delighting in lengthy intellectual debates.

One of the sorrows of Ehrenfest's life was his son, Vassik, who was
born in 1917 and suffered from Down's syndrome. Much to Ehrenfest's regret, in 1932 Vassik was placed in an institution in Amsterdam. Albert
tried to comfort his friend by saying, "Valuable individuals must not be
sacrificed to hopeless things." Though he was referring to Ehrenfest and
his son, he just as easily could have been thinking of himself and Eduard—and possibly Lieserl.

A year later, Paul Ehrenfest and Tatyana, his wife and colleague, separated. Ehrenfest was bereft. On September 27, he went to visit their
sixteen-year-old son. He entered Vassik's room, and a short while later
two shots rang out. Ehrenfest had shot his son in the face, then turned
the gun on himself. They both died instantly.

✧

The Ninth Commandment instructs, "Thou shalt not bear false witness
against thy neighbor." In Vojvodina this commandment is embraced as a
solemn promise to tell the truth. *Obećanje je dužnost,* a promise is a duty,
they say.

If a Serb does reveal a guarded secret, it is usually after many years of
silence, and then he will cite another Biblical code of honor: "In the
mouth of two or three witnesses shall every word be established." Every
witness I interviewed prefaced his or her testimony with a statement
about honor and the truth. This code of conduct is discussed in *Testimony:
Crises of Witnessing in Literature, Psychoanalysis, and History* by Shoshana Felman
and Dori Laub: "To testify is . . . not merely to narrate but to commit
oneself, and to commit the narrative, to others: *to take responsibility*—in
speech—for history or for the truth of an occurrence."

The metric tradition of Serbian folk ballads has also cultivated a reverence for careful listening—an ear for memory—as an oral recitation of spiritual and moral truths becomes a poetic form. Hence, the unwritten record of the Serbian experience "follows a trust in the value of individual witnesses" and gives them a unique credibility.

In Lieserl's story there are seven witnesses who have honorably testified: Dragiša Marić, a second cousin once removed, who confirmed that Lieserl lived with her grandparents when Mileva returned to Bern; Dragiša's mother, Ljubica Marić, who told me a German-speaking woman came and took Lieserl away; Jovan Ružić, Mileva's second cousin, who had never spoken of Lieserl until it "just slipped from my memory into my mouth"; Sofija Galić Golubović, Mileva's first cousin, who personally knew Lieserl but denied any knowledge of her to Hans Albert, thus preserving her vow of silence; Milenko Damjanov, whose parents were close friends of the Marić family and said that Mileva's baby was not one-hundred percent right because she had tried to hide her pregnancy by wearing tight corsets; Grete Markstein, who somehow knew about the existence of a daughter; and finally, Dr. John Phillips, the psychoanalyst who reported Erick von Kahler's saying that Einstein's first child was a "Mongoloid idiot."

The criteria for determining a truth is to establish the facts and nuances that agree—or disagree. There are many threads of agreement that weave through Lieserl's story. All the witnesses agree that she was the child of Mileva and Albert, that she was born in Vojvodina, and that Mileva and Albert were not yet married at the time of her birth. They all agree that she was born in 1902. Most of them agree that Mileva's parents cared for the child while Mileva was living in Bern. They all agree that Lieserl had scarlet fever. Ljubica Marić and Mira Alečković remembered that a German-speaking woman came to take her away. Damjanov and Phillips testified to Lieserl's "problems." They all agree that she disappeared when she was about two years old.

In addition, Alečković, a Serbian children's poet, wrote the following statement for Milan Popović's book on March 29, 1997: "I remember that my mother, Milica Marić, close relative of Miloš Marić, father of Mileva Einstein-Marić, said that Mileva's illegitimate child was christened in the Kovilj Monastery near Novi Sad. The child was then taken by Julka, sis-

ter of Miloš Marić, and given to a German woman so she could learn
how to speak German. I heard from my grandmother that the child died
in 1903. They called her Lizerel [sic]."

But Slavica and I had searched the eighteenth-century Kovilj
Monastery, situated between Novi Sad and Titel, with the help of one of
the monks residing there. The monk went through every record in the
archives and could find no trace of Lieserl's birth, christening, or death.

The story of Lieserl was not common knowledge in the community.
It was not bruited about as gossip. Even family members like Ana Milić,
Mira Gajin, and Branka Galić knew nothing. Dr. Laza Marković hid the
story from his own family—although a few of his seven daughters remembered "a peculiar cloud of silence regarding Mileva." The people
who were either direct or indirect witnesses to Lieserl's existence bore
what Felman and Laub call "the solitude of responsibility." Or, as Slavica
would say, *"Jezik za zube,* you put your tongue behind your teeth—you
shut up. You honor your promise."

It has taken almost ninety years, and two or more generations, for
residents of Vojvodina to speak what they know about Lieserl. The publication of the love letters seemed to give them permission. Even so, they
did not offer hearsay. They took the mandate of a question seriously and
revealed only what they knew for sure.

✧

On January 17, 1904, on a late Sunday afternoon, when Mileva was five
months pregnant with Hans Albert, she attended a lecture on alcoholism
by Dr. Gustav von Bunge at the French Church in Bern. At the church
she bought a pamphlet entitled "Alcoholism and Degeneration"—the
pamphlet tucked into the copy of *The Sexual Question* that Mira Gajin had
found among Mileva's papers and given to Slavica and me.

In the early part of the century, there was a movement in the medical profession to prohibit the consumption of alcohol. In 1916, Albert
was treated by a doctor named Otto Juliusburger who was an anti-alcohol
activist, and even he "agreed with his doctor that mankind was being
stultified by hard liquor," although he confessed to a "love of good food
and drink." The following year, when he was recovering from an ulcer,

Albert wrote to Michele Besso, "I am committing myself to do everything else [to get well]—which is unbelievable—to abstain from drinking, etc., in short to perform the rites of medicine loyally and piously."

And Mileva herself seems to have been worried about her sister Zorka's drinking. By the time of her 1907 visit to Mileva in Bern, Zorka was already showing a propensity for drink. "Perhaps you will take a sip of wine for me. I have heard that you have wine from your vineyard. Do not drink up everything before I come," Zorka wrote on a postcard to friends in Sremski Karlovci. She was twenty-four years old, and already people had begun to see her as a *mirna ludakinja,* a "quiet loony."

✧

When the von Bunge pamphlet fell out of Mileva's copy of *The Sexual Question,* I had noticed that some of the text was underlined. People underline words or phrases in books for many reasons. The Oxford English Dictionary says that underlining is to "catch the eye more readily." It also stresses a beautiful phrase or a meaningful turn of language. It is a kind of mute conversation, a way of teaching yourself something that you had not known before. Underlining emphasizes a point, triggers an idea. It is an act of creating a symbiotic relationship with an author's point of view, an author's way of feeling. Your thoughts are suddenly supported by someone in the outside world.

The yellowed von Bunge pamphlet is only eight pages long, and although the underlining was scant, what it emphasized was revealing. The first passage marked by Mileva read:

The human being with healthy blood will be able to overcome all kinds of diseases, such as TB and the bacteria which destroy the stomach and the gall bladder. On the other hand, if the cells of the organs are weakened, the bacteria will be the monsters of the body.

Mileva may have feared that wine had tainted her blood when she was pregnant with Lieserl and perhaps now with Hans Albert. The fetus was already struggling, having to form itself around her left hip like a comma. To alleviate pain, it was customary to take small glasses of wine, sometimes *rakija.* In many instances, wine provided a better variety of relief than the medically approved tincture of opium, laudanum.

A few paragraphs later, Mileva underlined: *It is a misfortune that the sick*

*blood which the child will inherit from its degenerated mother will create a future problem
with a most fundamental and important function—breast-feeding. If the mother retains her
capability to breast-feed, but then gives the child away for artificial nutrition, the child will
still develop normally. However, if the mother is not capable of breast-feeding and gives it
to even the best wet nurse, the child will develop a disposition toward alcoholism. Then the
child will pass this disposition on to his children and thus, his great grandchildren. Because
the inability to breast-feed is a symptom of a general degeneration, the capability to breast-
feed will be lost to all future generations.*

Mileva had not been able to breast-feed her first two children. Several
conditions might prevent a woman from breast-feeding, including mas-
titis, a staphylococcal infection of the breast, which at the turn of the
century would have had to run its course—there being no penicillin—
or childbed fever, a puerperal infection of the vagina or the uterus, caused
by unsanitary childbirth conditions or other factors, such as anemia, prolonged labor, traumatic delivery, and again, breast infection. Mileva might
have been just too sick to feed Lieserl. Calling in a wet nurse (which she
did) would have been an acceptable alternative.

Breast-feeding the infant was of particular importance to Albert. Before the baby was born, he had said that Lieserl "should not be stuffed with
cow's milk, because it might make her stupid. I believe yours would be
more nourishing, what do you think?"

✧

The other item of Mileva's produced by Mrs. Gajin, the 596-page book *Die
Sexuelle Frage*, has a torn brown paper jacket. On it is a drawing of a nude
man standing in front of a gnarled tree. He holds a hatchet, raised next to
his head. He looks as if he is going to cut down the tree of knowledge, but
the illustration may also represent the act of felling old notions and prim-
itive superstitions.

The passages Mileva had underlined were few relative to the length
of the book. But the selections were a revelation. "You need to understand
Mileva in order to find Lieserl," Slavica had said. After years of searching,
of trying to get inside the mind of Mileva, I never felt closer than I did
when reading the notations written in her own hand.

✧

Five years after the birth of Hans Albert, when Mileva was thirty-four years old, she found herself pregnant for the third time. Her life with Albert was disintegrating. Once a brilliant student, she was now a mother and a housekeeper. It was probably at this point in her life that she came across Forel's book.

On the title page, next to "The Sexual Question," she wrote in Serbo-Croatian, *"The source of the truth."* Among the first passages she underlined was one that followed the statement "When a sperm and egg unite, they are totally equal to each other in value." Mileva underscored: *"This coupling symbolizes the social equality and the rights of the two sexes!"* The next sentence reads: "In the course of development, the conjugated nuclei divide again into two cells. Each of these two cells contains almost the same quality of paternal and maternal chromatin." Mileva underlined: *"The impact on the child is more or less equally divided by the mother's and the father's chromosomes."*

By 1909, Albert was cold, distant, and interested in other women. The Einsteins' sex life, once so passionate and exciting, lay almost dormant. "We become idle when we are inactive," Forel wrote, "for the mind's resistance accumulates, and idleness renders the renewal of the corresponding activity more difficult." Mileva underlined: *"If you stop having sex for a long time, then your urge for sexuality diminishes. At the same time, if you have a lot of sex it will increase your urge."*

✧

In a chapter on female homosexual love, Mileva marked: *"A very typical feature of female homosexuality is that women are much more interested in the aura, the softness, of the other woman. Whereas with men, they are more fixated on a woman's genitals."* She further underscored: *"young normal girls often like to sleep together in the same bed, to caress and kiss each other, which is not the case with normal young men. In the male sex such sensual caresses are nearly always accompanied and provoked by sexual appetite. This is not the case of women."* Whether Mileva was interested in women as sexual partners is impossible to determine from this distance. Perhaps she was reading with her sister, Zorka, in mind, who had never displayed an interest in men.

In 1901, Mileva and Albert had read Forel's *Der Hypnotismus*. She told Albert that she had "finished reading the book by Forel," and she thought he was a quack. Her response was most likely due to a course in basic psychology that she had taken in the winter of 1896 and to the influence of Albert's skepticism. Her professor had taught that Forel's theory of hypnosis was "an immoral thing," and she had believed him.

However, by the time she read *The Sexual Question*, Mileva seemed to have revised her opinion. In the margin of the book she had written **"MDF,"** for Medical Doctor Forel, alongside, *"one should strive for a combination of art and knowledge with honesty and altruism. A lot of doctors care too much about the written word and do not think independently."* She appeared to appreciate his opinions. Her interst in psychology and the unconscious had matured.

✧

In the chapter "The Influences of Repeated Sexual Excitations," in a section concerning pornography, Mileva read that "prostitution produces normal intercourse in man." She underlined: *Today's culture has developed in a way that distorts genuine sexuality. For example, prostitution. With paid sex, a prostitute who does not even feel anything learns how to artificially stimulate her clients. The problem is that she often brings, along with her expertise, sexual diseases. These diseases can become part of our inherited sexuality.*

This highlighted passage about venereal disease suggests that Mileva apparently worried about Albert's sexual life outside their bedroom. Furthermore, Einstein historians believe that Albert frequented prostitutes before he married, and that Mileva may have been aware of it.

Dr. János Plesch had maintained that Albert contracted syphilis sometime between leaving Mileva and marrying Elsa. But Albert could have contracted the disease prior to 1910, when he began to exhibit active interest in other women.

If Albert had contracted syphilis before Mileva became pregnant with Eduard, in November 1909, or even before Lieserl was born, in 1902, he might have passed the syphilis to Mileva, who could have been a latent carrier. She, in turn, could have passed it to a baby *in utero*. The closer to conception that the mother is infected, the greater the risk of congenital syphilis in the fetus, which can result in a variety of birth defects from skin lesions to a failure to thrive, to an enlarged liver and spleen, to mental retardation. But with a mother who is a latent carrier, a healthy child can be born between two syphilitic children. Hans Albert, Mileva and Albert's only healthy offspring, was a middle child.

"I think I can confirm," Mileva read on page seventy-eight, in a section called "The Sexual Appetite," "that generally a man is able to distinguish between natural desire and obsessive sexual appetite." The next sentence she underlined with a newly sharpened pencil point: *"By serious and persevering work and by avoiding all means of excitation, the sexual appetite can usually be kept within the bounds of moderation. . . .* We have mentioned in the sentence before that pornographic art is one of the means which artificially excite the sexual appetite."

Mileva drew her pencil back and forth, underlining thickly, *"The artificial stimulation of the libido, including pornography and prostitution, is especially (sic) for simple people. We have mentioned above that pornographic art is one of the means which artificially excite the sexual appetite, especially for simple people. This connection between prostitute and customer is a winning situation for both people. Money and sex. Exploitation of the sexual appetite is the source of all evil."* Mileva was so struck by this statement that she turned to the title page of the book and wrote in the lower left-hand corner "S.78"—refer back to page seventy-eight.

She next underlined, *"the sexual appetite contrasts sharply with the feelings of higher love."* And then, *"it may also happen that love precedes appetite, and this often leads to the most happy sexual relationships. . . . Marriage law stems often from religious customs, which themselves have their origins in barbaric rituals. This simple truth about marriage shows that we are deeply caught within the wire snare of these rituals."*

Albert told a friend that "each personal tie was a form of torture for him, that each bond was often intolerable." Mileva may have been feeling the "wire snare" herself. Certainly, it would have been emotionally debilitating to live with a husband who later said, "[I] married Mileva Marić because I felt sorry for her. Mileva was unlikable, she was ugly, she limped, and generally, no one wanted anything to do with her." She must have been desperate to find solace. Still, she did not seek comfort in the church, even though she seemed to be religious in her own fashion. From interviews that I conducted, it seems that she sought comfort in an abstract exploration of philosophical and psychological concepts and in her relationships with her children.

And yet, throughout her passionate attachment to Albert, Mileva had been adamant in her feminist beliefs. Those beliefs, though generally accepted among her female university friends, were unusual for the time. Forel wrote, "a woman has an instinctive admiration for men of high intellect and lofty sentiments and she strives to imitate those men who provoke her admiration and she tries to carry out their ideas." Mileva drew a vertical line in the margin alongside the lines *"Let us therefore give women their proper rights, equal to ours. And at the same time we must give them a higher education and the same free instruction as ourselves. We shall see them abandon the obscure paths of mysticism to devote themselves to social progress."*

The next entry Mileva underlined: *In a marriage, the housework of a wife should not be seen as an independent performance but as real work which she should be just as much paid for as her husband. Because of this, married couples should not have just one bank account. The wife should be paid for her housework. Maybe a divorce could be prevented if they had separate bank accounts. And if the marriage is happy, in the case they have separate bank accounts, the extravagance of one of the partners could not ruin the whole family.*

In a section called "Utopian Ideas on the Ideal Marriage of the Future," Mileva read that those people who are brought up with equal rights will be aware of their differences in their life tasks. She noted with vertical lines in the margins, *They will have learnt to find the truest satisfaction in the accomplishment of their different duties, and in their work in common for the benefit of society. They will also have learnt to despise frivolity and luxury, to attach no importance to personal property and to put all their ambition into the quantity and quality of their work.*

"I am convinced," Forel wrote and Mileva underscored, *"that it is only by the introduction of the scientific spirit, of a philosophical manner of thinking, into our schools and among the masses, that we shall be able to contend competently with the routine and parrot-like repetitions which are rooted in the worship of old authoritative doctrines and prejudices."*

"Men who are useful from the social point of view, and those who take pleasure in work, and those who are good tempered, peaceful and amiable, should be induced to multiply," she read. Then she highlighted in the margin the following lines: *"If men are endowed with clear intelligence and an active mind, or with an intellectual or artistic creative imagination, they constitute excellent subjects for reproduction."*

✧

Albert was impossible with money. He often lost it. Sometimes he gave it away. When Mileva became angry about his extravagance, he accused her of henpecking, of being parsimonious. "When marriage is consummated on the basis of free reciprocal consent," Forel wrote, "when both parties know exactly to what they have pledged themselves," Mileva underlined, *"when the corrupting influence of money is eliminated,* then love and mutual respect, combined with a healthy sexual appetite, will constitute the intimate and personal ties of marriage."

Albert's mother, Pauline, would never acknowledge that Mileva's family was quite wealthy while the Einsteins were quite poor. She also refused to give Mileva credit for cleverly handling the family finances. Mileva had managed to save a good percentage of Albert's salary. With this money, she invested in stocks, but never speculated. And yet, perhaps recalling Pauline's opposition, Mileva marked in the book's margin, *"Look at the indignation of parents when their children become betrothed to persons whom they consider to be beneath them in social position, or who possess too little money!"* Nevertheless, Albert refused to allow Mileva to use her dowry of 10,000 Swiss francs during their years together.

"I did not marry your daughter for money," Albert told Miloš Marić around 1904, "but because I love her, because I need her, because the two of us are one."

Mileva began to mark another paragraph when her pencil point broke, and so she resumed her underlining with a fountain pen. In black ink she marked that it is *"necessary to remunerate the wife for her work as mother and housekeeper, as the husband is remunerated for his work,"* and a few pages later, *"A man who is healthy in mind and body, hardworking and full of ideas, finds a suitable companion. Instead of leading an easy life, they both undertake as much work as possible, especially social duties. Then they procreate at sufficient intervals as many children as they can without injury to the health of the wife. This is an ideal combination of positive altruism and posi-*

tive egoism." Mileva marked this line as her own, inscribing a very large, clear **"M."** in the margin.

❖

In "The Art of Loving Long," Mileva returned to her penciled notations. On the far left-hand side, toward the gutter of the book, she drew a long line, almost the length of the page. The passage must have been disturbing for her to read: "When amorous sexual intoxication is over, the husband no longer finds any charm in his wife. He becomes enamored of other women to whom he devotes his attention. He reserves his bad temper for his wife, while the latter takes no more trouble to please him." Then Mileva emphasized, *"I agree that a man cannot for long conceal his true nature—we are what we are by heredity."*

Albert's bad temper was well known in his family. Evelyn Einstein told me in 1995 that she remembered when "we played together, he was like another child. He was wonderful. But on the other hand, he threw me down the stairs! It happened one day in 1949 when we were visiting him in Princeton."

Evelyn had been taught early on never to touch anything in her grandfather's study. But one day she could not resist the temptation of entering it. She stood in the middle of the room with her hands clasped behind her back and looked around.

"He saw me in his study. He didn't know that I had been trained not to touch anything on anybody's desk."

All of a sudden she heard a shout from behind her—and before she could turn around, her grandfather had grabbed her by the shoulders and was shoving her out of the room. She tripped and "skidded down the stairs. He had a kind of rage that hit fast and was uncontrollable."

❖

"If the feminine mind is generally wanting in intellectual imagination, it is all the more powerful in the practical intuition of its judgment and in sentimental imagination," Forel wrote. Mileva underlined, *The female soul has a certain feeling for aesthetics and poetry. This feminine soul is the true and warm sun of a fortunate family. . . . The husband and children too often enjoy a mother's work without fully realizing the devoted labor, the love and the pains which she has given to create an array of sunlight—in which warming light, peace and joy awake.*

Forel continued, "the husband should not only regard his wife as the incarnation of all the domestic virtues, but he should also continue to imagine her as the Venus of his early love." Mileva accented, *"This condition may be realized even when youth has passed away, provided the deep sympathetic sentiments of an ideal love have truly existed and are maintained. The wife will then continue to be for her husband the goddess she has always been."*

✧

In a chapter entitled "Emanations of the Sexual Drive," Mileva read that "a true woman rejoices at the progress of her pregnancy. The last pains of childbirth have hardly ceased before she laughs for joy and pride at hearing the first cries of the newly born." Mileva marked the next lines: *"The instinctive outburst of maternal love toward the new-born child corresponds to the natural right of the child, for the child needs the continual care of the mother—so-called doting love. Nothing is so beautiful in the world as the radiant joy of a young mother nursing her child. And nothing, nothing is more degenerate than giving her child into strange hands."* Like Forel's and van Bunge's "degenerate," Mileva had abandoned her baby in Vojvodina to a wet nurse, her mother, and her sister.

Forel recounted a situation that Mileva might have actually followed in the newspaper in 1904. It was the case of Frieda Keller from the canton of St. Gall in Switzerland. As a result of a rape, she gave birth to a daughter in 1899 at the age of twenty-five. Twelve days after the birth, Frieda took her daughter to the foundling hospital at St. Gall. Frieda was under tremendous financial stress, having to provide five francs a week for the daughter's upkeep and pay her sister thirty-four francs for her own room and board.

Five years went by. After the fifth Easter, the foundling hospital informed Frieda that they could not keep the child any longer. She would have to come and fetch her. Frieda brought the girl to a lonely spot in the woods and sat down while the child played. In a while, with her hands and shoes she dug a grave, then strangled the child with string, using such force that it was difficult to untie the knot on the dead body afterward. Within two months, the rain had washed away the grave and the little girl's body was found. The mother immediately confessed. Forel wrote, "How is it that such a brave and industrious woman can feel such repulsion toward her own child? If the judges had asked themselves this question and had replied to it without prejudice, they would not have had the courage to condemn her at all." Here Mileva underlined, *"for their conscience would have clearly shown them the true culprits—masculine brutality, our hypocritical sexual customs and our unjust laws, which inspire terror in a frail brain."* Mileva did not have a frail brain. But by the time she was engaged in this private reading, she had certainly experienced the social injustices perpetrated on women.

✦

In a chapter entitled "The Right to Live of Monsters, Idiots, or the Deformed," Forel wrote, "Large asylums are built for idiots, and there is much joy when after many years of persevering effort some devoted person succeeds in teaching these beings, whose mentality is far inferior to that of a monkey, to repeat words like a parrot, to scribble some words or to repeat a prayer mechanically with their eyes turned toward heaven!" And here Mileva underlined, *"Honestly spoken, the self-sacrificing caretakers and teachers of these idiots would do better by letting them die. They would do more good for themselves by giving birth to their own healthy and capable children."* This echoes what Albert said to Paul Ehrenfest about his Down's syndrome son: "valuable individuals must not be sacrificed to helpless things."

I recalled another reference to idiots in the von Bunge pamphlet about alcoholism. On page six of the pamphlet, Mileva had underlined two times in black ink, with a heavy hand, *"It will not take very much education until people will understand that giving birth to a sick and handicapped child will be the worst crime that human beings are capable of doing."*

Those were the last lines Mileva had underlined in the von Bunge pamphlet. Her resonant notations in Forel's book and von Bunge's pamphlet revealed her feminist beliefs, her sexual concerns, her private worries about her relationship with her husband, and ultimately the story of Lieserl. Mileva had unwittingly left a record of her life.

The next time she traveled to Vojvodina, in 1913, she brought the book and the pamphlet with her and left them in a cabinet in the family home in Novi Sad. Eighty-two years later, they were taken down from Mira Gajin's attic and placed in my hands.

✧

At the very beginning of my search for Einstein's daughter, I had considered and researched the possibility of Lieserl's having been mentally retarded or having had Down's syndrome.

Early on, in an interview with the elderly Ljubica Marić in Kać, I was offered a tantalizing piece of the puzzle.

"Mrs. Marić," I had asked, "can you remember any children born into this family who were odd like Zorka and your aunt?"

"You mean idiots?" she asked. She thought for a moment, then replied, "I know of two children born in the early sixties who were very introverted and only good at mathematical figures. I am not sure what happened to these children. I think they were sent to a special school." Although this information alone is far from enough to prove even a congenital propensity toward mental retardation or Down's syndrome in the family, speculation and discussion of an idiotic child, a damaged child, kept recurring over the course of my search.

Ultimately, I came to believe that it was precisely Mileva's decision to leave her baby that was the key to the mystery of Lieserl. Mileva had allowed herself this act of abandonment because there was absolutely nothing she could do for the child. In those days, a simpleton child was considered ineducable. The child was merely placed in a corner and told to be quiet. If the child was agitated, she or he would be tethered by a wrist or an ankle, or shut in a closet.

Serbian custom prevented Mileva from placing the child for adoption or sending her to an orphanage. In Vojvodina, there was no greater disgrace than giving up a child to strangers. Adoptions were so rare that stories of such cases have never found their way into folk tales or local lore.

After five years of research, there is no doubt in my mind that Lieserl was severely mentally handicapped and that Mileva and her family arranged to shelter her at home. Mileva could not bring an abnormal child back to Bern. Albert was on the cusp of his remarkable career, they had no money to care for her, no social system to support them. It was best to leave her hidden in the fold of the Marić family.

I submit that it was Lieserl's affliction that made Albert's tone of voice so cool and dispassionate in his letter of September 19, 1903: "I am very sorry about what has happened to Lieserl. Scarlet fever often leaves some lasting trace behind." Besides Lieserl's mental handicap, it was now apparent to him that she was suffering physical problems as well.

We know that when Mileva returned to Albert in Bern in September 1903, she was forever changed. She insisted that whatever happened "was too personal" and kept it a secret all her life.

✧

Toward the end of my research, I found a friend and a confidante in a man who was close to the Gajin family and who had spent time in their house while Mileva was still alive. I voiced my theory to him—that Mileva's father had taken specific and decisive steps to draw a curtain around Lieserl's history; that, to the extent he was able, Miloŝ Marić had arranged it so that no official records about her life remained in any governmental or church repositories. Those things beyond his control, letters or minor scraps of evidence, were lost to wars or the passage of time. My source agreed—the first time anyone with knowledge of the events of Lieserl's short life confirmed my suspicions.

None of the four women I researched—Julka Savić-Popović, Nada Marić (Sister Teodora), Anka Streim, and Grete Markstein—can be conclusively proven to be Lieserl. It is my belief that Lieserl Einstein-Marić, born with a mental handicap, died at the age of twenty-one months of scarlet fever aggravated by secondary invasive infections, such as septic shock or endocarditis or pneumonia, on September 15, 1903, the day of a solar eclipse, when the sun disappeared from the sky.

Endnotes

PROLOGUE

"with open arms": MM to HS, second half of May 1901. John Stachel, ed. *The Collected Papers of Albert Einstein, Volume One: The Early Years: 1879–1902*, trans. Dr. Anna Beck. (Princeton: Princeton University Press, 1987), 109.

"promised herself to preserve": MM to HKS, second half of May 1901. Stachel, *CPAE*, no. 109.

"had to nail their shoes": MM to HKS, May 1901. Stachel, *CPAE*, no. 109.

"it was snowing so gaily all the time": MM to HKS, May 1901. Stachel, *CPAE*, no. 109.

"produced avalanches": MM to HKS, May 1901. Stachel, *CPAE*, no. 109.

"when I was allowed to press": AE to MM, second half of May 1901. Stachel, *CPAE*, no. 107.

PART I

"It is better to suffer": Ruth Farnam. *A Nation at Bay: What an American Woman Saw and Did in Suffering Serbia* (Indianapolis: Bobbs-Merrill, 1918), 40.

four cosmic mountain tops: Traian Stoianovich, *A Study in Balkan Civilization* (New York: Alfred A. Knopf, 1967), 43.

a beard was rarely seen: Alec Brown, *Yugoslav Life and Landscape* (London: Elek, 1955), 14.

"tell their beads": Miloš Tsernianski, *Migrations* (New York: Harcourt Brace & Company, 1994), 59.

a grand ceremony: Interview with Dragiša Marić. 10 March 1995, Kać.

English-style cape: Živko Marković. Paper, "Contribution of Mileva Marić Einstein to Science," presented at the *Symposium Mileva Marić Einstein,* October 1995, Novi Sad.

Titel's newly built church: Interviews with Jovan Ružić, March 1995 and 10 February 1998, Novi Sad.

live on into eternity: Woislav M. Petrovitch, *Serbia: Her People, History and Aspirations* (London: George G. Harrap, 1915), 22.

the verb used: Olive Lodge, *Peasant Life in Jugoslavia* (London: Seeley, 1941), 172.

almost always affected the left hip: A. Czeizel, M.D. and G. Tusnády, C.Sc. *Isolated Common Abnormalties in Hungary* (Budapest: Akadémiai Kiadó, 1984), 158.

traditional swaddling practices: G. Th. M. Bossers, "Congenital Anomalies of the Hip Joint" in Huffstadt, A.J.C., ed. *Congenital Malformations* (Princeton: Excerpta Medica, 1980), 285. With proper attention at birth, the problem can be repaired. The treatment may consist of a gentle manipulative reduction of the head into the socket. Reduction is maintained by splinting the abduction for a period of two to six months.

legs bound tightly together: Bossers, 287.

"eldest woman": Milka Bajić Poderegin. *The Dawning* (New York: Interlink Books, 1995), 114.

School documents from Glavni imenik Kraljevske male realke u Mitrovici (The Main Register of the Royal High School), Ispitno Izvješće Pučke škole u Ruma (The Exam Report of the Elementary School in Ruma), and Matica Srpska.

She was . . . grudgingly allowed: Senta Troemel-Ploetz, Ph.D., *Mileva Marić: The Woman Who Did Einstein's Mathematics.* "Women's Studies International Forum," Vol. 13, no. 5, 35, 1990.

"1.76 meters tall": János Plesch and Peter H. Plesch *Some Reminiscences of Albert Einstein.* (London: The Royal Society, 1995), 310. Carl Seelig, trans. Mervyn Savill. *Albert Einstein: A Documentary Biography,* (London: Staples Press Limited, 1956), 58.

varicose veins: Military Service Book, 13 March 1901, Stachel, *CPAE,* no. 91.

"I am very happy about your intention": AE to MM, 16 February 1898. Stachel, *CPAE,* no. 39.

"the Marić girl visits us often": Correspondence from Milana Bota Stefanović to her mother, 1898. Collection of Ivana Stefanović.

"this morning Miss Marić came": Correspondence from Milana Bota Stefanović to her mother, 1898. Collection of Ivana Stefanović.

"my business": ME-M to HKS, 20 March 1903. John Stachel Collection. All translations for this collection are by Eilin Merten.

their relationship became intimate: Concluded from AE to MM, early August 1899. Stachel, *CPAE*, no. 50.

"to be like a wild street urchin": AE to MM, 1 August 1900. Stachel, *CPAE*, no. 69.

"my wild little rascal": AE to MM, 20 August 1900. Stachel, *CPAE*, no. 73.

"my little beast": AE to MM, 13? September 1900. Stachel, *CPAE*, no. 75.

"the philistine life any longer": AE to MM, 3 October 1900. Stachel, *CPAE*, no. 79.

"is this not a journeyman's": AE to HK, 11 October 1900. Stachel, *CPAE*, no. 81.

"Mica and I rarely get together": Correspondence from Milana Bota Stefanović to her mother, 3 June 1898. Collection of Ivana Stefanović.

"From the series of our joint experiences": MM to AE, after 10 August—before 10 September 1899. Stachel, *CPAE*, no. 53.

"read [her] letter in the quiet little chamber": AE to MM, 6 August 1900. Stachel, *CPAE*, no. 70.

"home with [her] good old lady": AE to MM, 1 August 1900. Stachel, *CPAE*, no. 69. Slavica Dokmanović and I found this poem among Mileva's belongings "on the ceiling" in Mrs. Gajin's house. Actually it is a poem set to music, also composed by Mileva, in her handwriting on traditional printed sheet music paper. I have researched its origins, assuming it was written by someone else, but have found nothing to support this assumption.

"One kisses equally well": AE to MM, 23 March 1901. Stachel, *CPAE*, no. 93.

"According to our theory": AE to MM, 12 December 1901. Stachel, *CPAE*, no. 127.

"our paper": AE to MM, 4 April 1901. Stachel, *CPAE*, no. 96. (Although Albert gave the professor their paper, it was published under Albert's name alone. Albert Einstein. *Folgerungen aus den Capillaritätserscheinungen.* Annalen der Physik 4 [1901]: 513–523.)

"Why? We are . . . only, . . . one stone!": Gjurić Trbuhović, trans. Miloš Dokmanović.

"happy and proud I will be": AE to MM, 27 March 1901. Stachel, *CPAE*, no. 94. (Note: Curiously, Einstein's statement does not elicit a citation from the editors of *CPAE*.)

Senta Troemel-Ploetz, 419. Marity is the Hungarian spelling for Marić. Until 1988, Swiss law required women to put their husbands' names first in their double names, 418.

Peter Michelmore, *Einstein, Profile of a Man.* (New York: Dodd, Mead & Company, 1962), 45.

"[Mileva] would be most qualified": Desanka Gjurić Trbuhović, *U senci Alberta Ajnstajna* (Kruševac: Bagdala, 1969), 100, trans. Karlo Baranj, copyright Alan Adelson. Used with permission.

"how proud I will be": AE to MM, 13? September 1900. Stachel, *CPAE*, no. 75.

without further examination: Interview with Senta Troemel-Ploetz, 16 April 1995 and Stachel, no. 75, note 5.

"innocently": AE to MM, 23? July 1900. Stachel, *CPAE,* no. 68.

"mama threw herself": AE to MM, 23? July 1900. Stachel, *CPAE,* no. 68.

"she is a book like you": AE to MM, 23? July 1900. Stachel, *CPAE,* no. 68.

"she is not healthy": AE to MM, 30 August or 6 September 1900. Stachel, *CPAE,* no. 74.

"they both love me and are so disconsolate": AE to MM, 30 August or 6 September 1900. Stachel, *CPAE,* no. 74.

"They were happy that a beautiful man": Interview with Milenko Damjanov, February 1998. Novi Sad.

"Better to know to behave": Prince Lazarovich-Hrebelianovich, with Princess Lazarovich-Hrebelianovich (Eleanor Calhoun) *Serbian People: Their Past and Their Destiny.* (New York: Scribner's, 1910), 52.

"neither of us two have gotten a job": AE to HK, 11 October 1900. Stachel, *CPAE,* no. 81.

applied for a teaching position: AE to MM, 30 April 1901. Stachel, *CPAE,* no. 102.

"soon I will have honored all the physicists from the North Sea": AE to MM, 4 April 1901. Stachel, *CPAE,* no. 96.

"But it is only because of nervousness": AE to MM, 30 April 1901. Stachel, *CPAE,* no. 102.

"robs me of all desire": MM to AE, 2 May 1901. Stachel, *CPAE,* no. 103.

We do not know what forms of birth control Mileva and Albert used. However, during that time, it was common practice in Serbia to wash out the vagina after intercourse with pure vinegar made from wine. Lodge, 301.

"One has to be patient": AE to MM, 28? May 1901. Stachel, *CPAE,* no. 111.

"If only we could be together": AE to MM, 4? June 1901. Stachel, *CPAE,* no. 112.

They were afraid of him: Interview with Dragiša Marić. 10 March 1995, Kać.

Jews of the Austro-Hungian Empire: ed. Slavo Goldstein, trans. Mira Vlatković and Sonja Wild-Bićanić. *Jews in Yugoslavia* (Zagreb: Muzejski prostor, 1989), 142. A partial equality of Jews was granted in 1849. Full emancipation of Hungarian Jewry was granted 22 December 1867, Law no. XVII.

"That woman cannot gain entrance": AE to MM, 29? July 1900. Stachel, *CPAE,* no. 68.

"If she gets a child": AE to MM, 29? July 1900. Stachel, *CPAE,* no. 68.

"By fathering a child before marriage": Lewis Pyenson, article: "Einstein's Natural Daughter," *Science History Publications, History of Science,* XXVIII, 1990, 375.

There was never a question: Interview with Dragiša Marić. 10 March 1995, Kać.

the man was not required: Vera St. Erlich, *Family in Transition: A Study of 300 Yugoslav Villages* (Princeton: Princeton University Press, 1966), 159.

Suicide among pregnant unmarried women: Conversation with Slavica Dokmanović, March 1996. Suicides persisted as a culturally silent solution until the 1960s.

"get any silly ideas": AE to MM, 28? May 1901. Stachel, *CPAE,* no. 111.

drink a boiling-hot: Lodge, 301.

provisional position: AE to MM, 15 April 1901. Stachel, *CPAE,* no. 101.

"I will look immediately *for a position":* AE to MM, 7? July 1901. Stachel, *CPAE,* no. 114.

mother is weeping: Conversation with Slavica Dokmanović, April 1997, Sremski Karlovci.

"stepped on a snake's tail": Barbara Halpern-Kerewsky. *Watch Out for Snakes! Ethnosemantic Misinterpretations and Interpretation of a Serbian Healing Charm.* Anthropological Linguistics 25 (Fall 1983), 321.

"she must live illegally with him": Interview with Dragiša Marić, 10 March 1995, Kać.

"I cannot help but love him very much": MM to HKS, 23 November–mid-December 1901. Stachel, *CPAE,* no. 125.

"My parents are now probably": MM to AE, 8 July 1901. Stachel, *CPAE,* no. 116.

"Good luck on your exams": AE to MM, 22? July 1901. Stachel, *CPAE,* no. 119.

"I am joyfully waiting": MM to AE, 8? July 1901. Stachel, *CPAE,* no. 116.

"does not suspect the mixed feelings": MM to AE, 31? July 1901. Stachel, *CPAE,* no. 121.

"parents the necessary news": MM to AE, 31? July 1901. Stachel, *CPAE,* no. 121.

"You should be happy": MM to HKS, October 1901. Collection of John Stachel.

"My dear one is far away": MM to HKS, October 1901. Collection of John Stachel.

"On the day of the feast": Lodge, 166.

"passed her doctorate": Correspondence from Milana Bota to her mother, 4 November 1901. Collection of Ivana Stefanović.

she had left the university: Correspondence from Silvana Bolli, ETH Rektoratskanzlei. 20 May 1996.

"doesn't get married": Correspondence from Milana Bota to her mother, 4 November 1901. Collection of Ivana Stefanović.

four-story stone rectangle: Correspondence from Dr. Michel Guisolan, archivist, Stadtarchiv, Stadt Stein am Rhein, Switzerland, 6 June 1997.

"I am angry with the cruel fate": MM to AE, 13 November 1901. Stachel, *CPAE,* no. 124.

"I'll write to Helene": MM to AE, 13 November 1901. Stachel, *CPAE,* no. 124.

"I've already stored up": MM to AE, 13 November 1901. Stachel, *CPAE,* no. 124.

"A smart, good-looking young man": Zastava, list Srpske narodne radikalne stranke, The Newspaper of the Serbian People's Radical Party. 16 November 1901.

"I am unspeakably happy": Presumed from letter, AE to MM, 28 November 1901. Stachel, *CPAE,* no. 126.

"Their Miezel [Mileva] will get a good husband": AE to MM, 28 November 1901. Stachel, *CPAE,* no. 126.

"You were so nice": AE to MM, 12 December 1901. Stachel, *CPAE,* no. 127.

"The only problem": AE to MM, 12 December 1901. Stachel, *CPAE,* no. 127.

"I would not like": AE to MM, 12 December 1901. Stachel, *CPAE,* no. 127.

"my dear mother-in-law": MM to HKS, 23 November–mid-December 1901. Stachel, *CPAE,* no. 125.

"Long live impudence": AE to MM, 12 December 1901. Stachel, *CPAE*, no. 127.

"present their parents with": AE to MM, 7? July 1901. Stachel, *CPAE*, no. 114.

On a Sunday afternoon: Náše Vreme (Novi Sad newspaper), *15 December 1901.*

not keep a black cat: P. Kemp. *Healing Ritual. Studies in the Technique and Tradition of the Southern Slavs.* (London: Faber and Faber, 1935), 44.

sight of a hare: Lodge, 265.

"there is no longer any doubt": AE to MM, 19 December 1901. Stachel, *CPAE*, no. 130.

Naše Doba (Novi Sad newspaper). Sunday, 16 December 1901. Issue 140.

"Mr. Djurić's apricot tree": Zastava 25 December 1901. Issue 288.

Serbian children traditionally: Mila Bosić. *Godišnji običaji Srba u Vojvodini.* (Annual Customs of the Serbs in the Vojvodina.) (Novi Sad: Muzej Vojvodine, 1996), 441.

"intimate winter solitude": AE to MM, 19 December 1901. Stachel, *CPAE*, no. 130.

"Have I already told you": AE to MM, 28 December 1901. Stachel, *CPAE*, no. 131.

"[Ehrat] talks about it": AE to MM, 28 December 1901. Stachel, *CPAE*, no. 131.

Serbs believed: Bosić, 442.

the weather was still springlike: Naše Doba, Our Times. No. 143. Sunday, 30 December 1902, Novi Sad.

St. Stefan was born a Jew: Svetaca Za Decembar 1977. Manastir Sveti Ćirilo kod Valjeva.

five times more likely: Czeizel and Tusnády, 155.

"big tweezers": Conversation with Marija Dokmanović, 3 May 1998, New York.

crucial point: Nicholson J. Eastman and Louis M. Hellman. *Williams Obstetrics, 13th Edition* (New York: Appleton-Century-Crofts, 1961), 1120.

weakened by the birth: ME-M to HKS, 15 May 1904. Martin J. Klein, A.J. Kox and Robert Schulmann, eds. *The Collected Papers of Albert Einstein, Volume Five: The Swiss Years: Correspondence, 1902–1914.* trans. Dr. Anna Beck; Don Howard, consultant. (Princeton: Princeton University Press, 1933), letter no. 19. In 1904, after giving birth to her second child, statistically an easier birth than the first, Mileva wrote Helene that she "was very weakened by the birth and greatly in need of good care." medically, it can be assumed the same happened with her first confinement.

more than half: Erlich, 181.

infant mortality rate: Czeizel and Tusnády, 157. According to Czeizel and Tusnády, "Congenital dislocation of the hip, or CDH, is a condition that was named and described by Hippocrates. However, in general, CDH means merely a genetic liability, which becomes manifest as a consequence of pre- and postnatal triggering factors."

approximately sixty percent: Czeizel and Tusnády, 157.

familial cluster: Czeizel and Tusnády, 165.

"his mother was shocked": Maja Winteler-Einstein. *Albert Einstein—Biographical Sketch.* Excerpted in Stachel, *CPAE*, xviii.

"stupid": Albrecht Fölsing, *Albert Einstein: A Biography,* trans. Ewald Osers (New York: Viking, 1997), 11.

"turn completely yellow": Winteler-Einstein, in Stachel, *CPAE,* xviii.

"Poor, poor sweetheart": AE to MM, 4 February 1902. Stachel, *CPAE,* no. 134.

From interviews conducted on the main street of Titel by the author in 1995 and 1998.

"One could hold a meeting": AE to MM, 4 February 1902. Stachel, *CPAE,* no. 134.

"This Miss Marić": Pauline Einstein to Pauline Winteler, 20 February 1902. Stachel, *CPAE,* no. 138.

"private means": Stadtarchiv Bern. Bern, Switzerland. Mileva Marić's name is listed in Bern's record series, intermediate registration control for foreigners E 2.2.1.4./004.

"how tenderly I think of you": AE to MM, 28 June 1902 or later. Klein, et al., no. 1.

fabulous view: Seelig, 59.

"cheerful, lightheaded mood": AE to Hans Wohlwend, 15 August–3 October, 1902. Klein, et al., *CPAE,* no. 2.

Mileva's return to Bern: Michelmore, 42. This quote came from HAE to the writer, Michelmore. However, when HAE was interviewed by Michelmore around 1960, he already knew about Lieserl.

"Albert Einstein/Mileva Marić": Hope Mayo, ed. and trans. *The Einstein Family Correspondence, Including the Albert Einstein–Mileva Marić Love Letters* (New York: Christie's, 1996), *28.*

"the civil registrar proclaimed": Marriage certificate, 6 January 1903. Klein, et al., no. 4.

"We have been married for $2\frac{1}{2}$ months": ME-M to HKS, 20 March 1903. Collection of John Stachel, trans. Eilin Merten.

"This, may you forgive me": Farnam, 27.

"I have become": ME-M to HKS. 20 March 1903. Collection of John Stachel, trans. Eilin Merten.

"Albert cannot go before July": ME-M to HKS, trans. Dr. Anna Beck. Popović, no. 15.

Swiss citizens: Interview with the Kanton Polizei, 3 November 1998, Bern. *Deutsches Passgesetz,* German Passport Law was ratified 12 October 1867 and allowed citizens of any of these countries to travel freely to any of the others.

"German States": Interview with Marianne Howald at the Stadtarchiv, 2 November 1998, Bern. Switzerland did not give women the right to vote until 1971.

Arlberg train: All train schedules were generously provided by Dr. Ljubomir Trbuhović from *Guide Internationale de la Compagnie* for the summer of 1903.

"now even dynamite": *Magyar Szó,* Jewish Hungarian newspaper published in Novi Sad, 28 August 1903.

"Budapest, Thursday, August twenty-seventh": ME-M to AE, 27 August 1903. Klein, et al., no. 12.

"Listen to all of this advice": Ženski Svet (Women's World) 11, 1 November 1903.

high fever: Merck Manual, 1901, (New York: Merck, 1901), 237.

"I'm not at all angry": AE to ME-M, 19? September 1903. Klein, et al., no. 13.

According to Swiss law: Article 25, paragraph 5 of the Bernese Civil Code. Courtesy of the Department federal des Affaires etrangerès, Bern, Switzerland.

"Now come back to me soon": AE to ME-M, 19? September 1903. Klein, et al., no. 13.

"Personal matters never occupied": Ronald W. Clark, *Einstein: The Life and Times* (New York: The World Publishing Company, 1971), 31.

PART II

"poor little Helene": AE to MM, 19 September 1900. Stachel, *CPAE,* no. 76.

"carry her in his large": MM to HK, 11 October 1900. Stachel, *CPAE,* no. 81.

"rejoice with you": MM to HKS, 11 December 1900. Stachel, *CPAE,* no. 83.

"become a nimble, capable little housewife": AE to HK, 11 October 1900. Stachel, *CPAE,* no. 81.

"Dear Mrs. Savić": AE to HKS, 20 December 1900. Stachel, *CPAE,* no. 86. To the best of the translator's knowledge, this is a mathematical joke referring to Helene's pregnancy.

"at the women's hospital": Birth certificate number 618, Tübingen, 30 October 1901, Registrar, Griesshaber; trans. Constance Frank.

"the child of the married couple Savić": Birth certificate number 618, Tübingen, 30 October 1901, Registrar, Griesshaber; trans. Constance Frank.

it is unclear: MM to HKS, October 1901, Saturday. Collection of John Stachel.

"so pleased to hear the news": ME-M to HKS, 20 March 1903, Collection of John Stachel.

"Do you think people": ME-M to HKS, 20 March 1903, Collection of John Stachel.

"[I] was very weakened by the birth": ME-M to HKS, 20 March 1903, Collection of John Stachel.

"when [he] was born": Milan Popović, *A Friendship—Letters Between Mileva and Albert Einstein and Helene Savić* (Montenegro: CIP Podgorica, 1998), 14 June 1904, no. 18, trans. Dr. Anna Beck.

"little treasure": ME-M to HKS, 14 June 1904. Popović, no. 18.

"Albert assumes quite a fatherly dignity": ME-M to HKS, 14 June 1904. Popović, no. 18.

"just before we left for Novi Sad": Elizabeth Roboz-Einstein, *Hans Albert Einstein: Reminiscences of His Life and Our Life Together* (Iowa City: Iowa Institute of Hydraulic Research, 1991), page 94.

"not against moderate alcohol consumption": Dr. Dusan Popov, Enciklopedija Novog Sada, vol. 2 (Novi Sad: Novosadski Klub: Prometej, 1994), 137.

"friendly reception": ME-M to HKS, December 1906. Popović, no. 20.

"I often think with pleasure": ME-M to HKS, December 1906. Collection of John Stachel.

"I do not have a passport": ME-M to HKS, 1906. Popović, no. 19. The Bern Archive only keeps passport and visa records for fifty years. Thus by 1953 the clues to Mileva's travels had been destroyed.

"very bad for the poor men": ME-M to HKS, 29 March 1909. Collection of John Stachel.

"little ones would feel": ME-M to HKS, 29 March, 1909. Collection of John Stachel.

"I was very distressed to hear": ME-M to HKS, 25 June 1909. Collection of John Stachel.

"one of your children": ME-M to HKS, 25 June 1909. Collection of John Stachel.

"our guest": ME-M to HKS, 1909. Popović, no. 22.

"You can trust me": ME-M to HKS, 1909. Popović, no. 22.

"I can reassure you": ME-M to HKS, 3 September 1909. Collection of John Stachel.

"I don't need to tell you": ME-M to HKS, 3 September 1909. Collection of John Stachel.

"I wrote you in Vienna": ME-M to HKS, 3 September 1909. Popović, no. 26.

"I am sorry that I caused you distress": AE to Georg Meyer, 7 June 1909. Klein, et al., no. 166.

"uncommon ugliness": AE to the daughter of Anna Meyer-Schmid, 27 July 1951. Roger Highfield and Paul Carter, *The Private Lives of Albert Einstein* (New York: St. Martin's Press, 1993), 125.

"the mental balance": AE to Michele Besso, 17 November 1909. Klein et al., no. 187.

it was warm: Gjurić Trbuhović, 119.

"You see": ME-M to HKS, 1909 or 1910. Popović, no 28.

"the picture of your children": ME-M to HKS, 1909. Popović, no. 24.

"neither a brother nor a sister": ME-M to HKS, 1909. Popović, no. 24.

"we expect a third ally": ME-M to HKS, 1909. Popović, no. 28.

"How much I am suffering now": MM to AE, 8 July 1901. Stachel, *CPAE,* no. 116.

"you know yourself what dangers": AE to HAE, 6 October 1932. Mayo, *EFC,* 81.

"I nursed him myself": ME-M to HKS, February 1911. Popović, no. 30.

"love and its effects": Highfield and Carter, 132.

"of rare beauty and charm": Highfield and Carter, 132.

"It is not what it used to be": ME-M to HKS, undated. Popović, 116.

trying hard: Gjurić Trbuhović, 118.

did not want to go: ME-M to HKS, February 1911. Popović, no. 30.

"I think": ME-M to HKS, February 1911. Popović, no. 30.

"Little Eduard": ME-M to HKS, 1913. Popović, no. 31.

"The hygienic conditions are:" ME-M to HKS, 1913. Popović, no. 31.

"With good care": Dr. Laza Marković, *Books for the People. Marriage: Or How Will a Nation Achieve Good Progeny,* vol. 149, trans. Dr. Marija Stajić, (Novi Sad: Matica srpska, printed by Djordje Ivković, 1913), 37–38.

"my youngest": AE to Heinrich Zangger, 24 July–7 August 1915. Robert Schulmann, A.J. Kox, Michel Janssen, Józes Illy, eds., *The Collected Papers of Albert Einstein. Volume Eight. The Berlin Years: Correspondence, 1914–1918,* trans. Ann M. Hentschel; Klaus Hentschel, consultant. (Princeton: Princeton University Press, 1998), letter no. 101.

"I am depressed": AE to Michele Besso, December 1916. Highfield and Carter and Speziali 1972, 101.

"had shown their backs": ME-M to HKS, 1913. Popović, no. 31.

"Paula's behavior displeased me": AE to Elsa Löwenthal, 30 April 1912. Klein, et al., no. 389.

"underestimate": AE to Elsa Löwenthal, 10 October 1913. Klein, et al., no. 476.

"is the most sour": AE to Elsa Löwenthal, after 21 December 1913. Klein, et al., 497.

Albert was known: Dimitri Marianoff with Palma Wayne, *Einstein: An Intimate Study of a Great Man* (New York: Doubleday Doran, 1944), 186.

"by nature": AE to Elsa Löwenthal, 27 December 1913–4 January 1914. Klein, et al., no. 498.

"My great Albert": ME-M to HKS, December 1913. Popović, no. 31.

"the Serbian heroine": AE to HKS, after 1 January 1913. Klein, et al., no. 424.

"I treat my wife": AE to Elsa Löwenthal, before 2 December 1913, and AE to Elsa Löwenthal, after 2 December 1913. Klein, et al., nos. 488 and 489.

"Even though my eyes have seen": Marković, 4.

"have been staying here": AE to Heinrich Zangger, 20 September 1913. Klein, et al., no. 474.

"at the end of the month": AE to Elsa Löwenthal, 11 August 1913, Klein, et al., no. 466.

"Steinli": Roboz-Einstein, 29.

"There was": HAE to Djordje Krstić, 5 November 1970. Elizabeth Roboz Einstein, 97.

"What a woman does": Petar Petrovitch Nyegosh (*The Mountain Wreath,* London: George Allen & Unwin, 1930).

"Little Swiss of Serbian Orthodox Faith": *Zastava,* Serbian Radical party newspaper, 21 September 1913, trans. Miloš Dokmanović.

"Tell me": AE to Elsa Löwenthal, 11 August 1913. Klein, et. al., no. 465.

"my wife goes there": AE to Elsa Löwenthal, 11? August 1913. Klein, et al., 465.

"You will see to it": AE to ME-M, April 1914. Mayo, *EFC,* 34.

"Life without my wife": AE to Henrich Zangger, 10? April 1915. Klein, et al., *CPAE,* no. 73.

"In personal respects": AE to Heinrich Zangger, 7 July 1915. Klein, et al., *CPAE,* no. 94.

"All the powers": S. L. A. Marshall, *World War I* (Boston: Houghton Mifflin, 1964), 33.

Ninety percent of Serbia: R. G. D. Laffan, *The Serbs: The Guardians of the Gate* (New York: Dorset, 1989), 242.

hoarding her dowry: AE to Michele Besso, before 28 June 1918. Klein, et al., *CPAE*, no. 572.

"constant attempts": AE to ME-M, 12 January 1915. Klein, et al., *CPAE*, no. 46.

"I remember": ME-M to AE, 5 November 1915. Klein, et al., *CPAE*, no. 135.

"The attempts": AE to Heinrich Zangger, 26 November 1915. Klein, et al., *CPAE*, no. 152.

"revealed": Michelmore, 73.

"turn our now well-tested": AE to ME-M, 6 February 1916. Klein, et al., *CPAE*, no. 187.

only ten days earlier: AE to ME-M, 8 April 1916. Klein, et al., *CPAE*, no. 211.

"Now I see you developing": AE to Michele Besso, 21 July 1916. Klein, et al., *CPAE*, no. 238.

"We men are deplorable": AE to Michele Besso, 21 July 1916. Klein, et al., *CPAE*, no. 238.

"get away from here": AE to HAE, 25 July 1916. Klein, et al., *CPAE*, no. 241, and Mayo, *EFC*, 38.

"Without hesitation": AE to Heinrich Zangger, 25 July 1916. Klein, et al., *CPAE*, no. 242.

Helene came to Zurich: AE to HAE, 10 March 1951. Mayo, *EFC*, 115.

"I believe": AE to Michele Besso, 24 August 1916. Klein, et al., *CPAE*, no. 251.

"very sorry": AE to Heinrich Zangger, 25 July 1916. Klein, et al., *CPAE*, no. 242.

"any more with": AE to Michele Besso, 6 September 1916. Klein, et al., *CPAE*, no. 254.

"their father": AE to HKS, 8 September 1916. Klein, et al., *CPAE*, no. 258.

"to feel sorry": AE to HKS, 8 September 1916. Klein, et al., *CPAE*, no. 258.

"is and will forever remain": AE to HKS, 8 September 1916. Klein, et al., *CPAE*, no. 258.

"suffering from severe anxiety": ME-M to HKS, 1917. Popović, no. 85.

"I will most probably": ME-M to HKS, 15 October 1916. Popović, no. 33.

"she is very worried": AE to HAE, 13 October 1916. Klein, et al., *CPAE*, no. 263.

"Your father's path": AE to HAE, after 31 October 1916. Klein, et al., *CPAE*, no. 271.

"Why I have to suffer": ME-M to HKS, 1 January 1917. Popović, no. 34.

"My wife": AE to Michele Besso, 7 May 1917. Klein, et al., *CPAE*, no. 335.

"Lard, meat, and sugar": Antonia Vallentin, *The Drama of Albert Einstein* (Garden City, NY: Doubleday & Company, 1954), 72.

"managed to find food": Vallentin, 144.

"I cannot come up with": AE to Michele Besso, 22 September 1917. Schulmann, *CPAE*, no. 381.

"the sister would assume": Heinrich Zangger to AE, 21 February 1918. Klein, et al., *CPAE,* no. 469.

"Just put yourself in my place": AE to ME-M, 12 March 1918. Mayo, *EFC,* 39.

"Yesterday, suddenly": Ilse Löwenthal Einstein to Georg Nicolai, 22 May 1918. Klein, et al., *CPAE,* no. 545.

"How the children": AE to Paul and Maja Winteler-Einstein and Pauline Einstein, 23 September 1918. Klein, et al., *CPAE,* no. 621.

"renewed divorce offensive": Heinrich Zangger to AE, 4 March 1918. Klein, et al., *CPAE,* no. 473f.

"I cannot tell you": ME-M to HKS, 1918. Popović, no. 236.

safe keeping: Popović, no. 236.

"I am very eager": AE to ME-M, undated, 1918. Mayo, *EFC,* 41.

"no accusations against the plaintiff": Bezirksgericht Zürich. Divorce document between Frau Mileva/Einstein geb. Marity and Professor Dr. Albert Einstein.

"destroyed at his request": Albrecht Fölsing, page 617, Friedrich Herneck, *Einstein privat, Herta Waldow erinnert sich an die Jahre 1927 bis 1933,* (Berlin: Buchverlag, Der Morgen, 1978), 146f.

"wife will keep": AE to ME-M, 23 July 1920. Mayo, *EFC,* 52.

"She has a sparkling": AE to Heinrich Zangger, 7 November 1911. Klein, et al., no. 303.

"talk about you": Plesch and Plesch, 319.

"vague seignorial loyalty": János Plesch, *János, The Story of a Doctor,* trans. Edward Fitzgerald. (London: Victor Gollanez Ltd., 1947), 34.

Max Reinhardt: as shown in a telegram dated 1917 congratulating Plesch on his marriage. Archives of János Plesch.

"was saddened": Michelmore, 89.

"could live better": AE to ME-M, 15 December 1920. Mayo, *EFC,* 52.

"your opposition": AE to ME-M, 15 December 1920. Mayo, *EFC,* 52.

"This is the famous Albert Einstein": Vallentin, 101.

"Above all things": AE in *The New York Times,* 8 July 1921.

"How are you": ME-M to HKS, 1924. Popović, no. 49.

"You are familiar": ME-M to HKS, 1924. Popović, 49.

"What you have confided": ME-M to HKS, 1922. Popović, no. 47.

She began practicing: Physicians' Society for Serbia, Vojvodina and Srem. No. 2070, 10 March 1929. Archive of Belgrade.

Helene remained the matriarch: Interview with Dr. Milan Popović, March 1995, Belgrade.

"most honored Herr Professor": HKS to AE, 9 November 1939. Albert Einstein Archives, nos. 53–6.

"replanting of older people": AE to HKS, 6 December 1939. Popović, no. 69.

"It made me quite sad": ME-M to HKS, 1931–1932. Popović, no. 67.

"reconciled himself": ME-M to HKS, 1932. Popović, no. 68.

"I am very sad": ME-M to Stana Kosanin, 23 July 1940. Popović, no. 70.

PART III

"Be patient as an ox": Reverend Father Nicholai Velimirović, *Serbia in Light and Darkness* (New York: Longmans, Green and Co., 1916), 107.

when a girl was born: Tihomir Djordjević, *Deca u verovanjima i običajima našega naroda* (Belgrade: Idea, 1990), 274.

"The love for mathematics": Interview with Dragiša Marić, 10 March 1995, Kać.

remarkable ability: Halpern-Kerewsky, 302.

sold one of the properties: The original property sales papers were given to me by Mira Gajin to give to Evelyn Einstein.

real estate money: Gjurić Trbuhović, 195.

When Kiš died: Conversation with Dragica Petrović, 17 September 1995, Belgrade.

"manuscripts, copyrights": Stachel, *CPAE*, xi.

"comply, as the agent": E-mail from Robert Schulmann, 13 February 1997.

"only the first four": Klein, et al., no. 424f. [ALSX. 73–751]

'I made some research about Lieserl . . .' *Mileva Marić's Love*. Television show in Belgrade. Journalist: Mira Adanja Polak, 24 November 1996.

"Do you know where": Interview with Milan Popović. 25 September 1995, Belgrade.

contemporary composer: *Performed Readings and Plays by Writers from Croatia, Macedonia, Slovenia, Serbia and Montenegro* (Belgrade: Tricycle Theatre, August 1993), 8.

"I have a good appetite": Correspondence from Milana Bota to her parents, 1900. Collection of Ivana Stefanović.

"God only knows": Milana Bota to her mother, 4 November 1901. Collection of Ivana Stefanović.

"Because of circumstances": MM to HKS, December 1901. Collection of John Stachel.

"almost dead and so dry": Milana Bota to her mother, 17 February 1902. Collection of Ivana Stefanović.

"Not a word": Interview with Ljubomir Trbuhović, 26 February 1995, Zurich.

PART IV

"First I will ask you": Interview with Jovan Ružić, 12 March 1995, Novi Sad.

"whose whereabouts were unknown": Farnam, 224.

"some difficulty": Ana Milić (pseudonym) to HAE, January 1955. Albert Einstein Archives, no. 82–974–1.

"quite a long time ago": Sofija Galić Golubović to HAE, 25 April 1957. Albert Einstein Archives, no. 82–971–1.

"on the drums": Interview with Branka Galić Koraksić, 8 February 1998, Belgrade.

alongside their Marić cousins: Gjurić Trbuhović, 119.

"I am definitely willing": HAE to Tima Galić, 1 December 1951. Albert Einstein Archives, no. 82–977.

"Your mother left": Tima Galić to HAE, 1 December 1951. Albert Einstein Archives, no. 82–977.

"every time I go to Novi Sad": Sofija Galić Golubović to HAE, 25 April 1957. Albert Einstein Archives, no. 82–971–1.

most of the furniture and belongings: Tima Galić to HAE, 1951. Albert Einstein Archives, no. 82–977.

"found yellowed and wrinkled . . ." Gjurić Trbuhović, 164.

eventually became: In 1996, the Einstein Family Correspondence, including the Albert Einstein–Mileva Marić Love Letters, which were part of the property of the Einstein Family Correspondence Trust, was placed for auction at Christie's in New York. Although the Love Letters sold to an unidentified buyer, a good portion of the remaining corpus went unsold. These letters were distributed among the Einstein family.

"we have recently": Sofija Galić Golubović to HAE, 11 June 1957. Albert Einstein Archives, no. 82–969–1.

"Her name": At Mrs. Milić's request, I used the pseudonym Nada. However, Nada's actual birth surname was Marić.

"A family member": Correspondence from Eva Meili-Sonderegger to the author, 18 August 1995, Zurich.

"I used to visit our Serbian monasteries": From the archives of Krušedol Orthodox Monastery.

"for not one penny": Document from Matica Srpska, courtesy of Zoran Budimlija.

"Forel differs from a quack": MM to AE, 13 November 1901. Stachel, *CPAE,* no. 124.

"I was asked by a circle": Milica Stefanović to her mother, Milana Bota Stefanović, 1929. Collection of Ivana Stefanović.

"Tonight I had a horrible vision": Stefanović, np. and Collection of Ivana Stefanović.

"If you are a star": Desanka Maksimović, *Greetings From the Old Country* (Toronto: Yugo-Slavia Publishers, 1976), np.

PART V

deposited in her name: AE to ME-M, 23 May 1923. Mayo, *EFC,* 52.

"pregnant with a house": AE to ME-M, undated, c. 1926–1929. Mayo, *EFC,* 64.

"pay their rent and not annoy you": AE to ME-M, 17 June 1924. Mayo, *EFC,* 52.

"his very good scientific knowledge": Boris E. Javrlov, Moscow. Correspondence to Dr. Heinz Lutstorf, ETH Library, Zurich, 17 October 1986.

"[I]t sounds wonderful": AE to HAE and Eduard Einstein, 26 March, ny. (1923). Mayo, *EFC,* 55.

"you will notice": AE to ME-M, undated, c. 1928. Mayo, *EFC*, 68.

"public scandal it would cause": AE to ME-M, undated, c. 1923. Mayo, *EFC*, 55.

two armed: Vallentin, 114.

imprisoned at Landsberg: Otto Friedrich, *Before the Deluge* (New York: Harper, 1995), 141.

"here [in Berlin]": AE to Eduard Einstein, c. March 24, 1921. Mayo, *EFC*, 55.

"Nazism was born": Vallentin, 190.

"ceased speaking ill": AE to ME-M, 19 April 1924. Mayo, *EFC*, 54.

"Nothing I do is appreciated": AE to ME-M, October 1925. Mayo, *EFC*, 61.

"laugh with your threat of your memoirs": AE to ME-M, October 1925. Mayo, *EFC*, 61.

"a nervous disturbance": Gjurić Trbuhović, 214.

mounting debts: Michele Besso to Heinrich Zangger, 12 January 1936. Heinrich A. Medicus, "The Friendship Among Three Singular Men: Einstein and His Friends Besso and Zangger" *Isis* 85 (1994), 471.

to promote a better understanding: Medicus, 475.

"It was only because I was afraid": AE to ME-M, 1 November 1928. Albert Einstein Archives, no. 75–697.

"When you come to visit": AE to Eduard Einstein, 8 October 1932. Mayo, *EFC*, 79.

casting a shadow: Michelmore, 146.

"would not have noticed [Mileva]": Marianoff, 12.

"Men are like bicycles": AE to Eduard Einstein, 5 February 1930. Mayo, *EFC*, no. 75.

"cunning female": Highfield and Carter, 234.

"a dear, seriously ill child": ME-M to AE, c. 1932–33. Mayo, *EFC*, 81.

"I am not in favor of": AE to ME-M, 20 August 1932. Mayo, *EFC*, 78.

"ruined my brother": Roboz-Einstein, 25.

"hopeless mental case": Helen Dukas, FBI file, SAC, Newark (199–29614, 100–32986.) Subject: Internal Security, 9 March 1955, pp. 1–8. Brian, 478.

"I have come to realize that Freud's": AE to Eduard Einstein, 10 April 1936. Mayo, *EFC*, 92.

"I gave you the Nobel Prize money": AE to ME-M, c. 1932. Mayo, *EFC*, 81.

"do what you think is right": AE to HAE, 6 October 1932. Mayo, *EFC*, 81.

"There is a difference of age": AE to HAE, November 1925. Mayo, *EFC*, 64.

"such significant faults": AE to ME-M, 15 October 1926. Mayo, *EFC*, 53.

"business with [Hans] Albert": AE to ME-M, 28 January 1926. Mayo, *EFC*, 62.

"If you had let Hans Albert go to Munich": AE to ME-M, 13 February 1926. Mayo, *EFC*, 63.

"If they would never": AE to ME-M, 6 March 1926. Mayo, *EFC*, 63.

"[Hans Albert] will visit in July": AE to ME-M, 5 May 1928. Mayo, *EFC*, 65.

"pleasantly surprised": AE to ME-M, undated, c. 1928. Mayo, *EFC*, 65.

"I am sorry to hear": AE to ME-M, undated, c. 1929. Mayo, *EFC*, 65.

"overactive thyroid disorder": Denis Brian, *Einstein: A Life* (New York: John Wiley, 1996), 153.

"content, I myself": AE to HAE, 23 February 1924. *EFC,* 58.

"as if in his own home": Gjurić Trbuhović, 208.

"turning off his emotions like a tap": Interview with Evelyn Einstein in Highfield and Carter, 223.

"roll up his sleeves and improvise on the piano": Gjurić Trbuhović, 208.

"filled with a spiritual charm": Gjurić Trbuhović, 208.

"glowed with an inner fire . . ." Gjurić Trbuhović, 208.

on the thirty-first of December: Gjurić Trbuhović, 247.

"perhaps she has hidden the cash": AE to HAE, 7 June 1948. *EFC,* 103.

"demented minds": Berislav M. Berić and Dušan Miškov, *Proceedings of the 12th Scientific Meeting* (Bač: The Scientific Society for History of the Culture of Health for Vojvodina, 9–10 November 1984), 80–91.

in the spring of 1941: Interview with Pavle Stanojević, Director of the Vojvodina Archive, 11 February 1998.

"As far as I know": Interview with Hofrat Doctor Peter Broucek, Director of the *Kriegsarchiv* (War Archive) in Vienna, 8 March 1997.

"You must understand": Interview with Dr. Grozdana Čonak and Aleksandar Roslavljev, 11 February 1998, Novi Sad.

"Of course, I remember Mileva": Interview with Milenko Damjanov, 10 February 1998, Novi Sad.

PART VI

Grete and her two siblings: Grete's brother Leopold seems to have led a conventional life. In 1913, he married another Grete, Grete Schneider, who was also from Vienna. Leopold became a salesman and, later, a citizen of Hungary. He and Grete did not have children.

Leopold and his wife had only five years together. On 15 September 1918, Leopold died in Südtirol, a German-speaking region of Italy. He was thirty-two years old and probably died in the flu epidemic. His wife stayed in Vienna until 1939, never remarrying. Then, as a stateless widow, Grete Sara Markstein emigrated to New York aboard the S.S. *Conte di Savoia* in 1939. ("Sara" was not her real middle name; one of the ways that the Nazis branded Jews was by forcing them to use Sara or Israel as their middle names.) She claimed "housewife" as her profession.

Grete Markstein, the wife of Leopold, and Grete Markstein, the sister of Leopold, confused my research for a while. When I found that a Grete Markstein from Vienna had entered the United States in both 1924 *and* 1935, I thought the story was going to go in an entirely different direction. I thought that I could find "my" Grete in my own backyard. It was the U.S. Department of Justice Freedom of Information Act that set me right: When the material that I requested from them concerning both of the Grete Markstein journeys to America arrived, I discovered that there had been two Grete Marksteins.

"jüdische Eigenschaften": Steven Beller, *Vienna and the Jews 1867–1938: A Cultural History* (Cambridge: Cambridge University Press, 1989), 211.

A few years later: Correspondence to the author from Herbert Koch, archivist of the Magistrat der Stadt Wien, 18 January 1997. Grete's last address was in the ninth district at Widerhofergasse 5/13 in Vienna. According to a statement from a bureaucratic institution, probably the police, on 12 April 1920, "officially she moved out a while ago."

worked with Lola Stein: Some biographical information on Lola Stein comes from the World Jewish Relief, London; Luisa Biasiolo, Director.

"just before the end of the war": Grete Markstein to Leopold Jessner. Geheimes Staatsarchiv Preußischer Kulturbesitz, 21 June 1920.

"all actors, if they were lying": Interview with Dr. Lothar Schirmer, Director, Landesmuseum für Kultur und Geschichte Berlins. 30 January 1997.

"filth, lice": George Grosz in Friedrich, 37.

abundance of young actresses: Anthony Read and David Fisher, *Berlin: The Biography of a City* (London: Pimlico, 1994), 183.

daring recreations: Friedrich, 248.

to have been hired: Interview with Dr. Lothar Schirmer, Director, Landesmuseum für Kultur und Geschichte Berlins. 30 January 1997.

"a young female lover": Schauspielhaus contract for Grete Markstein, 1 September 1921. Geheimes Staatsarchiv Preußischer Kulturbesitz.

"twenty-five hundred marks": Grete Markstein to Leopold Jessner, 21 June 1920. Geheimes Staatsarchiv Preußischer Kulturbesitz.

was to be deducted: Contract between Grete Markstein and Schauspielhaus, notary no. 257, 28 June 1920. Geheimes Staatsarchiv Preußischer Kulturbesitz.

"the problem of Eastern Jewish refugees": The New York Times, 16 January 1921.

"foreign profiteering Jews": The New York Times, 15 March 1921.

"the evil spirit": Vossche Zeitung, 1 January 1922.

"very important matters": Grete Markstein to Leopold Jessner, December 1920. Geheimes Staatsarchiv Preußischer Kulturbesitz.

"I take the liberty": A. C. Steinhardt to Direktion des Staatstheaters, 30 January 1922. Geheimes Staatsarchiv Preußischer Kulturbesitz.

"On principle we do not give out any information": Direktion des Staatstheaters to A.C. Steinhardt, 3 February 1922. Geheimes Staatsarchiv Preußischer Kulturbesitz.

"Because I had a feeling": Grete Markstein to Leopold Jessner, 18 December 1922. Geheimes Staatsarchiv Preußischer Kulturbesitz.

"My dear Fräulein Markstein": Leopold Jessner to Grete Markstein, 28 December 1922. Geheimes Staatsarchiv Preußischer Kulturbesitz.

"Fräulein Grete Maria Markstein is being treated": Dr. Herzberg to the theatre, 29 December 1922. Geheimes Staatsarchiv Preußischer Kulturbesitz.

"After my period of illness": Grete Markstein to theatre, 23 January 1923. Geheimes Staatsarchiv Preußischer Kulturbesitz.

"Dear Mister Theatre Manager Jessner": Grete Markstein to Leopold Jessner, 27 September 1923. Geheimes Staatsarchiv Preußischer Kulturbesitz.

"at this time Herr Jessner": Theatre to Grete Markstein, 5 October 1923. Geheimes Staatsarchiv Preußischer Kulturbesitz.

make a movie: Archives of the Motion Picture Academy, the National Film Information Service, and the Screen Actors' Guild.

"President Rückelt": According to the ship's manifest, filed in the National Archives, New York City, Grete Markstein arrived on the S.S. *George Washington* from Bremen, Germany, on 27 November 1923.

an apprentice shoemaker: Interview with Margaret Rückelt, the granddaughter of Paul Rückelt's brother Otto, 7 July 1997, Berlin.

I was in such a hurly-burly": Grete Markstein to Leopold Jessner, 6 February 1924, Geheimes Staatsarchiv Preußischer Kulturbesitz.

wishful thinking or outright fantasy: Jessner resigned from the Berlin theatre in 1930. He died in 1943 as the result of a dog bite.

"heavy state of exhaustion": Dr. Rehfisch to the Staatstheater, 31 March 1924. Geheimes Staatsarchiv Preußischer Kulturbesitz.

"Fräulein Grete Markstein is still suffering": Dr. Rehfisch to the Staatstheater, 16 April 1924.

"The creditor is entitled": Berlin-Lichterfelde to the Staatstheater, 15 February 1928.

"regarding the Distress Warrant": To the attorney Max Goldstücker. Richard Kaschner was the director of a real estate firm.

"One summer, Jim Bibo": Courtesy of Berthold Leimbach.

"melting pot of everything that is evil": Read and Fisher, 189.

was a liberal: Friedrich, 215.

"The yellow press": Friedrich, 216.

six-page paper: Friedrich, 220.

"Many of us regard this": Max Born in Friedrich, 220.

"Why do you want me to go": Vallentin, 87.

"Party Books": János Plesch collection, Jüdisches Museum, Berlin.

opulent stag parties: Plesch, 148.

"All my guests": Plesch, 149.

Einstein was his: Fölsing, 601.

"Because of the endorsement": Elsa Einstein to Grete Markstein, 28 November 1930. Albert Einstein Archives, no. 47–594. After checking with both the Princeton University Press and Robert Schulmann, at the time of this printing I have been unable to determine an executor of Elsa Einstein's estate.

"the female storyteller": AE to An die Berliner Handelsgesellschaft, 29 September 1932. Albert Einstein Archives, no. 51–043.

money paid to Grete: Plesch, 202.

Elsa's prettiest feature: Vallentin, 142.

"intellectual women": Vera Weizmann, *The Impossible Takes Longer* (London: H. Hamilton, 1967), 102–103.

complained to him: AE to Elsa Löwenthal, after 11 August 1913. Klein, et al., no. 466.

"I love living in the little house": Fölsing, 612.

"left the field clear": Herneck, Friedrich. *Einstein privat, Herta Waldow erinnert sich an die Jahre 1927 bis 1933. (Einstein in Private: Herta Waldow Recalls the Years 1927 to 1933.)* (Berlin: Buchverlag, Der Morgen, 1978), 123.

Ludek bears a strong resemblance: Michael Specter, front page, *The New York Times,* 22 July 1995.

"solemn vow" Specter, *The New York Times,* 22 July 1925.

nor Margarete: Highfield and Carter, 214.

Shortly after Georg was born: Interviews with Jacqui Lyons, 2 February 1997, London, and Richard Markstein, 28 March 1998, New York.

"Victorious, we are going to defeat France!": Read and Fisher, 199.

"In view of Hitler": Fölsing, 659.

"only live in a country": New York World Telegram, 11 March 1933.

"Good News": Fölsing, 661.

"I did not know": Peter A. Bucky, *The Private Albert Einstein* (Kansas City, MO: Andrews and McMeel, 1992), 60.

"You made me really happy": AE to ME-M, 29 April 1933. *EFC,* 82.

Quai d'Orsay: Abraham Pais, *Einstein Lived Here* (New York: Oxford University Press, 1994), 193.

"life [was] more burdened": Mayo, *EFC,* 81.

"You have gone mad": Pais, 80.

"I have been": AE to Max Planck, 6 April 1933, Fölsing, 666.

"personally": AE to Michele Besso, 5 May 1933, Fölsing, 666.

unnamed doctor: Vallentin, 236.

"Both children": Vallentin, 236.

German Jewish refugees: Yehuda Bauer, *My Brother's Keeper: A History of the Joint Distribution Committee 1929–1939* (Philadelphia: The Jewish Publication Society of America, 1974), 138.

twelve hundred: Bauer, 149.

By June 1934: From "Report of the German Commission of the National Committee." June 27, 1934. From the archives of the American Jewish Joint Distribution Committee, New York.

"I trust that I shall not be thought immodest": Plesch, 409.

"I fear": AE to Frederick Lindemann, 22 January 1935. Chewell Papers, The Library, Nuffield College, Oxford.

Alfred Einstein: Interview with Judy Tsou, Research Librarian, University of California at Berkeley Music Library, 26 January 1999.

her registration: Correspondence from Lieselotte Montague, World Jewish Relief, London, 20 November 1996. (In the research materials there are a variety of spellings of this name. For clarity I have settled on Zygmunt Herschdoerfer.)

The problem is: Correspondence from Lieselotte Montague, World Jewish Relief, 6 January 1999.

Herschdoerfer was born: Public Record Office, Great Britain, file HO45/15814.

Jews were encouraged to register: Interview with Lieselotte Montague, World Jewish Relief, 20 November 1996.

"MRS. HERSCHDOERFFER [sic] PRETENDING": Frederick Lindemann to Hermann Weyl, 23 November 1935. Albert Einstein Archives, no. 51–044.

"Do not contact us": Interview with Mrs. Herschdoerfer, 12 August 1996, London.

"the matter of your pseudo-daughter": Max von Laue. Archive HS 1973–6, 137. Deutsches Museum, von Meisterwerken der Naturwissenschaft und Technik. Munich.

"disavowed all knowledge": Highfield and Carter, 302.

"have been lost or removed": Highfield and Carter, 302.

"assistance of other friends": Plesch, 221.

hire a detective: Historians have read "Biel" as "Bial." The author checked the handwriting with an expert and was advised that the correct spelling is "Biel."

"Jewish detective": F. Biel to Helen Dukas, 19 August 1936, Vienna. Albert Einstein Archives, no. 51–046.

"bad reputation was described to me": F. Biel to Helen Dukas, 19 August 1936, Vienna. Albert Einstein Archives, no. 51–046.

"All my friends are hoaxing me": AE to János Plesch, 1936. Albert Einstein Archives, no. 31–541.

"Joyful may be children's": János Plesch to AE, 9 September 1936, trans. Prof. P. H. Plesch. Used with permission. Albert Einstein Archives, no. 31–540.

"In the county of Chester": Courtesy of Mrs. Zygmunt Herschdoerfer, September 1996.

"Georg G. Markstein": Lola Stein to AE, 6 May 1947. Albert Einstein Archives, no. 58–470.

"already had very funny experiences": AE to Lola Stein, 15 May 1947. Albert Einstein Archives, no. 58–471.

a famous writer: Interviews with Jacqui Lyons, George Markstein's literary agent, 28 March 1997, London, and Richard Markstein, 6 April 1997, New York.

"a special honor": Lola Stein to AE, 6 July 1947. Albert Einstein Archives, no. 58–472.

"I am looking forward to receiving your biographical book": János Plesch Archives, 3 February 1944. Jüdisches Museum, Berlin, trans. Dr. Stefan Elfenbein.

"You are so right": János Plesch to AE, 10 May 1944. János Plesch Archives, Jüdisches Museum, Berlin, trans. Prof. P. H. Plesch. Used with permission.

"himself has vetted the chapter": Correspondence from Edward Fitzgerald to János Plesch, 18 September 1945. Jüdisches Museum, Berlin.

"The manuscript has been destroyed": Correspondence from Prof. P. H. Plesch, 4 February 1998.

"If my Ilse": Vallentin, 241.

"like a lost soul": Vallentin, 240.

"was surely invented": Plesch and Plesch, 310.

"Bury her": Highfield and Carter, 216.

"Everything conspires": AE to HAE, 4 January 1937. *EFC,* no. 92.

"ne": Interview with Marie Grendelmeier, 9 March 1995, Zurich.

"If you see your mother again": AE to HAE, 11 July 1948. Mayo, *EFC,* 103.

found it under the mattress: Interview with Marie Grendelmeier, March 9, 1995, Zurich.

"You have probably wondered": AE to Carl Seelig, 4 January 1954. Highfield and Carter, 257.

"chains of the merely personal": Jeremy Bernstein, *Einstein* (New York: Penguin, 1976), 77.

"I always get by best": AE to Heinrich Zangger, 17 May 1915. Schulmann, *CPAE,* no. 84.

"perfectly suited": Bucky, 133.

"Einstein died": Bucky, 133.

"weak vascular system": Plesch and Plesch, 309.

"You can imagine how I feel": Plesch and Plesch, 309.

"My aim lies": Sachi Sri Kantha, *An Einstein Dictionary* (Westport, CT: Greenwood Press, 1996), 199.

"let it burst": Plesch and Plesch, 307.

PART VII

"valuable individuals must not be sacrificed": AE to Paul Ehrenfest. Berlin, c. August 1932. Fölsing, 673.

Ehrenfest was bereft: Brian, 250.

"in the mouth of two or three witnesses": 2 Corinthians 13:1.

"To testify is . . . not merely to narrate": Shoshana Felman and Dori Laub, M.D., *Testimony: Crisis of Witnessing in Literature, Psychoanalysis, and History* (New York: Routledge, 1992), 204.

poetic form: J. W. Wiles, *Serbian Songs and Poems: Chords of the Yugoslav Harp* (London: George Allen & Unwin, 1918), 12.

"follows a trust": James McConkey, ed. *The Anatomy of Memory* (New York: Oxford University Press, 1996), 152.

"I remember that my mother": Popović, 50.

"a peculiar cloud of silence": Interview with Dr. Karmensita Berić, 9 September 1998, Toronto.

"the solitude of responsibility": Felman and Laub, 3. From Paul Celan's verse, *"No one bears witness for the witness."*

"agreed with his doctor": Fölsing, 406.

"a love of good food and drink": Clark, Ronald W. *Einstein: The Life and Times.* (New York: World Publishing, 1971), 349.

"I am committing myself": AE to Michele Besso, 13 May 1917. Klein, et al., *CPAE,* no. 339.

"Perhaps you will take a sip of wine for me": Correspondence from Zorka Marić to Jovan Bogdanović, 1 January 1907. Courtesy of Nikola and Slavica Dokmanović.

"The human being with healthy blood": Gustav von Bunge, "Alcoholism and Degeneration," trans. Dr. Stefan Elfenbein (Bern: Abstinence Society of the Sober People of Bern, 1904), 5.

"the sick blood": von Bunge, 4.

"should not be stuffed": AE to MM, 12 December 1901. Stachel, *CPAE,* no. 127.

fed cow's milk: Laza Marković, *Reč nad otvorenim grobom* (Novi Sad: Braća M. Popović Publishing, 1904), 9.

"when a sperm and egg unite": Auguste Forel, *Die sexuelle Frage. Eine naturwissenschaftliche, psychologische, hygienische und soziologische Studie für Gebildete,* trans. Dr. Stefan Elfenbein (Munich: Reinhardt, 1905), 13.

"In the course of development": Forel, 12.

"We become idle when we are inactive": Forel, 77.

"A very typical feature of female homosexuality": Forel, 257.

"young normal girls often like to sleep together": Forel, 85.

"finished reading the book by Forel": MM to AE, 13 November 1901. Stachel, *CPAE,* no. 124.

"one should strive for a combination of art": Forel, 410.

"The idea of the unconscious immediately calls to mind": Forel, 496.

"prostitution produces normal intercourse in men": Forel, 75.

Albert frequented prostitutes: Professor Res Jost interview with Otto Stern, a colleague of Einstein's in Prague, 1961, ETH.

passed it in utero: Interview with Dr. Gerald Rodriguez, 24 August 1998, Santa Fe, NM.

a healthy child: Merck Manual, 1901, 1623.

"I think I can confirm": Forel, 78.

"the artificial stimulation of the libido": Forel, 78.

"the sexual appetite contrasts": Forel, 82.

"it may also happen": Forel, 100.

"each personal tie": Bucky, 104.

"I felt sorry for her": Bucky, 101.

"an instinctive admiration": Forel, 128.

"In a marriage, the housework": Forel, 361.

"they will also have learnt": Forel, 529.

"I am convinced": Forel, 517.

"Men who are useful": Forel, 523.

"When marriage is consummated": Forel, 420.

quite wealthy: AE to Michele Besso, before 28 June 1918. Klein, et al., *CPAE,* no. 572.

"handling the family finances": Michelmore, 59.

"the indignation of parents": Forel, 444.

"I did not marry your daughter for money": Gjurić Trbuhović, 100.

"necessary to remunerate the wife": Forel, 468.

"a man who is healthy": Forel, 445.

"amorous sexual intoxication": Forel, 533.

"we played together": Interview with Evelyn Einstein, 3 April 1995.

"if the feminine mind": Forel, 127.

"the husband should . . . regard his wife": Forel, 535.

"a true woman rejoices": Forel, 125.

"The instinctive outburst": Forel, 125.

"with her hands and shoes": Forel, 415.

"How is it that such a brave": Forel, 413.

"for their conscience would have clearly shown": Forel, 415.

"Large asylums are built for idiots": Forel, 400.

"It will not take very much education": von Bunge, 6.

"was too personal": Michelmore, 42.

Selected Bibliography

Adam, Helen Pearl Humphry. *Paris Sees It Through: A Diary, 1914–1919.* London: Hodder and Stoughton, 1919.

Adamic, Louis. *The Native's Return: An American Immigrant Visits Yugoslavia and Discovers His Old Country.* New York: Harper & Brothers, 1934.

Allen, Roy F. *Literary Life in German Expressionism and the Berlin Circles.* Ann Arbor, MI: UMI Research Press, 1972.

Allport, Gordon W., and Postman, Leo Joseph. *The Psychology of Rumor.* Cambridge: Cambridge University Press, 1988.

Ambrozič, Matija. *Smrtnost dece u našoj zemlji (Mortality of Children in Our Country).* Two volumes from the collection of papers from the First Congress of Doctors in the Federative People's Republic of Yugoslavia, Belgrade, 1949.

American Jewish Committee. *The Jews in the Eastern War Zone.* New York: American Jewish Committee, 1916.

American Jewish Historical Society Journal 53 (1964). Published by the American Jewish Historical Society, Waltham, MA.

American Jewish Joint Distribution Committee, New York. *Report of the German Commission of the National Committee,* 27 June 1934.

American Jewish Yearbook, 1940. Philadelphia: Jewish Publication Society, 1940.

Amtliches Fernsprechbuch für Berlin und Umgegend Oberpostdirektion Berlin. Berlin: Oberpost-direktion, 1920–1933.

Amurelli, Kario. *A Book for a Penny: Getting Off the Throne.* Belgrade: Smiljevo [publishing house of Pera Todorović], 1889.

Andrić, Ivo. *The Bridge on the Drina.* Chicago: The University of Chicago Press, 1977.

————. *The Dammed Yard and Other Stories.* London: Forest Books, 1992.

Barsley, Michael. *The Orient Express.* New York: Stein and Day, 1966.

Bauer, Yehuda. *My Brother's Keeper: A History of the American Joint Distribution Committee 1929–1939.* Philadelphia: The Jewish Publication Society of America, 1974.

Beckerle, Monika. *Dachkammer und literarischer Salon: Schriftstellerinnen in der Pfalz (The Garret and the Literary Salon: Women Writers in Pfalz).* Landau: Pfalzische Verlagsanstalt, 1991.

Beller, Steven. *Vienna and the Jews 1867–1938: A Cultural History.* Cambridge: Cambridge University Press, 1989.

Benson, Larry D. *Orphaned Children: A Bibliography.* Monticello: Larry D. Benson, 1991.

Berić, Berislav M., and Miškov, Dušan. *Proceedings of the 12th Scientific Meeting.* Bač: The Scientific Society for History of the Culture of Health for Vojvodina, 9–10 November 1984.

————. *An Overview of the History of Hospitals in Novi Sad, 1730–1981.* Novi Sad: Newsletter of the Scientific Society for History of Culture of Health in the Vojvodina.

Bernstein, Jeremy. *Einstein.* New York: Penguin, 1976.

————. "Einstein When Young." *The New Yorker* (6 July 1987): 77–80.

————. "A Critic at Large: Besso." *The New Yorker* (27 February 1989): 86–92.

Bertaut, Jules. *Paris 1870–1935.* London: Eyre and Spottiswoode, 1936.

Bojović, Snežana. *Sima Lozanić u srpskoj nauci i kulturi (Serbian Science and Culture).* Beograd: MNT, 1993.

Bosić, Mila. *Godišnji običaji Srba u Vojvodini (Annual Customs of the Serbs in Vojvodina).* Novi Sad: Muzej Vojvodine, 1996.

Bossers, G. Th. M., "Congenital Anomalies of the Hip Joint" in Huffstadt, A.J.C., ed. *Congenital Malformations.* Princeton: Excerpta Medica, 1980.

Bowlby, John. "The Making and Breaking of Affectional Bonds." *British Journal of Psychiatry* 130 (1977): 201–10.

Bradshaw's Overland Guide, 1902. Manchester: Bradshaw & Blacklock, 1902.

Brian, Denis. *Einstein: A Life.* New York: John Wiley, 1996.

Brittain, Vera. *Testament of Youth: An Autobiographical Study of the Years 1900–1925.* London: Victor Gollancz, 1933.

Brodzinsky, David, and Schechter, Marshall D., eds. *The Psychology of Adoption.* New York: Oxford University Press, 1990.

Brown, Alec. *Yugoslav Life and Landscape.* London: Elek, 1955.

Brown, Mabel Webster. *Neuropsychiatry and the War.* New York: War Work Committee, The National Committee for Mental Hygiene, 1918.

Bucky, Peter A. *The Private Albert Einstein*. Kansas City, Missouri; Andrews and McMeel, 1992.

Budke, Petra. *Schriftstellerinnen in Berlin, 1871 bis 1945: ein Lexikon zu Leben und Werk*. Berlin: Orlanda Frauenverlag, c. 1995.

von Bunge, Gustav. *Alkoholismus und Degeneration: die Abstinenz-gessellschaft der Berner nüchternen Menschen*. "Alcoholism and Degeneration." Lecture given for the Abstinence Society of the Sober People of Berne, January 1904.

Bunović, Dragutin; Protić, Žarko; and Vasić, Lazar. *Dobro dosliu Novi Sad* (Welcome to Novi Sad). Trans. Jelena Dejanović-Rebić. Novi Sad: Forum, 1990.

Cajkanović, Veselin. *Rečnik srpskih narodnih verovanja o biljkama (Dictionary of Serbian Plant Lore)*. Beograd: Srpska akademija nauka i umetnosti, Srpska književna zadruga, 1985.

Canfield, Dorothy. *Home Fires in France*. New York: Henry Holt, 1918.

Carter, C. O. *The Inheritance of Common Congenital Malformations. Medical Genetics*, vol. 4. New York: Grune and Stratton, 1965.

Chemicalage Directory, Who's Who. London: Benn Brolkers, 1963.

Clark, M. E. *Paris Waits*. London: Smith, Elder, 1915.

Clark, Ronald W. *Einstein: The Life and Times*. New York: World Publishing, 1971.

Čolović, Ivan. *Divlja književnost: etnolingvistiĉko prouĉavanje paraliterature (Literature, Epitaphs, Obituaries, Folk Songs)*. Beograd: Nolit, 1984.

Conrad, Joseph. "Magic Charms and Healing Rituals in Contemporary Yugoslavia." *Southern Europe* 10 (1983): 99–120.

Cookridge, E. H. *Orient Express: The Life and Times of the World's Most Famous Train*. New York: Random House, 1978.

Co-operative Reconstruction: A Report of the Work Accomplished in Serbia. Serbian Child Welfare Association of America: New York, c1924.

Cook's Continental Time Tables, 1901. London: Thomas Cook & Son, 1901.

Čurčija-Prodanović, Nada. *Heroes of Serbia*. London: Oxford University Press, 1963.

Czeizel, A., M.D., and Tusnády, G., C.Sc. *Isolated Common Congenital Abnormalities in Hungary*. Budapest: Akadémiai Kiadó, 1984.

Dabizić, Miodrag. *Staro jezgro Zemuna (The Old Nucleus of Zemun)*. Zemun: Štamparija "Sava Mihić," 1967.

Djilas, Milovan. *Memoir of a Revolutionary*. New York: Harcourt Brace Jovanovich, 1973.

Djordjević, Tihomir. *Deca u verovanjima i obiĉajima našega naroda (Children in the Beliefs and Customs of Our People.)* Beograd: Idea, 1990.

————. *Veštica i vila u našem narodnom verovanju i predanju (The Witch and the Fairy in the Lore of Our People)*. Beograd: Narodna biblioteka Srbije, 1989.

Djurić, Antonije. *Žene—Solunci govore (World War One: The Saloniki Women Veterans Speak)*. Beograd: NIRO "Književne novine," 1987.

Djurić-Milojković, Jelena. *Tradition and Avant-Garde: Literature and Art in Serbian Culture: 1900–1918*. New York: East European Monographs, 1988.

Dordević, Vladimir, R. *Ogled srpske muziĉke bibliografije do 1914 (Serbian Music Bibliography Until 1914)*. Beograd: Nolit, 1969.

Dudić, Nikola. *Stara groblja i nadgrobni belezi u Srbiji (Old Graveyards and Gravestones in Serbia)*. Beograd: Republicki zavod za zaštitu spomenika kulture, 1995.

Dundes, Alan. *Essays in Folklore Theory and Method*. Madras: Cre-A, 1990.

————. *Parsing Through Customs: Essays by a Freudian Folklorist*. New York: Garland, 1981.

————. *Interpreting Folklore*. Madison: University of Wisconsin Press, 1987.

Durham, Mary E. *Through the Land of the Serbs*. London: Edward Arnold, 1904.

Durrell, Lawrence. *White Eagles Over Serbia*. New York: Arcade, 1957.

Eastman, Nicholson J., and Hellman, Louis M. *Williams Obstetrics, 13th Edition*. New York: Appleton-Century-Crofts, 1961.

von Eckardt, Wolf, and Gulman, Sander, L. *Bertolt Brecht's Berlin*. Lincoln: University of Nebraska Press, 1993.

Einstein-Roboz, Elizabeth. *Hans Albert Einstein: Reminiscences of His Life and Our Life Together*. Iowa City: Iowa Institute of Hydraulic Research, 1991.

Einstein-Winteler, Maja. *Albert Einstein—a Biographical Sketch*. Excerpted in *The Collected Papers of Albert Einstein* vol. 1.

Epstein, C. J., ed. *The Morphogenesis of Down Syndrome*. New York: Wiley-Liss, 1991.

Explanatory Report on the European Convention on the Adoption of Children. Strasbourg: Council of Europe, 1967.

Farnam, Ruth S. *A Nation at Bay: What an American Woman Saw and Did in Suffering Serbia*. Indianapolis: Bobbs-Merrill, 1918.

Felman, Shoshana, and Laub, Dori, M.D. *Testimony: Crises of Witnessing in Literature, Psychoanalysis, and History*. New York: Routledge, 1992.

Fermi, Laura. *Illustrious Immigrants: The Intellectual Migration from Europe, 1930–41*. Chicago: The University of Chicago Press, 1971.

Filipović, Milenko, S. *Among the People, Native Yugoslav Ethnography: Selected Writing of Milenko S. Filipovic*. Ed. E. A. Hammel. Ann Arbor: Michigan Slavic Publications, Department of Slavic Languages and Literatures, c. 1982.

————. "Symbolic Adoption Among the Serbs." *Ethnology Journal* 4 (Jan. 1965): 66–71.

Flückiger, Max. *Albert Einstein and Switzerland*. Bern: Albert Einstein-Gesellschaft, 1991.

Fölsing, Albrecht, trans. Osers, Ewald. *Albert Einstein: A Biography*. New York: Viking, 1997.

Footman, David. *Balkan Holiday*. London: Heinemann, 1935.

Forel, Auguste. Trans. H. W. Armit. *Hypnotism; or, Suggestion and Psychotherapy: A Study of the Psychological, Psycho-Physiological and Therapeutic Aspects of Hypnotism*. London: Rebman, 1906.

————. *The Sexual Question: A Scientific, Psychological, Hygienic and Sociological Study*. New York: Rebman, 1908.

————. *Die sexuelle Frage. Eine naturwissenschaftliche, psychologische, hygienische und soziologische Studie für Gebildete*. Munchen: Reinhardt, 1905.

Frank, Philipp. *Einstein: His Life and Times*. New York: Knopf, 1947.

Freidenreich, Harriet Pass. *The Jews of Yugoslavia.* Philadelphia: The Jewish Publications Society of America, 1979.

Frenzel, Herbert A., and Moser, Hans Joachim. *Kurschners biographisches Theater-Handbuch: Schauspiel, Oper, Film, Rundfunk, Deutschland, Osterreich, Schweiz (Kurschner's Biographical Theatre Handbook: Theatre, Opera, Film, Radio in Germany, Austria, Switzerland).* Berlin: Gruyter, 1956.

Freud, Sigmund. *Totem and Taboo.* New York: Vintage, 1946.

Friedrich, Otto. *Before the Deluge.* New York: Harperperennial Library, 1995.

Fussell, Paul. *The Great War and Modern Memory.* London: Oxford University Press, 1977.

Gilbert, Sandra. "Soldier's Heart: Literary Men, Literary Women and the Great War." *Signs: Journal of Women in Culture and Society* 8 (3) (1983): 422–50.

Goldstein, Slavko, ed. *Jews in Yugoslavia.* Trans. Mira Vlatković and Sonja Wild-Bićanić. Zagreb: Muzejski prostor, 1989.

Green, Neil E., *Skeletal Trauma in Children.* Philadelphia: Saunders, 1994.

Guide Internationale de la Compagnie Internationale des Wagons-Lits et des Grands Express Européans (International Guide of the International Wagon-Lit and European Grand Express Company). Paris: CIWL, 1903.

Hagen, Randi L., and Kahn, Arnold. "Discrimination Against Competent Women." *Journal of Applied Social Psychology* 5, 4 (1975): 362–76.

Halpern-Kerewsky, Barbara. "Genealogy as Oral Genre in a Serbian Village." *Oral Tradition in Literature,* 301–21.

———. "Watch Out for Snakes! Ethnosemantic Misinterpretations and Interpretation of a Serbian Healing Charm." *Anthropological Linguistics* 25, (Fall 1983): 309–25.

———. "The Power of the Word: Healing Charms as an Oral Genre." *Journal of American Folklore* 91 (Oct.–Dec. 1978): 903–24.

Halpern, Joel, and Halpern-Kerewsky, Barbara. *A Serbian Village in Historical Perspective.* New York: Holt, Rinehart and Winston, 1972.

Halpern, Joel M. *Family in Transition: A Study of 300 Yugoslav Villages.* Princeton: Princeton University Press, 1966.

Heilbron, J. L., and Wheaton, Bruce R. *Literature on the History of Physics in the 20th Century.* Berkeley: Office for History of Science and Technology, 1981.

Herneck, Friedrich. *Einstein privat, Herta Waldow erinnert sich an die Jahre 1927 bis 1933 (Einstein in Private: Herta Waldow Recalls the Years 1927 to 1933).* Berlin: Buchverlag, Der Morgen, 1978.

Highfield, Roger, and Carter, Paul. *The Private Lives of Albert Einstein.* New York: St. Martin's Press, 1993.

Hillgruber, Andreas. *Germany and the Two World Wars.* Cambridge, MA: Harvard University Press, 1981.

Hoffmann, Banesh, with Helen Dukas. *Albert Einstein: Creator and Rebel.* New York: New American Library, 1972.

Hogg, Garry. *Orient Express: The Birth, Life and Death of a Great Train.* New York: Walker and Company.

Holmes, L. B., et al. *Mental Retardation: An Atlas of Diseases with Associated Physical Abnormalities.* New York: Macmillan, 1972.

Holton, Gerald. *Einstein, History, and Other Passions.* Woodbury, New York: American Institute of Physics, 1995.

————. "Of Love, Physics and Other Passions: The Letters of Albert and Mileva, Part One and Two." *Physics Today* (August 1994): 23–29, 37–43.

Horecky, Paul L. *East Central and Southeast Europe: A Handbook of Library and Archival Resources in North America.* Los Angeles, California: Clio Press, c1976.

Hronika jedneljubari (The Chronicle of a Love Story). Pogledi Magazine, January 1944.

Huffstadt, A.J.C. *Congenital Malformations.* Amsterdam: Excerpta Medica, 1980.

Hufton, Olwen. *The Prospect Before Her: A History of Women in Western Europe.* New York: HarperCollins, 1995.

Huston, Nancy. "Tales of War and Tears of Women." *Women's Studies International Forum* 5 (3/4) (1982): 271–82.

Illy, József. "Albert Einstein in Prague." *Isis* 70 (252) (1979): 76–84.

Imrey, Ferenc. *Through Blood and Ice.* New York: Dutton, 1930.

Janković, Barbara Velman. *Dungeon.* Belgrade: Dereta, 1996.

Jelavich, Barbara. *History of the Balkans, Twentieth Century.* Cambridge: Cambridge University Press, 1995.

Jerković, Vera, ed. *Cirilske rukopisne knjige Biblioteke Matice srpske (Cyrillic Manuscript Books of the Matica Srpska Library).* Novi Sad: Biblioteka Matice srpske, 1991.

Jerrold, Walter. *The Danube.* New York: Frederick A. Stokes, 1947.

Jones, Ernest. *The Life and Works of Sigmund Freud,* vols. 2 and 3. New York: Basic Books, 1953.

Josephs, Jeremy. *Swastika Over Paris.* New York: Little, Brown, 1989.

Kantha, Sachi Sri. *An Einstein Dictionary.* Westport, CT: Greenwood Press, 1996.

Karadžić, Vuk Stefanović. *Narodne Poslovice (Folk Proverbs).* Belgrade: Državna Štamparija Kraljevine Jugoslavije, 1933.

————. *Život i običaji naroda srpskog (The Life and Customs of the Serb People).* Vienna, 1867.

Kemp, P. *Healing Ritual. Studies in the Technique and Tradition of the Southern Slavs.* London: Faber and Faber, 1935.

Kirk, H. Davis. *Shared Fate: A Theory of Adoption and Mental Health.* London: Free Press of Glencoe, 1964.

Kiš, Danilo. *The Encyclopedia of the Dead.* New York: Penguin, 1989.

————. *Garden, Ashes.* New York: Harcourt Brace Jovanovich, 1975.

Klein, Martin, J., Kox, A. J., and Schulmann, Robert, eds. *The Collected Papers of Albert Einstein, Volume Five: The Swiss Years: Correspondence, 1902–1914.* trans. Dr. Anna Beck; Don Howard, consultant. Princeton: Princeton University Press, 1993.

Kmietowicz, Frank A. *Slavic Mythical Beliefs.* Windsor, Ontario: F. Kmietowicz, 1982.

Konstantinov, Miloš. *Prilozi i publikacije archivarskih radnika Jugoslavije (Contributions and Publications of Archivists in Yugoslavia).* Sremski Karlovci: Archiv Vojvodine.

Konstantinović, Nikola. *Selo Beogradskog pašaluka do polovine XVII veka: feudalna privreda, privreda neposrednih proizvodjača, život na selu (The Village in the Beograd Province Up to the Mid-Seventeenth Century: Feudal Economy, and Economy of the Direct Producers, and Life in the Village).* Beograd: M. St. Duricić, 1969.

Koonz, Claudia. *Mothers in the Fatherland: Women, the Family and Nazi Politics.* New York: St. Martin's Press, 1987.

Košutić, Slavko, ed. *Novi Sad Through Memories of Old Post Cards.* Novi Sad: Futuro, 1996.

Krlĕza, Miroslav. *The Return of Philip Latinowicz.* Evanston, IL: Northwestern University Press, 1995.

————. *On the Edge of Reason.* London: Quarter Encounters, 1987.

Krstić, Djordje. "The Wishes of Dr. Einstein." *Dnevnik* 28 (9) (1974).

————. *The Education of Mileva Marić Einstein: The First Woman Theoretical Physicist at the Royal Classical High School in Zagreb at the End of the Century. Collected Papers on the History of Education,* 9: 111, 1975.

————. *Prva teoretska fizičarka na svetu (The First Woman Theoretical Physicist of the World).* Belgrade: Dnevnik, 1978.

Kultura tradycyjna w zyciu wspolczesnej rodziny wiejskiej: z polskich i serbskich baden etnologicznych (Traditional Culture in the Life of Poles and Serbs). Poznan: Wydawn. Nauk. Uniwersytetu im. Adama Mickiewicza w Poznaniu, 1986.

Laffan, R. G. D., C. F. *The Serbs: The Guardians of the Gate.* New York: Dorset Press, 1989.

Lampe, John R. *Modernization and Social Structure: The Case of the Pre-1914 Balkan Capitals.* Southeastern Europe / L'Europe du Sud-Est (1979): 11–32.

Larsen, Steen, F. "Remembering Without Experience: Memory for Reported Events," in *Remembering Reconsidered: Ecological and Traditional Approaches to the Study of Memory.* Neisser, Ulrich and Winograd, Eugene. Cambridge: Cambridge University Press, 1988.

Lazarovich-Hrebelianovich, Prince, with Princess Lazarovich-Hrebelianovich (Eleanor Calhoun). *Servian People: Their Past and Their Destiny.* New York: Scribner's, 1910.

Leimbach, Berthold. *Tondokumente der Kleinkunst und ihre Interpreten, 1889–1945 (Sound Documents from Cabarets and Their Interpreters in Germany, 1889–1945).* Gottingen: Hubert, 1991.

Lessner, Erwin. *The Danube: The Dramatic History of the Great River and the People Touched by its Flow.* New York: Doubleday, 1961.

Lewanski, Richard. *The Slavic Literatures.* New York: F. Ungar, 1967.

Lifton, Betty Jean. *Journey of the Adopted Self: A Quest for Wholeness.* New York: Basic Books, 1994.

Lodge, Olive. *Peasant Life in Jugoslavia.* London: Seeley, Service & Co., 1941.

Lukas, John. *Budapest: A Historical Portrait of a City and Its Culture.* London: Weidenfeld & Nicolson, 1988.

Macure, Miloš. *Problemi politike obnavljanja stanovništva u Srbiji (Migration, Demography, Population).* Beograd: Srpska akademija nauka, 1989.

Magyar Szó, Jewish Hungarian newspaper, Novi Sad.

Maksimović, Desanka. *Greetings from the Old Country.* Toronto: Yugo-Slavia Publishers, 1976.

Marianoff, Dimitri, with Wayne, Palma. *Einstein: An Intimate Study of a Great Man.* New York: Doubleday, 1944.

Marković, Laza. *Reč nad otvorenim grobom (A Word Before an Open Grave).* Novi Sad: Braća M. Popović, 1904.

————. *Books for the People. Marriage: Or How Will a Nation Achieve Good Progeny?* Volume 149. Novi Sad: Matica srpska, printed by Djordje Ivković, 1913.

Marković, Zivko, *Symposium Mileva Marić Einstein.* Paper presented October, 1995, in Novi Sad, Yugoslavia.

————. *Novosadjani o Milevi Marić-Ajnštajn (The Novi Sad People on Mileva Marić-Einstein).* Belgrade: Dnevnik, 1996.

Markstein, George. *Chance Awakening.* New York: Ballantine, 1977.

————. *The Cooler.* London: Pan, 1975.

————. *Ferret.* New York: Ballantine, 1983.

————. *The Goering Testament.* London: Pan, 1979.

————. *The Man From Yesterday.* London: Pan, 1977.

————. *Soul Hunters.* London: New English Library/Hodder and Stoughton, 1987.

————. *Tara Kane.* New York: Dell, 1979.

————. *Traitor for a Cause.* London: The Bodley Head, 1979.

————. *Ultimate Issue.* New York: Ballantine, 1982.

Marshall, S.L.A. *World War I.* Boston: Houghton Mifflin, 1964.

Massie, Robert K. *The Romanovs: The Final Chapter.* New York: Ballantine, 1995.

Mathieu, W. A. *The Musical Life.* Boston: Shambhala, 1994.

Maticki, Miodrag. *Bibliografija srpskih almanaha i kalendara (Bibliography of Serbian Almanacs and Calendars).* Beograd: Republički zavod za zaštitu spomenika kulture, 1995.

Mayer, Gyula. *Budapest Anno . . .* Text: Mesterházi Lajos, 1979.

Mayo, Hope, ed. and trans. *The Einstein Family Correspondence, Including the Albert Einstein–Mileva Marič Love Letters.* New York: Christie's, 1996.

McConkey, James, ed. *The Anatomy of Memory.* New York: Oxford University Press, 1996.

McCagg, William O. *A History of the Habsburg Jews: 1670–1918.* Bloomington: Indiana University Press, 1989.

Medicus, Heinrich A. "The Friendship Among Three Singular Men: Einstein and His Friends Besso and Zangger." *Isis* 85 (1994): 456–78.

Meichle, Adolf W. *Albert Einstein's Years in Berne: 1902–1909.* Berne: Albert Einstein-Gesellschaft, 1993.

Melina, Lois Ruskai. *Adoption: An Annotated Bibliography and Guide.* New York: Garland, 1987.

Mendelsohn, Ezra. *The Jews of East Central Europe: Between the World Wars.* Bloomington: Indiana University Press, 1987.

Merck Manual, 1901. New York: Merck, 1901.

Metcalf, Walter Bradford. *Tuberculosis of the Lymphatic System.* New York: 1919.

Michelmore, Peter. *Einstein, Profile of a Man.* New York: Dodd, Mead, 1962.

Mieder, Wolfgang, and Dundes, Alan. *The Wisdom of Many: Essays on the Proverb.* New York: Garland, 1981.

Mihailović, Todor. *Raonička buna (Peasant Uprisings, Land Tenure, 1804–1918).* Beograd: Ljubodrag T. Mihailović, 1970.

Mijatović, Čedomir. *A Royal Tragedy: Being the Story of the Assassination of Alexander and Queen Draga of Servia.* New York: Dodd, 1907.

Mikić, Petar, G. *Zapisi o radjanju i umiranju dece u Novom Sadu i Vojvodini tokom XIXi XX reka (On Birthrate and Mortality of Children in Vojvodina in the 19th and 20th Centuries).* Novi Sad: Matica srpska, 1989.

Milich, Zorka. *A Stranger's Supper.* New York: Twayne, 1995.

Misailović, Milenko. *Mudrost narodnog humora (The Wisdom of Folk Humor).* Titovo Užice: Vesti, 1987.

Morris, Joseph, E. *Beautiful Europe: The Lake of Como.* London: A. & C. Black, 1919.

Mügge, M. A. *Serbian Folk Songs, Fairy Tales and Proverbs.* London: Dranes, 1916.

Neisser, Ulric, and Winograd, Eugene. *Remembering Reconsidered: Ecological and Traditional Approaches to the Study of Memory.* Cambridge: Cambridge University Press, 1988.

Nenin, Milivoj. *Stefanovićevo "Biti il' ne biti."* Pokušaj biografije *(Stefanović's "To Be or Not to Be": An Attempt at Biography).* Novi Sad: Svetovi, 1993.

———. *Epistolarna biografija Svetislava Stefanovića (The Epistolary Biography of Svetislav Stefanović).* Novi Sad: Matica srpska. 1987.

———. *Svetislav Stefanović: Preteča modernizma (Svetislav Stefanović: The Forerunner of Modernism).* Novi Sad: Svetovi, 1985.

Neu, R. L. "D-D Translocation in a Boy with Mental Retardation and Congenital Dislocation of the Hip." *Ann. Genet.* 12, pp. 250–265.

Niles, Reg. *Adoption Agencies, Orphanages and Maternity Homes: An Historical Directory.* Garden City, NY: Phileas Deigh, 1981.

Nyegosh, Petar Petrovitch. *The Mountain Wreath.* London: George Allen & Unwin, 1930.

Otović, Vladmir. *Manastir Grgeteg (Eastern Orthodox Monasteries).* Novi Sad: Matica Srpska, 1990.

Pais, Abraham. *Einstein Lived Here.* New York: Oxford University Press, 1994.

———. *"Subtle Is the Lord . . ." The Science and the Life of Albert Einstein.* New York: Oxford University Press, 1982.

Pavlovich, Paul. *The History of the Serbian Orthodox Church.* Toronto: Serbian Heritage Books, 1989.

P.E.N. *Schriftstellerlexikon, Bundesrepublik Deutschland (The Writers Encyclopedia, German Federal Republic).* Munich: Piper, c. 1982.

Performed Readings and Plays by Writers from Croatia, Macedonia, Slovenia, Serbia and Montenegro. Belgrade: Tricycle Theater, August 1993.

Perrault, Gilles. *Paris Under the Occupation.* London: A. Deutsch, 1989.

Perutz, M. F. "A Passion for Science." *New York Review of Books* (20 February 1997): 39.

Petranović, Anka. *Fondovi i zbirke Archiva Srbije (Archives of Serbia.)* Beograd: Archiv Srbije, 1967.

Petrovich, Michael Boro. *A History of Modern Serbia, 1804–1918.* New York: Harcourt Brace Jovanovich, 1976.

Petrovitch, Woislav M. *Serbia: Her People, History and Aspirations.* London: George G. Harrap, 1915.

————. *Hero Tales and Legends of the Serbians.* New York: Farrar & Rinehart, and London: George G. Harrap, 1914.

Plesch, János. *János, The Story of a Doctor.* Trans. Edward Fitzgerald. London: Victor Gollancz Ltd., 1947.

Plesch, János, and Plesch, Peter H. *Some Reminiscences of Albert Einstein.* The Royal Society, London, 49 (2) (1995): 303–28.

Poderegin, Milka Bajić, *The Dawning.* New York: Interlink Books, 1995.

Popov, Dr. Dušan, ed. *Enciklopedija Novog Sada,* vol. 2. Novi Sad: Novosadski Klub, Prometej, 1994.

————. *The Autonomous Province of Vojvodina Yesterday and Today.* Novi Sad Office of Information, 1965.

————. *Vojvodina, Socialist Autonomous Province.* Trans. Madge Phillips-Tomasević. Beograd: Jugoslovenska revija, 1980.

Popović, Milan, ed. *A Friendship: Letters Between Mileva and Albert Einstein and Helene Savić.* Montenegro: CIP Podgorica, 1998.

Popović, Nikola B. *Ilustrovana istorija Srba (Illustrated History of the Serbs).* Beograd: Litera, 1991.

Pore, Renate. *A Conflict of Interest: Women in German Social Democracy, 1919–1933.* Westport, CT: Greenwood Press, 1981.

Prokop, Ana. *Porodično pravo: usvojenje (Family: Law Adoption in Yugoslavia).* Zagreb: Pravna biblioteka, 1970.

Prokschi, Rudolf. *Ein neuer Aufbruch bei den Nonnen in der Serbischen Orthodoxen Kirche im 20. Jahrhundert (A New Beginning of the Nuns in the Serbian Orthodox Church in the 20th Century).* Würzburg: Augustinus-Verlag, 1996.

Pupin, Michael I. *From Immigrant to Inventor.* New York: Scribner's, 1960.

Pupin, Michael Idvorsky. *Serbian Orthodox Church.* London: John Murray, 1918.

Pyenson, Lewis. *Einstein's Natural Daughter.* Science History Publications, History of Science, xxviii 1990.

————. *The Young Einstein: The Advent of Relativity.* Bristol and Boston: Adam Hilger, 1985.

Rafalovich, S. "The Relationship of Parents of a Child with a Congenital Defect." *Reconstruction Surgery Trauma* 14 (154) (1974).

Rajković, Zorica. *Traditional Forms of Common-Law Marriage Among the Croats and the Serbs in the Light of the Concept of "Trial Marriage."* Trans. Vladimir Ivir. Zagreb: Istitut za narodnu umjetnost, 1975.

Raleigh, Donald J. *Revolution on the Volga: 1917 in Saratov.* Ithaca: Cornell University Press, 1986.

Read, Anthony, and Fisher, David. *Berlin: The Biography of a City.* London: Pimlico, 1994.

Reiser, Anton. *Albert Einstein: A Biographical Portrait.* New York: Albert & Charles Boni, 1930.

Renn, Jürgen, and Schulmann, Robert, eds. *Albert Einstein/Mileva Marić, The Love Letters.* Shawn Smith, trans. Princeton: Princeton University Press, 1992.

Reznikoff, Charles, and Engleman, U. Z. *Jews of Charleston.* Philadelphia: Jewish Publication Society, 1950.

Ribarić, Julka Radauš. *Yugoslavian/Croatian Embroidery: Design and Techniques.* New York: Van Nostrand Reinhold, 1979.

Richards, Gerald, I. D. "Fetal and Infant Mortality Associated with Congenital Malformations." *British Journal of Medicine,* 27 (1973): 85–90.

Robinson, George W. "Birth Characteristics of Children with Congenital Dislocation of the Hip." *American Journal of Epidemiology* 87 (2) (1968).

Roeder, Helen. *Saints and Their Attributes: With a Guide to Localities and Patronage.* London: Longmans, Green, 1955.

Rubin, David C. *Memory in Oral Traditions.* New York: Oxford University Press, 1995.

Ružić, Nikanor. *Tablice raznovrsnih primera srodstva (Ružić Family History).* Beograd: Kraljevsko-srpskó državna štampariji, 1816.

Sarvan, M. "Rana Smrtnost Odojčadi" ("Early Death Among Infants"). First Congress of Doctors in the Federative People's Republic of Yugoslavia, Belgrade, 1949.

Šaulić, J. "The Oral Women Poets of the Serbs." Trans. Alec Brown. *Slavonic and East European Review* 42 (Dec. 1963): 161–83.

St. Erlich, Vera. *Family in Transition: A Study of 300 Yugoslav Villages.* Princeton: Princeton University Press, 1966.

Samilson, Robert L.; Tsou, Paul; Aamoth, Gordon; Green, William M. "Dislocation and Subluxation of the Hip in Cerebral Palsy." *Journal of Bone and Joint Surgery,* 54A (4) (June 1972).

Schuder, Werner, ed. *Kürschner Deutscher Literatur—Kalender Nekrolog 1936–1970.* Berlin: Walter de Gruyter, 1973.

Schulmann, Robert, Kox, A. J., Janssen, Michel, Józes, Illy, eds. *The Collected Papers of Albert Einstein. Volume Eight. The Berlin Years: Correspondence, 1914–1918.* Ann M. Hentschel, trans. Klaus Hentschel, consultant. Princeton: Princeton University Press, 1998.

Sekulić, Ante. *Bački Hrvati—Bačka Croats.* Zagreb: Jugoslavenskalić, 1989.

Seelig, Carl. *Albert Einstein: A Documentary Biography.* Trans. Mervyn Savill. London: Staples Press, 1956.

Seitel, Peter. "Proverbs: A Social Use of Metaphor." In *The Wisdom of Many: Essays on the Proverbs.* Mieder, Wolfgang, and Dundes, Alan, eds. New York: Garland, 1981.

Senz, Josef Volkmar. *Totenbuch der Apatiner Gemeinschaft (Death Registry in Apatin).* Straubing: Apatiner Gemeinschaft, 1980.

700 godina medicine u Srba (700 Years of Medicine of the Serbs). Beograd: Srpska akademija nauka i umetnosti, 1971.

Shirer, William. *Berlin Diary: The Journal of a Foreign Correspondent, 1934–1941*. New York: Galahad Books, 1995.

Skrivanić, Gavro, A. *Putevi u srednjovekovnoj Srbiji (Roads in the Middle Ages in Serbia)*. Zemun: Štamparija "Sava Mihić," 1967.

Slack, Nancy G. and Pnina, G. A. *Creative Couples in the Sciences*. New Brunswick, NJ: Rutgers University Press, 1994.

Smith, I. Evelyn, ed. *Readings in Adoption*. New York: Philosophical Library, 1963.

Solovine, Maurice. *Letters to Solovine: Albert Einstein*. New York: Citadel Press, 1993.

Sorić, A. *Jews in Yugoslavia*. Trans. Mira Vlatković. Zagreb: MGC, 1989.

Šosberger, Pavle. *Novosadski Jevreji: iz istorije zajednice u Novom Sadu (The History of the Jewish Community in Novi Sad)*. Novi Sad: Književna zajednica Novog Sada, 1988.

Specter, Michael. "Einstein's Son? It's a Question of Relativity." *The New York Times*, 22 July 1995. Section A, p. 1.

Spence, Donald, P. "Passive Remembering." In *Remembering Reconsidered: Ecological and Traditional Approaches to the Study of Memory*. Neisser, Ulrich, and Winograd, Eugene, eds. Cambridge: Cambridge University Press, 1988.

Speziali, Pierre, ed. *Albert Einstein–Michele Besso Correspondence, 1903–1935*. Paris: Hermann, 1972.

Stachel, John, ed. *The Collected Papers of Albert Einstein. Volume One. The Early Years: 1879–1902*. Trans. Dr. Anna Beck; Peter Havas, consultant. Princeton: Princeton University Press, 1987.

—————. "The Scientific Relationship of Albert Einstein and Mileva Marić." Paper prepared for the Symposium on "Creative Couples and Gender Complementarity: Cross-disciplinary Perspectives," at the 1991 Annual Meeting of the AAAS, Washington, D.C., 15 February 1991.

—————. "Einstein and Ether Drift Experiments." *American Institute of Physics* (May 1997): 45–7.

Stader, Stefan. *Ortssippenbuch der Katholischen Pfarrgemeinde Jahrmarkt im Banat (Catholic Genealogy Register of the Banat)*. [Kaiserslautern: S. N.] 1985.

Stead, Alfred, ed. *Servian by the Servians*. London: Heinemann, 1909.

Stefanović, Josif. *Žrtve fašizma (World War, 1939–1945: Victims of Fascism)*. Leskovac: Josif Stefanović, 1970.

Stefanović, Pavle. *Eseji. Strofe i Ritmovi: 1912–1919 (Essays. A Collection of Essays and Poems: 1912–1919)*. Belgrade: Nolit. 1982.

Stein (Stern), Lola. *Lotti: eines Mannes Leidenschaft (Lotto: A Man's Passion)*. Leipzig-Stö: Stern Bücher Verlag, 1923.

—————. *People Like You and Me*. London: Lindsay Drummond, 1946.

—————. *Des Meisters Gefährtin (The Master's Mate)*. Berlin, Siwinna, 1919.

Stoianovich, Traian *A Study in Balkan Civilization*. New York: Knopf, 1967.

Strauss, Herbert A. and Möller, Horst. *International Biographical Dictionary of Central European Emigrés 1933–1945*. New York: K. G. Saur, 1983.

Stretenović, Miša. "The Love Between a Famous Scientist, Albert Einstein, and a Serbian, Mileva Marić." *Vreme* (23 May 1929).

Sulzberger, C. L. *A Long Row of Candles: Memoirs and Diaries, 1934–1954.* New York: Macmillan, 1969.

Tanić, Zivan. *Seljaci na evropskim raskrsnicama: analiza ekonomskih migracijie ("Peasants at European Crossroads: An Analysis of Economic Migration").* Beograd: Institut drustvenih nauka, 1974.

Tausanović, Olivera. *Istorijski Arhiv Beograda (Bibliographical References and Indexes).* Belgrade: Istorijski arhiv Beograda, 1984–81.

Taylor, A.J.P. *The First World War.* New York: G. P. Putnam's Sons, 1970.

Thurstan, Violetta. *Field Hospital and Flying Column.* New York: G. P. Putnam's Sons, 1915.

Tišma, Aleksandar. *The Use of Man.* New York: Harcourt Brace Jovanovich, 1988.

Todorova, Maria. *Imagining the Balkans.* New York: Oxford University Press, 1997.

Todorović, Kosta. *Golgota i vaskrs Srbije 1916–1918 (World War, 1914–1918, Personal Narratives, Serbian).* Beograd: Beogradski izdavačko-grafički zavod, 1971.

Trbuhović-Gjurić, Desanka. *U senci Alberta Ajnštajna.* Kruševac: Bagdala, 1969. trans. Karlo Baranj, copyright Alan Adelson.

Troemel-Ploetz, Senta, Ph.D. *"Mileva Marić: The Woman Who Did Einstein's Mathematics."* Women's Studies International Forum 13 (5) 1990: 415–32.

Trojanović, Sima. *Psihofizičko izražavanje srpskog naroda poglavito bez reči (Psychological mode of expression, mainly nonverbal, of the Serb people).* Beograd: Prosveta, 1986.

Tsernianski, Miloš. *Migrations.* New York: Harcourt Brace, 1994.

Turner, Ann Warren. *Rituals of Birth: From Prehistory to the Present.* New York: D. McKay, 1978.

Univerzitet u Novom Sadu. *Zbornik sa savetovanja: Doprinos Mileve Ajnštajn Marić nauci* (University of Novi Sad. *The Contribution of Mileva Marić Einstein to Science).* 1978.

Vallentin, Antonina. *The Drama of Albert Einstein.* Garden City, NY: Doubleday, 1954.

Velimirović, The Reverend Father Nicholai. *Serbia in Light and Darkness.* New York: Longmans, Green, 1916.

Visser, Jan. *Functional Treatment of Congenital Dislocation of the Hip.* Copenhagen: Munksgaard, 1984.

Vlahović, Mitar, S. *National Costumes of Serbia in the Ethnographic Museum in Belgrade.* Belgrade: "Jugoslavia," 1954.

Vujicic, Mil. *Recnik mesta u oslobodenoj oblasti Stare Srbije: po sluzbenim podacima (Directories, Historical and Geographical Material About the Cities and Towns).* Beograd: U Državna Štamparija Kraljevine Srbije, 1914.

Vukanović, T. P. *Narodne tužbalice: folkorna gradja sabrana u Srba poreklom iz Crne Core na Kosovu i Kosanici (Laments of the Serbs of Montenegro, Origins in Kosovo and Kosanica).* Vranje: Narodni muzej, 1972.

————. *Rečnik mesta u oslobodjenoj oblasti Stare Srbije: po službenim podacima (Directory of Cities and Towns in the Liberated Part of Old Serbia).* Belgrade: Državna Štamparija Kraljevine Srbije, 1914.

Warrington, E. K., and Sanders, H. I. "The Fate of Old Memories." *Quarterly Journal of Experimental Psychology,* 23:432–42.

Webster, Jancar Barbara. *Women and Revolution in Yugoslavia: 1941–1945.* Denver, Colorado Arden, 1990.

Weinreb, Maxine L. *The Psychological Experience of Women Who Surrender Babies for Adoption.* Thesis, Boston University, 1991.

Weizmann, Vera. *The Impossible Takes Longer.* London: Hamilton, 1967.

Wenger, William. *Eisenbahnen der Welt (Railroads of the World).* Lausanne: Mondo Editions, 1969.

West, Rebecca. *Black Lamb and Grey Falcon.* New York: Penguin, 1969.

Wheaton, Bruce. *Inventory of Sources for History of Twentieth-Century Physics.* Stuttgart: Verlag für Geschichte der Naturwissenschaften und der Technik, 1992.

————. *An Inventory of Published Letters to and from Physicists, 1900–1950.* Berkeley: Office for the History of Science and Technology, 1982.

————. *Catalogue of the Paul Ehrenfest Archive at the Museum Boerhaave.* Leiden: Museum Boerhaave, 1977.

Whitrow, G. J., ed. *Einstein: The Man and His Achievement.* New York: Dover, 1973.

Wiles, J. W. *Serbian Songs and Poems: Chords of the Yugoslav Harp.* London: George Allen & Unwin, 1918.

Wilson, Francesca M. *Portraits and Sketches of Serbia.* London: Swarthmore Press, 1920.

Wininger, Salomon. *Biographisches Lexikon berühmter Juden aller Zeiten und Länder: ein Nachschlagebuch für das jüdische Volk (Biographical Dictionary of Famous Jews of All Times and All Countries).* Czernowitz: Wininger, 1914.

Wolff, Larry. *Child Abuse in Freud's Vienna: Postcards from the End of the World.* New York: New York University Press, 1995.

Woodtli, Susanna. *Du feminisme a l'égalité politique: un siècle de luttes en Suisse, 1868–1971.* Lausanne: Payot, 1977.

Zarecka-Irwin, Iwona. *Frames of Remembrance; The Dynamics of Collective Memory.* New Brunswick: Transaction Publishers, 1994.

Zastava, list Srpske narodne radikalne stranke (The Newspaper of the Serbian People's Radical Party). 1901, 1902, 1903.

Zečević, Slobodan. *Kult mrtvih kod Srba (The Serbs' Cult of the Dead).* Belgrade: Vuk Karadzić: Etnografski muzej, 1982.

Ženski Svet *(Women's World* magazine*).* Novi Sad, 1901–3.

Acknowledgments

It is with gratitude and pleasure that I thank the following people for reading the myriad incarnations of my manuscript and offering their invaluable advice: Dr. Anna Beck, Christine Brooks, Henry Chalfant, Kathleen Chalfant, Joseph Dispenza, Marija Dokmanović, Miloš Dokmanović, Slavica Dokmanović, Dr. Stefan Elfenbein, Greg Glazner, Dee Ito, Ruth Lopez, Peter Nash, Alan Palmer, Dr. Judit Schulmann, Dr. Marina Stajić, Joan Tewkesbury, Ben Zackheim, and Victoria Zackheim.

    Charlie Ramsburg, my friend and husband, read this book more times than I can count. With love, he offered a clear eye for nonsense, constant grammar corrections, unwavering guidance, and sensitive encouragement. I am eternally grateful.

    After stringing and unstringing words together for five years, it is truly difficult to find the appropriate words to thank my friend and agent, Kathleen Anderson. She has read the manuscript in every manifestation, too many to count, and each time she has delicately suggested new paths toward clarity and resolution. Kathy has spent an extraordinary amount of time listening to me on the telephone from all over the world prattling on about my suppositions, clarifications, and personal anxieties—all the while gently, but firmly, guiding me toward the end of the search and the final version of the book. I embrace her with my gratitude. And I thank my European agent, Danny Baror, for his perseverance, kindness, and wry humor during this venture.

We have never had a direct conversation (although we once bungled through a morning without a translator in bad French), but I know Slavica Dokmanović, and she knows me. We share a kinship for which there is no language. The moment we met it was apparent that there was no need to declare what we believed or what we desired, it was all inherently evident. That first night, we smiled at each other across her table and proceeded as if we had been friends all our lives. I thank Slavica with all my heart for her help, guidance, and patience with this book, and most specifically for her trust and friendship.

From the beginning, my editor at Riverhead Books, Julie Grau, has encouraged me and entrusted me with what she called "an organic book." It took a great deal of patience and flexibility for Julie to stand by the book as, over and over again, it had to be rewritten as the story unfolded. Along with her perseverance, Julie's lyrical editing has not only enhanced the book, but has been an education, too. Her assistant, Hanya Yanagihara, has steadfastly, and with kindness, helped to organize and implement the complexities of guiding this book to press. I also want to thank Gina Anderson, legal counsel for Riverhead, who has kindly and patiently guided me through the labyrinthine tasks of clarifying legal issues and acquiring permissions.

Stefan Elfenbein met me at the train station in Berlin. There was no mistaking him, he towered above the crowd. From the moment I left the train, I was forever running to keep up with his gigantic strides. But that was the only difficult part of our relationship. Stefan began as my German translator and Berlin guide, but soon became my valued colleague. We worked together in Berlin looking for Grete Markstein, finding her, then tracking down her history. Because Stefan is such a fine journalist, his expertise was invaluable—and because Stefan is such a fine person, his friendship is precious.

When I first telephoned Evelyn Einstein and asked if I could interview her, she said, "You don't have to bother with me, Robert Schulmann knows more about my family than I do!" However, I am glad that I bothered with Evelyn. Walking into her home was like walking into a jumble of history. Over a five-year period, we spent many hours together while she guided me firmly past the standard version of the Einstein story, and into a complicated narrative of family strife, where there were no solutions. I value Evelyn's friendship and am grateful that this story brought her into my life.

I would like to extend a special hand of gratitude to Robert Schulmann, director of the Einstein Papers Project, for providing priceless help to me during this project. Over the years he has answered hundreds of questions and helped me to see more clearly the dynamic of the icon, Albert Einstein.

Richard Markstein did not know what hit him when I called him on the telephone. "I found your grandmother, Grete," I told him, and in the same breath, "and I need your permission to get her official records." Richard was unruffled. He leapt into the story with assistance and enthusiasm, and I am forever grateful to him for his confidence.

Vida Ognjenović has written about Mileva Einstein-Marić for the theatre and has unselfishly shared her findings, her musings, and her manuscript, too. Ivana Stefanović has generously and tenaciously assisted me, first from Belgrade, then from Damascus. Her collection of letters and photographs, along with her intuition regarding Serbian motherhood, helped to lead me toward the resolution of Lieserl's life.

I am enormously indebted to the translators who worked on this book. Their translations ranged from complicated legal documents, to obscure books, to personal letters, to handwritten scraps of paper that required a magnifying glass. Dr. Anna Beck, who was the translator for Volumes One through Five of *The Collected Papers of Albert Einstein* (published by Princeton University Press) did a remarkable job of translating from her astonishing range of languages, including Hungarian, German, and Serbo-Croatian. Katalin Thury was my translator in Hungary. Creatively and humorously, she dug our path through the bureaucracy of record offices and archives. Thanks to Karlo Baranj, of Sweden, who translated Desanka Djurić Trbuhović's biography of Mileva Einstein-Marić into English; Constance Frank, of Santa Fe, who was the first translator and encourager; Matthew Griffin, of New York City; Sharon Hill, of Santa Fe; Gregory Mehrten, of New York City; Eilin Merten, who gallantly worked with me on the spur of the moment; and Sonia Bonin, in Berlin, who helped with last-minute materials.

Miloš Dokmanović, Slavica's grown son, worked as our translator for two of my trips to Serbia. His intuition about his mother and his ease with language made his translating so fluent that oftentimes it was as if he were not there at all. Slavica's daughter, Marija Dokmanović, who attends university in America, did an exceptional job of translating a great deal of the material that I brought back from Serbia, including newspapers, books, and legal documents. She was so sensitive to the nuances of this book that her translations were often like poems. Nikola, the husband and father of this exceptional family, saw to it that I was well supplied with petrol and bottles of his homemade brandy.

Jelena Petrović is a family friend who traveled to Serbia with me on my last trip. We shared hotels and meals and days of traipsing through archives, record offices, and graveyards. I had been advised to be low-key, so instead of renting an English or French car that would have stood out in Belgrade, we rented a Yugo. It turned out to be a bright-gold Yugo with "AVIS" sparkling in fluorescent orange on its two doors. Jelena, with élan, dismissed my nervousness, staring down staring eyes and negative reactions.

I would like to extend a very special expression of gratitude to Dr. Ljubomir Trbuhović, who was exceptionally generous with his time and expertise and intuition.

At the beginning of my research, Grete Markstein had merely been the name of a bothersome woman in the Einstein Archives. Through the Menschik family, I found the writer George Markstein, not knowing if he was the right George or not. But I tracked him to his agent, Jacqui Lyons, in London and she confirmed that I had the right Markstein. From that point, and with considerable thoroughness and doggedness, Jacqui joined me in discovering the details of George and Grete Markstein's lives.

I wish to offer the following people my heartfelt gratitude for their support and encouragement: Alan Adelson; Marshall Arisman; Dr. Karmensita Berić; Frank Buchsbaum; Sanja Popović-Bogdanich; John Breakey and Bobbe Breakey; Alice Calaprice, who helped me face the daunting task of permissions; Chris Cover, of Christie's; Dr. Marion C. Diamond; Eva Einstein; Helena Finn; Deborah Garrison, of *The New Yorker* magazine, who kindly helped me get the story started; Linda Gillen; Dr. Radmila Group; Carey Harrison; Michael Herschdoerfer in Amsterdam; Robin Hoffman, who stood by with generosity; Myron L. Hoffmann; Dr. Don Howard; Dr. Mary-Claire King; Keryn Lane; Hanne Loewy; Herbert Lottman in Paris; Constanin Marić in Paris, Lelia Matthews and Paul Matthews; Judy Menschik, Joe Menschik, and Elliot Menschik, who led me to George Markstein; Zorka Milich; Vesna Mladenović; Connie Mutel; Paul Needham; Dr. Vesna Nafeld; Charlie Niles for being so graciously accommodating; Dr. Abraham Pais; the late Alan Palmer, whose friendship and confidence helped me over a hard place and whom I still miss; Sybille Pearson and Tony Pearson; Dina Perez; John Curtis Perry; Dr. Senta Troemel-Ploetz, who collegially and in friendship shared her materials on Mileva; Mark Porter at Christie's; Lisa Primiano; Dr. Sterling Puck; Dr. Lewis Pyenson, who was generous with his expertise and kind in his encouragement at just the right moment; Mark Recktman; Dr. Gerald Rodriguez, who was always industriously available to answer medical questions or to research them for me; Kathy Rodriguez, who struggled with early memories of her Serbian family to enable me to learn more about children in the Balkans; David Rubin, who offered me invaluable information about memory; Judy Siegel; Dr. John Stachel; Dr. Vera John Steiner; Judy Stern and Reuben Stern; Nadja Tesich; Jeff Williams; and Elizabeth Zackheim.

In Serbia, I am grateful to the following people for taking a stranger into their lives and offering me their stories. Zoran Budimlija, Novi Sad; Dušanka Siritović; Sremski Karlovci; Dr. Ana Frenkel, Novi Sad; Darko Hihnjec, Sremski Karlovci; Aleksandra Vavić-Horović, Novi Sad; Vladimir Horović, Novi Sad; Branka Galić Koraksić, Belgrade, for her clarity and kindness and hours spent going through her father's belongings; Father Jovica Jovanović, Titel; Father Djordje S. Krstić, Kać; Momir Lazić, Belgrade; Dragiša Marić and his mother, Ljubica Marić, Kać, who spent hours telling me their story; the late Branko Miškov, Titel; Dragica Petrović and Bogdan Petrović, Belgrade; Dr. Milan Popović, Belgrade; Jovan Ružić, Novi Sad, who kindly allowed himself to become one of the central figures of this story; Jusanka Ružić, Novi Sad; Vera Stefanović and Ana Stefanović, Belgrade, and Pavle S. Stanojević and his staff, who spent more than a week combing the Vojvodine Archives for records concerning Lieserl.

I wish to thank my friends in Budapest, Dr. Klára Ajkay and Leventhe Thury, who offered me comfort and encouragement and introductions to people who, in turn, were able to help me with the government. And my thanks to the esteemed writer Stojan Vujižić, who offered me the records and memories of the Budapest Serbian community.

I want to thank the following people in the United Kingdom for their help: In London, Alexander Baron, who did a remarkable job researching Grete Markstein through the British archive system; James Elias, researcher; Roy Faibish; Aurelia Herschdoerfer; Denise Markstein; Madeline Herschdoerfer Turki and Sylvia Herschdoerfer; Mark Taha, researcher; Lynne Silver Woolfson, Gerald Woolfson, Anne Marie Starr and Bob Starr; and Professor P. H. Plesch of North Staffordshire.

In Germany, Austria, and Switzerland, many people graciously participated in my research. I would like to thank in particular Giuseppe Castagnetti, Jurgen Renn, Ute Leinau, Dr. Fritz Lendemann, and Margaret Rückelt, Berlin; Walter Elfenbein, Frankfurt; Marie Grendelmeier, Martin Grendelmeier, Eva Meili-Sonderegger, and Dr. Werner Zimmerman, Zurich; and Hannah Lessing-Askapa, Vienna.

To the many archives, collections, libraries, consulates, and especially to the archivists and librarians, who helped so much in this project, I extend my sincere gratitude.

Ze'ev Rosenkranz and Judith Levy, The Albert Einstein Archives, Jerusalem; A. Meichle, Albert Einstein Gesellschaft, Bern; Jack Sutter, American Friends Service Committee, Philadelphia; Caroline Moseley and Jack Scott, American Institute of Physics; Julie Kerssen, American Jewish Joint Distribution Committee; Garrett Williams, American Museum of Historical Documents; Toni Siegenthaler, Amt für den Zivilstands und Bürgerrechtsdienst des Kantons Bern; Archiv für die Geschichte der Max-Planck Gesellschaft, Berlin; Archive of the Jewish Community, Novi Sad; Archives of The American Jewish Joint Distribution Committee,

New York City; Archiv Novi Sad; Arhiv Petrovaradin; Arhiv Rukopisno Odeljenje, Novi Sad; Arhiv Srbije, Belgrade; Arhiv Sremska Mitrovica; Arhiv Vojvodine, Novi Sad; Arhiv Vojvodine, Sremski Karlovci; Association of Jewish Refugees in Great Britain, London; Auswärtiges Amt, Ministère fédéral des Affaires étrangères, Bonn; Dr. Frank Mecklenburg and Ronald H. Axelrod, Leo Baeck Institute, New York City; Balch Institute; Office of the Bezirksbürgermeisterin von Berlin-Schöneberg; Francesca Burri, Bern Registry; Péter Heinermann, Biblioteka Matice Srpske, Novi Sad; Charles Niles, Archivist, Boston University Library, Department of Special Collections; Dr. Charles Cutter, Director, Brandeis University Library, Special Collections, Waltham, MA; Peter McInally, British Information Office, New York; British Library, Official Publications Library; British Library Sciences, Reference and Information Services, Aldwych; Imréné Benicz, Budapest Föváros Levéltára; Bundesarchiv, Koblenz; Herbert Gruber, Büro für Genealogie, Vienna; Central London Office of Land Registry; Central Archive for Private Hospital Records, Budapest; Lee S. Strickland, Central Intelligence Agency, Washington, D.C.; Central Registration Office, Budapest; S. Palmor, Central Zionist Archives, Jerusalem; Colindale Newspaper Library, London; Companies House, Department of Trade and Industry, London; Contemporary Scientific Archives Centre/National Cataloging Unit for the Archives of Contemporary Scientists, Oxford; E. Swinglehurst, Archivist, Thomas Cook, Ltd., London; Deutsches Museum, Munich; Directorate of International and Public Law, Bern; Eglise Orthodoxe Serbe Archives, Paris; Silvana Bolli, Irene Mendoza, Yvonne Voegeli, Eidgenössische Technische Hochschule Zurich; Paul Seger, Eidgenössisches Departement für Auswärtige Angelegenheiten, Bern; Maria Lauper, Einstein-Haus, Bern; Dr. Robert Schulmann, Annette Pringle, Michel Janssen, Anneli Mynttinen, The Einstein Papers Project, Boston University; Emilio Segré Visual Archives, College Park, MD; ETH Rektoratskanzlei, Swiss Federal Institute of Technology, Zurich; Diane Loosle, Sonja Nishimoto, Family History Library, Church of Jesus Christ of Latter-Day Saints, Salt Lake City and New York City; Family Records Centre, London; Farkasréti Temetö, Wolf Valley Cemetery, Budapest; Marion Fourestier, French Information Office, New York City; Dr. Iselin Gundermann, Geheimes Staatsarchiv Preußischer Kulturbesitz, Berlin; Hannelore Köhler, German Press Office, New York City; Glavni imenik Kraljevske male realke u Mitrovici, (The Main Register of the Royal Lower Grammar School, Mitrovica); Ulrike Schwerdtfeger, Goethe Institute Library, New York City and Berlin; Greek Orthodox Church, Budapest; Guidhall Library, London; Professor G. Brooser, Rector, Hajnal Imre University, Budapest; The Hebrew University, Jerusalem; Dr. Matthias Pfaffenbichler, Heraldisch-Genealogische Gesellschaft "Adler" Vienna; Sarah Ogilvie, Holocaust Museum, Washington, D.C.; Nicole Rona, Hungarian National Tourist Office, New York City; Immigration and Nationality Directorate, Liverpool; Immigration and Naturalization Service, Historical Reference Library, Washington, D.C.; Institute of Contemporary History and Weiner Library, London; Ispitno Izvješče Pučkeškole u Rumi (The Exam Report of the General People's School in Ruma); Mrs. H. Weiss, Israelitische Kultusgemeinde Wien; Istorijski Institut Srpske Akademije Nauka i Umetnosti, Sremski Karlovci; Luisa Biasiolo, Director; Lieselotte Montague, Jewish Refugees Committee, London; Johns Hopkins University Library, Special Collections, Aurel Wintner Papers; Jüdisches Museum der Stadt Wien Library, Vienna; Gisela Freydanck, Jüdisches Museum im Stadt Museum, Berlin; Doktor Peter Broucek, Director, Kriegsarchiv, Vienna, Krušedol Monastery; Bianca Welzing, Landsarchiv Berlin; Lenin Library, Moscow; Library of Congress, John von Neumann Papers, Washington, D.C.; London Metropolitan Archive; Herbert Kock, Archivist; Magistrat der Stadt Wien, Vienna; Rukopisno odeljenje (originalna dokumentacija Marić), Novi Sad; Matični Ured, u Novom Sadu, Rumi, Sremskoj Mitrovici, Titelu, Kaču, Knjige rodjenih, vencanih i umrlih; Dr. Volker Pellet, Spokesman, Ministry of Foreign Affairs, Bonn; Moscow City Archives, Russia; National Archives of the United States, National Personnel Records Center, Washington, D.C.; Lynda L. Mouchyn, National Archives, Northeast Region, New York City; National Down Syndrome Society, New York City; National Film Information Service, Hollywood; New Mexico State Library, Santa Fe; Frank Wright, Nevada State Museum; New York Academy of Medicine; Sister Dale Smith, New York Family History Center; New York Public Library, Tanya Gizdavčić, Slavic Division and the General and Map Divisions; Bosiljka Stevanovič, New York Public Library / Donnell; Eleanor Vallis, The Library, Nuffield College, Oxford; Novi Sad Records Office, Serbia; Office for National Statistics, General Register Office, Southport, England; Országos Pszichiátriai és Neurológiai Intézet, Budapest; Dr. Guiseppe Castagnetti, Marion Kazemi, Dr. Jürgen Renn, Max Planck Institut für Wissenschaftsgeschichte, Berlin; Polizei Direktion, Bern; Margaret Sherry, Princeton University Library, Rare Books and Special Collections; Daphne Ireland, Loan Osbome, Ben Tate, Princeton University Press; Probate Office, London; Public Record Office, Surrey, England; Rókus Kórhaz, Budapest; Royal Commission for Historical Manuscripts, London; Royal London Hospital Archives; Ruma Records Office; Šabac Museum; St. László Hospital, Budapest; Anatole Antonov, Press Office, Russian Consulate, Washington, D.C.; Alice Davis, Santa Fe Public Library; Srpska Akademija Naukei Umetnoto Archive, Sremski Karlovci; Savski Venać Records Office, Belgrade; Dr. Huldrych Gastpar, Schweizerisches Literaturarchiv, Bern; Bosko Jugović, Director, Serbisch-Orthodoxes Pfarramt Zum Hl. Sava, Vienna; Society of Genealogists, London; Staatsbibliothek zu Berlin; Marianne Howald, Margrit Zwicky, Stadtarchiv Bern; Stadtarchiv Zurich; Standesamt Tübingen; John Stachel Collection, Boston; Ivana Stefanović Collection, Belgrade; Dr. Michael Guisolan, Stadtarchiv Stein am Rhein; Evelyn Mock, Switzerland Tourism Office, New York City; Lásztity Péró, Szerb Országos Önkormányzat, Budapest; Temple of St. Sava, Belgrade; Új Köztemetö, New Public Cemetery, Budapest; Diane Currie, United States Department of Justice, Immigration and Naturalization Service, Washington, D.C.; United States Holocaust Memorial Museum, Washington, D.C.; Sarah Jones, United States Immigration and Naturalization Service, New York City; Marian Smith, Historical Reference Library, United States Immigration and Naturalization Service; Roswitha Haller, United States Information Resource Center, Vienna; Judy Tsou, University of California at Berkeley; Connie Mutel, University of Iowa, Institute of Hydraulic Research, Iowa City; University of Novi Sad, Medical School Archives; Vaznesenje Svih Svetih, All Saints Ascension, Sremska Mitrovica; Dr. Pavle S. Stanojević, Director, Vojvodina Archive, Novi Sad; Wellcome Library, London; Westminster Central Reference Library, London; Woburn House, Office of the United Synagogue, London; Dina Abrahamovic and Gunner Berg, YIVO, New York City; Petar Vico, Second Secretary, Yugoslav Mission to the United Nations; Zentral-und Landesbibliothek Berlin.

Credits / Permissions

Eduard and Hans Albert,1919. Courtesy Ivana Stefanović, Belgrade

Mileva. Courtesy Monolith Enterprises

Julka and Zora Savić. Courtesy Dr. Milan Popović, Belgrade

Julka Savić Popović. Courtesy Dr. Milan Popović, Belgrade

Nada Marić Lazić. Courtesy Ana Milić (pseudonym), Novi Sad

Sister Vera. © Michele Zackheim

Anka, Eduard, and Mileva. Courtesy Ivana Stefanović, Belgrade

Anka Streim. Courtesy Ivana Stefanović, Belgrade

Elsa and Albert Einstein. Courtesy Photoworld, provided by the American Institute of
    Physics, Emilio Segrè Visual Archives

Grete Markstein, 1922. Courtesy Stadtmuseum Berlin, Landesmuseum für Kultur und
    Geschichte Berlins

Paul Rückelt. Courtesy Margret Rückelt, Berlin

Grete Markstein, circa 1935. Courtesy Richard Markstein

János Plesch and Einstein. Courtesy Corbis-Bettmann, New York

Gustav Georg Markstein, Courtesy Richard Markstein

Branko Miškov. © Michele Zackheim

Marie Grendelmeier. © Michele Zackheim

Milan Popović. © Michele Zackheim

Dragiša Marić and mother. © Michele Zackheim

Jovan Ružić. © Michele Zackheim

Slavica Dokmanović. © Michele Zackheim

Milenko Damjanov. © Michele Zackheim

Slavica Dokmanović at graveyard. Courtesy Nikola Dokmanović

Mileva's home, Zurich. Courtesy Dr. Ljubomir Trbuhović, Zurich

Evelyn Einstein. Courtesy Monolith Enterprises

Mileva with Bernhard. Courtesy Monolith Enterprises

Albert, Mileva, and Eduard. Courtesy Monolith Enterprises

Speculative Lieserl. Courtesy Monolith Enterprises

The Spire. Courtesy Verlag Paul Haupt, Bern

PERMISSIONS

Various letters and other source material are excerpted from *The Collected Papers of Albert
    Einstein,* published by Princeton University Press.
    Volume 1: The Early Years, 1879–1902. Edited by John Stachel. Anna Beck, translator, and
        Peter Havas, consultant. © 1987 by The Hebrew University of Jerusalem.
    Volume 5: The Swiss Years Correspondence, 1902–1914. Edited by Martin J. Klein, A. J. Kox,
        and Robert Schulmann. Anna Beck, translator, and Don Howard, consultant.
        © 1993 by The Hebrew University of Jerusalem.
    Volume 8: The Berlin Years of Correspondence, 1914–1918. Edited by Robert Schulmann,
        A. J. Kox, Michel Janssen, and Illy Jósez. © 1998 by The Hebrew University of
        Jerusalem.
    All excerpts from the CPAE are reprinted with permission.

Forel, Auguste. *Die sexuelle Frage.* Munchen, Ernst Reinhardt Verlag, 1905. Reprinted by permission.

Excerpts from letters of Sofija Galić Golubović and Tima Galić are reprinted with permission of Branka Galić Koraksić.

Excerpts from Dr. Laza Marković's *Marriage, or How Will a Nation Achieve Good Progeny?* are reprinted with permission of Dr. Karmensita Berić Maskarel.

Excerpts from Svetislav Stefanović's *The Pain of the Unknown* and the letters of Milana Bota Stefanović are reprinted with permission of Ivana Stefanović.

Excerpts from Desanka Trbuhović Gjurić's *U Senci Alberta Ajnštajna,* © 1996, Alan Adelson and Karlo Baranj, are reprinted by permission. English translation by Karlo Baranj.

Excerpts from Grete Markstein's correspondence are reprinted by permission of Richard Markstein.

Excerpts from the writings of Dr. János Plesch, including excerpts from *János, The Story of a Doctor* (translations provided by Prof. P. H. Plesch), are reprinted with the permission of P. H. Plesch.

About the Author

A writer and visual artist, Michele Zackheim is the author of a novel, *Violette's Embrace*, based on the life of Violette Leduc. She lives in New York City.